THE COVER

This is a water color of the 1899/1930 section of Wilmington High School as it appeared in 1981. The painting was commissioned by the WHS Class of '81 as their class gift. It was painted by Dover, Vermont artist Betsy Fellows, mother of two former WHS students Dianne Fellows Guminak and Donna Fellows McPherson.

SMALL TOWN SCHOOL

SMALL TOWN SCHOOL

DAVE LARSEN

ONION RIVER PRESS

Onion River Press
89 Church Street
Burlington, VT 05401
info@onionriverpress.com
www.onionriverpress.com

ISBN: 978-1-966607-00-7
Library of Congress Control Number: 2025917006

CONTENTS

To the people of Wilmington, past and present

INTRODUCTION

I was hired to teach at Wilmington High School (WHS) in May, 1972. I met my first students four months later as the 1972-1973 school year began. At the time, I was only marginally aware that I was teaching in a building constructed at the end of the 19th century, and I certainly was not contemplating the possibility that I would continue teaching there into the first part of the 21st century.

Wilmington High School was a building steeped in history, with so many stories to tell. But during my teaching career (1972-2005), while I might have had an occasional interest in the history of the building, it was the demands of teaching and finding the time to meet them that prevented me from delving into that history. Now, some 52 years after my first week of teaching, this book is an attempt to rectify that.

In June, 2004, Wilmington High School as an institution officially closed. But there were no speeches and no closing ceremony, not even much time for sentimentality or reflection. There was much work to be done.

As a middle school teacher who had spent 32 years teaching at Wilmington Middle/High School, I was busy packing my teaching materials, books, and equipment for the move to my new school in Whitingham. My middle school colleagues were doing the same. In just two months, at the beginning of the 2004-2005 school year, the Wilmington Middle School program would merge with its counterpart in the Whitingham School to become Twin Valley Middle School.

Whitingham's high school faculty and students were preparing to reverse the process. They would move to the former Wilmington High School, and that building would now become Twin Valley High School.

Ten years later, in 2014, Twin Valley High School would move its students, teachers, and programs from the former Wilmington High School building to the newly renovated Whitingham School building where they would join the middle school to become Twin Valley Middle/High School.

With that exit of students in June, 2014, and the final closure of the Wilmington High School building as a school by any name, the echoes of exuberant student voices and the palpable intensity of their adolescent energy were gone forever. And the building stood empty.

Built in 1899, the school in many ways had served as the nucleus of the town. It was where generations of students had been educated and where countless memories had been created. Throughout its existence it had been the source of identity and pride for the entire town. The building had faithfully served the students and the community of Wilmington, Vermont for 105 years.

WHAT THIS BOOK IS (I HOPE) AND WHAT IT ISN'T

This book is intended to be the story of the school itself, first as Wilmington's Central School and later as Wilmington High School - a story that includes the building, its students, its staff, its educators, its programs, the Wilmington community, and to an extent, what and who came before the school's initial construction in 1899.

However, the book is by no means intended to serve as a definitive or comprehensive history of Wilmington's Central School, its high school, or its schools in general. Nor am I an expert on this subject. Early in my research I knew that the more I learned about the history of the school, the more I would realize how much *more* there was to learn about it. Whether this book does justice to the school's history, I will leave to others to decide.

THE SCHOOL: WHAT SHOULD WE CALL IT?

Even though the 1899 building and its 1930 and 1956 additions housed elementary grades until the construction of Wilmington's Deerfield Valley Elementary School (DVES) in 1970, it was often referred to as the high school. During my research I learned that it was also called the school house, the new public school, the village school, the graded school, or the central school.

In this book when referring to the school as it existed prior to 1970, I call it the Central School. If I quote someone and they refer to it as something else, "the high school," for example, I have honored that. So whether the building is referred to as the high school, the Central School, or something else, they are all one and the same. Note: *When DVES opened in 1970, the Central School became the high school, housing grades 7 - 12, and subsequently was always referred to as such.*

HOW THE BOOK IS ORGANIZED

The book is organized into three parts. Part One provides a description of the life of an educator (superintendent or teacher) during the latter half of the 19th century and into the early 20th century. Included in this section are chapters that describe what it took to become a superintendent of schools or a teacher, life as a teacher during this time, and the school calendar.

While some data, descriptions, and information in this section are nationally oriented, the focus of the section is on teaching conditions in Vermont and in Wilmington. The inclusion in Part One of national and state data and information is intended to provide a context for subsequent discussion of Wilmington's schools, educators, and general approach to education.

Part Two begins with a description of nineteenth century educational opportunities for Wilmington's children, including Wilmington's small district schools. It continues with and focuses on the construction of the Central School building in 1899, and then on the changes made to the building throughout the twentieth century by years of construction and renovation: 1930-1931; 1947 (proposed); 1955-1956; and 1981-1982.

As I did research for Part Two, my focus was on the building itself. However, it was impossible to ignore the experiences of everyone who was in some way associated with Wilmington's schools. Without including all of the interesting information I encountered while researching, I tried to balance the importance of stone, steel, bricks, and wood with the more human elements of a school that made it both special and memorable to the people who learned and worked there. For example, while not including an extensive exploration of the school's academic programs through the years, I do occasionally mention them as they pertain to the subject being described.

Part Three describes various elements of student life in the Central School and in Wilmington High School. Chapters in this section include student well-being, traditions, transportation, sports, technology, field trips, fundraising, and student activities. Woven into these chapters are anecdotes and information from my career at WHS.

HOW I WROTE THIS BOOK

As I wrote about the history of Wilmington's Central/High School, especially the building itself, I obtained information from both primary and secondary sources. Much of what is included in Parts One and Two of this book came from binders housed at the Pettee Memorial library in Wilmington. These binders are full of documents, newspaper articles, and photographs, all of them collected and organized by Margaret Greene of Wilmington. For many years, Mrs. Greene served as the town's librarian. Her efforts at documenting various aspects of Wilmington's history are both impressive and invaluable.

Note: *According to her obituary, before becoming Wilmington's town librarian, "Mrs. Greene began her teaching career in a one-room schoolhouse in East Dover. She then taught at the Cold Brook Schoolhouse in*

Wilmington, which was also a one-room schoolhouse. For many years, she had taught grades three and five at the Wilmington School."

My sources also included WHS literary publications and yearbooks (the *Mirror*), DVDs, photographs, books, annual town and school reports, my own letters and journals, communications with former students, various newspapers and other periodicals, and information on the Internet.

When it came to learning about the people and the culture of Wilmington's Central School and later its high school from 1899 until my arrival at WHS in 1972, I depended greatly on materials housed at the Historical Society of Wilmington. Its president, Julie (Crafts) Moore (WHS '81), was most helpful in providing and guiding me to many of the materials cited in this book. A general list of sources and a page of acknowledgements appear at the end of this book.

While I read and used many issues of the WHS *Mirror* and town reports, I did not use all of them. Therefore, it is inevitable that some relevant or important information is not included in this book. In addition, while I had conversations with many people about their experiences as students at Wilmington High School, I know I could have included more. It simply came down to trying to keep the book to a manageable length.

In describing or identifying various sections of the building, I am assuming that its front faces north.

Even though I chose not to include some of the minutiae of Wilmington High School's history, for anyone who's interested in it, a visit to Wilmington's Pettee Memorial Library will prove to be invaluable. I would recommend the binders that contain material provided by Mrs. Greene. I would also recommend reading the school reports in the collection of Wilmington's Town Reports, specifically the reports of the school directors, principals, and superintendents. They offer detailed and fascinating insights into the operation of the schools.

I would say the same about the Historical Society of Wilmington. It houses countless primary sources and artifacts that capture what living in Wilmington was like decades and centuries into the past. It is an absolutely fascinating place to visit. Of particular interest are copies of Wilmington High School's literary publication that eventually became its annual yearbook: the *Mirror*. They contain a wealth of information about the school and the town.

USING NAMES AND QUOTES

I identify adults and former students by their real names if their names are included in the public record or publicly available information (newspapers, Historical Society booklets, books, the *Mirror*, WHS yearbooks, town reports, etc.) or if I have their permission. Otherwise I use fictitious names.

I have included many quotes from various sources. In several of them there may be what appear to be typos or errors in grammar, spelling, or syntax. The syntax of decades ago had its own distinct style, as did spelling and punctuation, and I wanted to accurately portray that. I took great care to copy the quotes as they appeared in their original sources. I could have included any number of "sic" notations. However, for the sake of simplicity and flow, I decided instead to offer this explanation.

In some instances, I have added explanations to quotes or pieces of information. These appear in parentheses within the quote or at its end. In many instances, I have also added the notation, "Note," followed by an explanation or personal comment written in italics.

FINAL THOUGHTS

Parts of this book are meant to inform. Parts of it are meant to entertain. Parts of it may even bring back pleasant memories for former WHS students and employees. Parts of it may do all three. Most of all, however, I hope this book will serve as an interesting compilation of information that describes Wilmington's Central/high school and the people who were connected to it or by it.

Writing this book was a real "mom and pop" operation. I am not a professional writer. I used no professional editors or fact checkers. My wife, Kathy, devoted countless hours to reading this manuscript and offering suggestions on how to improve it. However, all final decisions about how this book was written were mine. So let me apologize in advance and assume responsibility for any awkward syntax, content omissions, factual inaccuracies, errors in punctuation, or anything else in my writing that could use some improvement.

That being said, I hope you enjoy reading what follows as much as I enjoyed writing it.

PART I

Educators in the 19th
& 20th Centuries

CHAPTER 1

School Superintendents

If we are to fully appreciate the education afforded to Wilmington's students in both the district schools and the Central School during the 19th century and into the 20th century, it helps to know the superintendents who were responsible for their education and the conditions in which they studied.

THE ROLE OF THE SCHOOL SUPERINTENDENT TODAY

Today's superintendents of schools report to a supervisory union board of school directors and are charged with overseeing the implementation of an increasing number of education-related state and federal laws and regulations. But that's not all.

Title 16 Vermont Statutes Annotated outlines the roles of today's school superintendents. According to Title 16 (Vermont's education laws), these roles include but are not limited to: carrying out the policies adopted by the local school board(s); preparing plans to achieve the educational goals and objectives established by the school district; nominating candidates for positions in the school district; hiring and supervising non-licensed supervisory union personnel; reporting to the secretary of education and the State Board of Education all required data and information from the school district; reporting on school district general and financial operations; arranging for teacher professional development; and providing general supervision of the schools in the district.

Although not specifically referenced in statute, there are additional areas of responsibility such as labor and contract disputes, personnel issues, supervising and evaluating central office personnel, intervening in extreme problems with students and/or parents, public relations, and external affairs with town and state governments.

The position of school superintendent, if done well, is demanding and time-consuming. In Vermont, a superintendent of schools usually has a doctorate or at least a Master's degree in education or a related field. The typical superintendent has classroom teaching experience and has also served as a school administrator, such as a principal, a district curriculum coordinator, or a district special education coordinator.

THE ROLE OF A 19TH CENTURY SCHOOL SUPERINTENDENT

By comparison, the job responsibilities and qualifications of a school superintendent in the 19th and early 20 centuries were considerably more limited. During this time, the role of the superintendent focused on supervising and evaluating the teachers in a town's school or schools. The superintendent reported to a single school board or, as was the case with district schools, to the individual board of each of several district schools in a town. Throughout much of the 19th century in Vermont, the town school superintendent of schools was elected or re-elected at town meeting for a one year term.

In his book, *History of Education in Vermont*, George Gary Bush, Ph. D. describes the role of Vermont school superintendents in the mid-to-late 19th century: "It is his duty to visit all legally organized common schools in town - the average number being 10 - at least once each year and give advice to the teachers respecting the government of the pupils and the courses of study; he must inspect the school buildings, and adopt all requisite measures for the inspection of the schools and the improvement of the scholars (students)." Note: *While the average number of small one-room district schools in Vermont was 10, Wilmington at one time had 16 such schools, each with its own board of directors.*

In addition, the superintendent had to assure that the school attendance register was properly maintained. He was also required to meet annually with other county superintendents and to "make a detailed report of the condition of the schools to be presented to the annual March meeting (of each town)."

With such an important role, one might reasonably assume that school superintendents were universally held in high regard. According to Bush, this was not necessarily the case. "The duties and compensation of the town superintendents were for a long time the occasion of much bitterness of feeling among the people."

Bush writes that this resulted in a "determination upon the part of many (superintendents) not to conform to the law. Teachers were legally required to obtain their teaching certificates from the town superintendent, but the law was disregarded by more than one sixth of the districts of the state."

Bush attributes this to the fact that superintendents were paid "$1 a day." And to make matters worse, "...the supervising and visiting of the schools was neglected, and doubtless many of the deficiencies then existing in the schools may be accounted for by this fact."

Bush continues: "The real seat of the trouble seems to have been that the State enacted the law that each town should choose a superintendent, and then required the town to pay for his services." Note: *When I was in the legislature, and most likely long before, this kind of directive from the State was referred to by some citizens as an unfunded mandate and was seen by them as an unwelcome expense and an unnecessary intrusion by the state into local affairs.*

TWO OF WILMINGTON'S 19TH CENTURY SCHOOL SUPERINTENDENTS

Unlike some of the school superintendents described in George Gary Bush's book, at least two of Wilmington's superintendents, Erastus A. Fitch in 1882 and Edward B. Buffum in 1885, appear to have been both competent and respected.

Mr. Buffum was born in 1851 and died in 1927. According to his obituary on Findagrave.com, "E. B. Buffum is most prominently associated in the public mind as a former esteemed teacher and as the affable salesman and confidential clerk in O. O. Ware's general store. Note: *O.O. Ware's store was located on the first floor of the building currently situated on the southeast corner of the intersection in downtown Wilmington.*

"He began teaching school at eighteen years of age and for more than a score of years was a successful teacher in this town (Wilmington) and three years superintendent of schools. In 1888 he moved to the village and became clerk for O. O. Ware and has here displayed great natural aptitude in the vocation of a salesman." Note: *Mr. Buffum was the uncle of Mary Buffum Maynard. Recollections of her time in the Castle School appear in this book in Chapter 7.*

Erastus A. Fitch was somewhat older than Edward Buffum. According to the *Deerfield Valley Times Reunion Edition - 1900*, Mr. Fitch was born in 1832, and during his boyhood "received the scant education afforded by the common and select schools of those days, supplemented by a course of study at the seminary of Springfield, Vt. This was followed or interspersed with teaching in his own town and at Weathersfield Bow, Vt." Note: *In addition to the so-called "normal schools" that were post-secondary schools designed to prepare teachers to instruct primary and secondary students, there were similar post-secondary schools or programs referred to as seminaries.*

Mr. Fitch was said to have been a lover of nature, a writer of literature and poetry, and well-versed in agriculture and education. He was an active citizen of Wilmington who was described in the *Deerfield Val-*

ley Times Reunion Edition as someone who apparently had an open mind: "Although loyal to his convictions, he holds no opinions so tenaciously that he cannot change when facts and reason dictate. This frame of mind has made him a learner all his life." Mr. Fitch died in 1915.

If the professional lives and qualifications of Mr. Buffum and Mr. Fitch are any indication, school superintendents in the 19th and early 20th centuries may not necessarily have been experts or college-trained in the field of formal education. However, one may assume that at least in Wilmington most superintendents were knowledgeable, well-rounded, and well-educated for their times and, absent information to the contrary, were well-regarded by the citizens they served.

CHAPTER 2

Becoming a Teacher

Today, depending on a state's laws and professional licensing requirements, teachers are generally required to have at least a bachelor's degree. Many, if not most, eventually earn graduate degrees that require an additional one or two years of study. In the mid-to-late 19th century and before, however, this was not the case.

Wilmington residents Margaret Greene and Rita Staib offered a contrast to current licensing requirements when they wrote in 1982 about the qualifications of teachers in the mid-to-late 1800s. "Very early, anyone who wanted to do so could be the teacher. It usually was a man who had received his education beyond elementary school at a 'Select School' or an out-of-town seminary."

It's true that in the earliest years of public education, teachers were almost exclusively men. However, in her paper, *The Vermont Schoolmarm and the Contemporary One-Room Schoolhouse*, author Jody Kenny writes that by the early 20th century this had changed dramatically. She cites the "Carnegie Commission Study of 1912-14." It reported that in Vermont in those years there were 1366 one-room schoolhouses. "Half of the teachers were between 20-30 years of age and had 2-7 years of experience. There were 256 male and 2,735 female teachers of whom slightly more than one-third had graduated from a normal school or college." Note:*"College," as it pertained to teachers training, usually meant some schooling after high school. In the 19th century and early 20th century, it rarely meant a two- or four-year degree.*

The Carnegie Commission Study concluded that circa 1914, "The typical rural school teacher is therefore a young woman of about twenty-three, who has been teaching about four years for $8.50 a week or $275 a school year. In many cases she teaches in her home town and either walks or drives from one to five miles to get to her school. She is a graduate of a four year high school, but has had no professional training. She either succeeds or fails in accordance with her native ability, and this fortunately is large."

Interestingly, Kenny offers evidence that in some ways the age and experience of the typical teacher in 1914 had not changed in the previous 70 years since the 1840s. She writes about an 1847 study of education in Vermont conducted by Horace Eaton who was serving concurrently as the state's governor and its first superintendent (commissioner) of education. Citing Eaton's study she writes, "A teacher of an average age of 22.4 years with 4.7 seasons of experience taught an average of twenty classes (probably lessons) a day."

In her 1941 essay, "Schools in Wilmington," Marilyn Howe adds some specific details. Applying to be a teacher was, she wrote, "a very simple procedure. Applicants were given an interview with the superintendent. The interview," she continues, "was followed by written examinations in arithmetic, history and civil government, grammar, geography, and physicology (physics)." These examinations were often created and administered by the local school committee or the local school superintendent.

Howe continues: "Legibility was considered one of the most important factors on a written examination. A passing average was sixty-five per cent with no mark below forty per cent on any one of the subjects. College degrees or normal school training were not required to become a school teacher."

According to the article, "Vermont Female Schoolteachers in the Nineteenth Century," written by Margaret K. Nelson, "This system of examination at the local level (in Vermont) persisted until 1889." However, according to Nelson, as early as 1845, other forms of certification emerged. Teaching certificates were issued by counties, and in the mid-1860s by normal schools. "Eventually," she writes, "State Board of Education certificates and teacher training programs in high schools and academies provided other means as well."

SOME OCCASIONAL CRITICISM

Vermont communities have a long-established tradition of support-ing their local schools and the people who work in them. And while teachers who labored in Vermont's one-room schoolhouses did not have the training and qualifications of today's teachers, within the context of the times, they were held in high esteem, perhaps even revered, by those in their communities who valued education.

However, in spite of local support and the publicly-acknowledged challenges faced by teachers in the 19th century and early-to-mid 20th century, there were occasionally state and local officials who were critical of their training and performance.

District superintendents during this time were almost exclusively men, and it was their responsibility to observe and evaluate the district's teachers. They, and what was called the superintending committee con-sisting of locally elected members similar to today's school board, had complete control over who was hired to teach and who was fired. Teacher evaluations were a "one-way street." Teachers had no contrac-tual right to appeal their job status, their teaching conditions, or what they perceived to be an unfair, inaccurate, or unnecessarily harsh evalu-ation by their superintendent.

One example of such an evaluation appears in Margaret Nelson's ar-ticle. She cites an unnamed Vermont superintendent who wrote to a "Miss M," a teacher under his supervision. Ms. Nelson quotes the su-perintendent: "Allow me to speak plainly of what I notice as defective in your school. You lack energy. In your manner you appear dull and stu-pid. Your heart beats too slowly; your blood runs sluggishly in its round of circulation; your eyes do not flash with enthusiasm; your voice falters, all indicating a want of earnestness in your work."

The superintendent then suggested that this teacher begin the day with a "cold bath in the morning, or an hour or two of vigorous Free Gymnastics . . . It would also be useful for you to dwell frequently and long upon the greatness and importance of your work, and the responsibility of your position...By some means, do wake up and stir yourself, or I must advise you to seek some more congenial employment."

Jody Kenny writes about Vermont's mid-19th century governor, Horace Eaton. As if to highlight the issue of undertrained, under-qualified, and underperforming teachers, "Eaton considered the 'paramount evil' of Vermont schools to have been 'the want of thoroughly trained teachers.'"

It appears that Governor Eaton's frustrations were shared 50 years later by Wilmington's school superintendent, Ernest A. Maynard. As superintendent, it was Mr. Maynard's primary responsibility to observe and then evaluate the performance of Wilmington's teachers, all of whom worked in the town's small district (one-room) schools.

In 1898, one year prior to the construction of Wilmington's Central School, Mr. Maynard was blunt in criticizing the quality of the town's district school teachers and, indirectly, the absence of requirements that assured quality instruction. He wrote in his annual report to the town, "The teachers, with a few exceptions, are much too poorly educated themselves...The idea is preposterous that a girl who has only studied in a district school is fully qualified for the responsibility of educating children properly."

Mr. Maynard pointed out that Massachusetts required teachers to be high school graduates with at least two additional years of normal school (teacher education) training. He continued: "It is not too much to expect that all teachers be capable of using tolerably correct English in the schoolroom. This, I find, that some are unable to do so."

He then commented on the teachers' lack of instructional skills and their overemphasis on rote learning: "With nearly all your teachers there is the tendency to overtrain the pupils' memory at the expense of reason. Pupils should be taught to think for themselves."

The superintendent concluded his comments by suggesting that some local teachers did a less than optimal job of planning their lessons or, even worse, that they failed to understand the importance of preparation. "The lack of proper preparation for their daily work is also evident. The teacher who 'takes no thought for the morrow,' but expects to be inspired on the spur of the moment with a way of overcoming difficulties, generally finds that perspiration, instead of inspiration, awaits her."

Note: *In my review of dozens of annual reports written by Wilmington's education leaders throughout the twentieth century, and during my more than 50 years living in Wilmington, I have never seen or been aware of similar public criticisms of anyone involved in any of Wilmington's schools. Superintendent Maynard's criticism of some of Wilmington's one-room district school teachers was candid to say the least, and especially so since it was expressed in such a public manner.*

It's difficult to determine whether Mr. Maynard's criticisms of some of Wilmington's teachers were well founded. However, it's possible, given that he wrote his comments the year before the construction of the Central School, he was attempting to establish a public rationale for increased school centralization and consolidation. This, of course, meant eliminating the district schools.

CHAPTER 3

Teachers and Gender

Teaching a group of students ranging in ages from five to the late teens, with a range of learning aptitudes just as wide, would test the abilities of any teacher past or present. And so would teaching in the small, confined space of an uninsulated building with only natural or lamp light and no indoor plumbing. Toss in various janitorial and maintenance responsibilities, and teachers in the 19th and early-to-mid 20th centuries had their hands full. And while lack of education, training, and experience may have hampered their effectiveness as teachers, at least in some cases there may have been another factor as well: gender.

In one of my graduate education classes at UVM in 1971, my professor suggested that the aspiring junior high and high school teachers in our class who were male would have a far easier time teaching and managing their future students than would the females in our class. A young male teacher, he said, would be deemed "cool" by his male students and "cute" and possibly even "crush-worthy" by his female students. The young female teacher, on the other hand, could be seen as a threat by her female students and as a pushover by the boys in her class.

I spent my elementary school years in the 1950s living and going to school in a typical middle class neighborhood in Rochester, NY. Throughout those years, and even in eighth grade in a large urban high school, I had only female teachers. The only exceptions were a male student teacher in fourth grade and male physical education teachers throughout my school years.

I remember all of those women as capable and kind but firm when it came to managing their classes. However, as firm as they might have been, very few fit the image of "schoolmarm."

According to Dictionary.com, a schoolmarm is a "female school-teacher, especially of the old-time country school type, popularly held to be strict and priggish." For many, this evokes the image of a stern, gray-haired unmarried woman, her hair tightly coiffed, wooden paddle in hand, commanding respect and obedience from her students, and confident in her abilities to teach all students and to discipline any who might challenge her authority.

But was the strict, controlling schoolmarm image rooted in fact? Or were women teachers during the 19th and early twentieth centuries in at least some of America's schools and even in some of Wilmington's district schools at a disadvantage because of their gender? There is some evidence that supports the latter possibility.

On the national level according to the 1992 PBS Series, *Only a Teacher*, "Even as they granted women moral superiority, reformers (in education) quietly worried over women's ability to maintain order in the classroom and discipline unruly children. In many schools, the new schoolmarms were young - some only fourteen or fifteen years old. They had finished the equivalent of eighth grade and, in some schools, that qualified them to teach. Their pupils might well be taller and older than they - at least when the farm boys put in their periodic appearances in the classroom. Nineteenth-century female teachers often complained that teaching was most challenging when the 'big boys,' who would either flirt or tease and defy them, arrived."

A VERMONT ISSUE?

There is at least some anecdotal evidence that age and gender placed young female teachers at a disadvantage in some of Vermont's class-rooms.

In a 1986 radio broadcast of the *Green Mountain Chronicles*, "School Consolidation: Farewell to the One-Room Schoolhouse," the narrator states, "From the teacher's point of view, there were some drawbacks (to the rural one-room schoolhouse or district school). Many of the older students were not much younger than the teachers themselves. Single-handedly maintaining discipline could challenge all of the new teacher's skills."

On the same broadcast, a former teacher, a female in a one-room schoolhouse near St. Johnsbury, Vermont, recalled one rather extreme example of those challenges: "We had a wood stove, a box stove, and I went out to get some wood, and when I came in, they (the older students) had the box cover up, and they were swinging a (younger) child over the open flames. Things like that you just couldn't allow, you know."

According to Margaret Nelson in her article, "Vermont Female Schoolteachers in the Nineteenth Century," in 1840s Vermont female teachers earned less than 40 percent of the wages paid to male teachers. This was because they tended to teach in the summer. These summer sessions "were considered easier to manage as no sixteen year-old boys attended." They were working on the farms.

In the May/June,1934 issue of the *Mirror*, WHS senior, Virginia Howe, offered her thoughts about the gender issue in the 19th century. She wrote, "People then thought as did Hamlet - 'Frailty, thy name is woman.' Consequently, a man was usually the lucky wage-earner in the winter term (of school), and a woman was engaged for the summer term. It was a long time before people could be convinced that a woman could handle the over-sized boys that came only in the winter when they were free from the tasks of the farm."

In their 1982 article, "Wilmington's Rural or District Schools," Wilmington residents Margaret Greene and Rita Staib added their perspective: "Teachers then as now, could be of either sex, however, if it was a hard school, male teachers were usually preferred. What do we mean by a 'hard school'? Sometimes children only four or five years old were sent to school, especially if the teacher was boarding at that home. Also sometimes boys as old as twenty or twenty-one attended...Sometimes the older boys only went to school to have some 'fun' and get out of doing so much work at home."

Virginia Howe, in her *Mirror* article, cited records from Wilmington's school district number ten, the Cutting district: "At one time the (school) committee voted to have a 'female teacher' in the winter. Then, on thinking the matter over, they decided it was too risky; so they had another meeting and agreed to cancel the former vote."

Miss Howe did not cite any specific published sources for information in her article. However, she did refer to her great-grandmother, Louise Snow, who taught "in the little red school house which stood very near the Dover road just below the Cold Brook bridge." Assuming that Miss Howe was 18 years old in her graduating year, 1934, it's conceivable that her great-grandmother was teaching in the 1870s or 1880s and, therefore, was a relatively reliable source of information for her *Mirror* article.

Whether some female teachers were disadvantaged by their gender or their small physical stature relative to that of some of their students is difficult to determine. However, given the comments of Margaret Nelson, Margaret Greene, Rita Staib, Virginia Howe, and others, that perception appears to have existed.

GENDER TRENDS IN WILMINGTON

Wilmington's annual school reports show that into the twentieth century an overwhelmingly disproportionate number of Wilmington's K-12 teachers were female. In 1935, males filled the roles of supervising principal and assistant principal. However, the 12 full-time teachers in the Wilmington school system were women. By 1951, however, a change in the teaching ranks had occurred. In the Wilmington school system there were as many male teachers as there were female teachers. This 1:1 ratio was essentially the same nine years later in 1960.

In 1971-1972, the year before I was hired, the female/male ratio in Wilmington High School had changed and was approximately 1:2 for teachers of grades 7-12. In 2003-2004, the final year of Wilmington High School, that had shifted to an approximate female/male ratio of 3:2.

Note: *During my time as a student at all levels, as well as my time teaching in Wilmington Middle/High School and my final year in Twin Valley Middle School, I never observed a pattern of gender ineffectiveness in either female or male teachers. Good teachers planned, prepared, and executed their lessons with knowledge and skill, and they cultivated meaningful relationships with their students. In my experience, none of this ever depended on a teacher's gender.*

CHAPTER 4

Teacher Pay and Benefits

APPRECIATING TEACHERS

In contrast to superintendent Maynard's 1898 criticisms of some of Wilmington's teachers in the district schools, WHS Principal H.H. Rice in his 1913 annual report wrote at length in support of teachers and their efforts to improve the lives of their students: "Quite a little is heard, indirectly, to the effect that teachers are being paid too much. This is usually from the inconsiderate, and those who class a teacher along with a day laborer at any other occupation...Trained and skilled teachers, like any skilled help anywhere, have a right to more re-muneration than the unskilled."

Mr. Rice, pointed out that the cost of "ordinary labor" had doubled in the past 50 years, as had the cost of living. He then asked, "Why should not the teacher's pay keep pace with such advances?"

And, he suggested, for those in town who were critical of teachers, why don't they "try their hand at teaching. The way is open, and there is certainly need of more teachers."

As far as the actual job of teaching was concerned, Principal Rice left no doubt where he stood: "Those who are not in the (teaching) work, and these are they who criticize most, know practically nothing of what must be done. It looks wondrously easy to one who has never tried it...Those who have tried it to any extent know that it is not so easy as it looks."

Finally, in an effort to explain why teachers teach, Mr. Rice wrote, "Most teachers who are really successful could easily make more pay in other forms of employment. Teachers...like the work. They like to see the young minds develop, and to help them to larger views and aspirations in life. They believe that teaching is one of the greatest, noblest, and most necessary occupations in which one can engage. I am sure that most of our townspeople, and all who are interested in the development of the young, do not consider teachers, as a whole, to be overpaid."

Thirty years later, in their 1943-1944 annual report, school directors C.A. Bayard, Juliet Adams, and Albert Cole, along with school superintendent Edward Boak, urged Wilmington's voters to demonstrate their appreciation for the town's teachers in at least two ways. One was financial. The school directors wrote, "Through the increase in our budget last year we were able to retain every one of the high school teachers and most of the elementary teachers. However, salaries are still going up (in neighboring school districts) and, if we are to maintain our present success, we must meet the competition. Our teachers receive better financial offers to go elsewhere, and often only loyalty to the town or a liking for the pupils or the teaching conditions has retained the teacher for us."

Note: *Even though Wilmington was able to pay its teachers a reasonable salary, at this time, according to the January 12, 1943 Windham Southwest District Bulletin, teachers and all Americans began to pay a so-called wartime Victory Tax which was a five percent deduction from their weekly salary checks on earnings over $12.*

But according to the school directors and Superintendent Boak, money wasn't the only consideration. Even a simple meal, it seems, could be a significant gesture of appreciation. They urged the citizens of Wilmington to "demonstrate the cordiality that you feel toward the teachers. A teacher who is invited out to supper for a pleasant evening feels very differently toward a town than one who is constantly being hectored because Johnnie got a 'C' when of course he should have had an 'A.' Among other kindnesses last fall, we were delighted when one lady issued a general invitation to any two teachers who were unable to return to their homes to have Thanksgiving dinner with her.ꞌꞌ

Two years after the end of World War Two, teachers' modest salaries continued to be an issue of concern. In his annual report in 1947, superintendent Boak wrote, "'The burning issue all over the nation,' to quote Ralph E. Noble, State Commissioner of Education, 'is the matter of teachers' salaries.' One can hardly pick up any newspaper or magazine without seeing some item in regard to teachers' salaries being increased or some campaign being conducted for that purpose."

That same year, WHS principal George Perry agreed with Mr. Boak. He cited in his report "ominous trends" in education, specifically the shortage of qualified teachers: "On the one hand we hear of the widespread breakdown in home discipline, with the school expected to take over this traditional task. On the other hand, just when we so badly need competent teachers, especially men, manning our schools we find thousands deserting the field, many others striking for a livable wage, and countless potential teachers training for every occupation except teaching."

He noted that, "One-fourth of all the teachers in Vermont are not professionally qualified to teach...this teacher shortage will last for many years more."

Because of these challenges, and citing the need to offer salaries that were competitive with larger school districts in and adjacent to Vermont, both Boak and Perry advocated for increased pay for Wilmington's teachers. According to their annual report, the school directors that year "granted a 10% cost-of-living increase in the salary of every school employee beginning in January, 1947."

In 1947, the first master contract for Wilmington teachers, which included salaries, benefits, working conditions, and other related items, was still 30 years away. However, Superintendent Boak and the school directors wrote that, "We are considering with the teachers a salary schedule for the next school year by means of which we hope to retain the great majority of our faculty."

ROOM AND BOARD BENEFITS IN WILMINGTON

In addition to salaries, teachers often received room and board as part of their remuneration. One local perspective regarding this is offered by writer Marilyn Wheeler who describes a common living arrangement for Wilmington's teachers. "Each family took turns in boarding a teacher. She stayed a designated number of nights at the home of each scholar (student). The number of nights per scholar was determined by the total attendance of the school. Consequently, the family with the most children had to board the teacher (the) longest."

According to the 1901 Wilmington Auditors Report, similar to today's annual Town Report, the cost of boarding was included in the pay Wilmington's teachers received from the school district. For example, the Central School principal, James Lobban, was paid $625 which included board for the school term. The salaries of some teachers, ranging from $132 to $270, also included board.

BOARDING AROUND

It was normal in 19th century Vermont for female (and less frequently for male) teachers to live with the families of their students or with a school official. Either as a legal requirement or a locally accepted practice, this arrangement was often referred to as "boarding around." Margaret Nelson in her article, "Vermont Female Schoolteachers in the Nineteenth Century," writes that boarding around was a common practice because "only occasionally did a school district allow the teacher to select his or her own place to board or did the teacher live close enough to (her family's) home that she could remain there."

For several reasons boarding around could be viewed as a benefit for teachers. Instead of living with total strangers or living alone, which was frowned upon, especially for females, teachers lived with families who resided in the district and who had children in the local school.

In addition, writes Nelson, "The practice also was said to better acquaint the teacher with the scholars (students). In isolated regions families probably found it a treat to have a respectable visitor in the home for a week or so" (or longer).

As young women in their late teens and early twenties, teachers certainly could not afford to purchase a home, nor in many cases could they afford to rent even the most modest room or apartment. Boarding around provided teachers the opportunity to live within their financial means, especially if they were charged no or very minimal room and board. But for all the advantages of boarding around, there were also drawbacks. Nelson points to several.

Boarding around allowed the district school board, if it was their choice, to put out to bid the hosting of a teacher. The family that offered the lowest bid would be chosen by the board to host the district's teacher for that term. This was seen as a cost saving approach for the taxpayers. However, in such situations, little or no attention might be paid to how comfortable a teacher was with their living arrangement or conditions.

Sometimes a teacher lived with a family without having to pay room and board. However, when that was the case, according to Nelson, "Not infrequently, one of the homes would be that of the district superintendent who had absolute power over the teacher. Boarding, by definition, left the woman dependent. As long as the teacher did not have to pay the families with whom she boarded, she could not negotiate the terms of the arrangement. Sleeping quarters might be shared with other family members, and the routine household responsibilities which fell on women in the household would be expected of the female boarder as well."

In addition, the expectation that teachers would live with local families tended to isolate teachers from their teaching peers or contemporaries. Nelson writes, "At a time when the distinction between woman's work and man's work was becoming more extreme and women increasingly came to rely on each other for emotional and intellectual support, the isolation from close friends, colleagues and family must have been painful for some."

Finally, in Vermont when it came to being hired as a teacher and then keeping her job, "Morals came first, literary qualifications second." According to Nelson, "Without an independent set of credentials (a state-issued teaching license), teachers necessarily depended on community definitions of suitability. The law required the observation of teachers, and society demanded this observation during the teacher's leisure time." This scrutiny was intended to assure a community that a teacher's morals and behavior were consistent with those in that particular community.

While this arrangement might have been reassuring to a particular community, living with families, especially under real or imagined scrutiny, could cause a teacher to feel observed and ultimately judged in a very personal way. When morality was the major criterion by which teachers were hired, retained, or fired, biased judgments by a hosting family, especially if it was a locally prominent one, could unfairly jeopardize a teacher's employment.

For these and other reasons, the practice of boarding around became less common in the latter decades of the 19th century. In general, teachers began to be viewed as professionals with professional needs of adequate time and space to prepare their lessons and perform their duties.

Note: *While they might have been regarded as professionals, as recently as the 1930s in Wilmington, female teachers could not get married and expect to keep their jobs. Wilmington teacher Margaret Greene is quoted in Bernice Barnett's article, "Growing Up In Wilmington," published in the 1990 Old Home Week edition of the Cracker Barrel: "My teaching career ended (in 1939) when I married Kendrick Greene because in those days if you were married you couldn't be a teacher." However, she continued, "During World War II teachers were scarce, so married women were allowed to teach."*

In addition to teachers being viewed more and more as professionals, boarding around became less common because the manner of paying for education was changing. Instead of only families with children in the schools, or families in general, paying for those schools, the Vermont legislature passed a law in 1864 that would fund a district's school based upon its grand list. According to Nelson, "This legislation was part of a larger policy to redistribute the cost of maintaining education to make it fall proportionate to real property rather than the number of children who used the schools." Note: *This system of taxing property continues in some form throughout the United States and, of course, here in Vermont.*

As the 19th century came to a close, even though boarding around was no longer a required or expected practice, teachers in Vermont and most likely in Wilmington continued to lead a frugal life. Margaret (Covey) Greene was one such teacher. In Bernice Barnett's article, Mrs. Greene recalled, "My first school was the East Dover North Street School. I boarded with the Clarence Moore family and walked about one mile one way, except in stormy weather when I would get a ride on the milk team."

THE PAY AND GENDER GAP

In her article about the pay received by Wilmington's teachers, Marilyn Howe wrote that in the latter part of the 19th century, "The teachers average salary was $57.97 a year, which was about $4.83 weekly, plus his or her board. These figures are only average wages; some teachers received as little as $2 a week with their board."

On a national level, and throughout the 19th century and the first half of the 20th century, teacher salaries were consistently modest. Teaching was a less lucrative occupation than most others. For example, according to the National Bureau of Economic Research (NBER), in 1880, males as blacksmiths earned on average approximately $57 per month. In contrast, in *History of Education in Vermont,* author George Gary Bush, Ph.D. reports that in 1878, male teachers in Vermont were earning only $30.44 per month and in 1883, only $34.32 per month.

Also, according to the NBER, in the 1880s, female teachers were at a double disadvantage when it came to pay. They were paid only $20 per month, and their pay was comparable to that of unskilled female mill workers who earned $23 per month.

Comparing statistics like these can be tricky. The data cited above on male and female earnings in non-teaching jobs are national data. They are approximations and they are averages. The data in Bush's book are from Vermont. And even though it might seem like we're "comparing apples and oranges," a basic examination of the data clearly demonstrates that in the latter 1800s, male teachers were paid considerably less than males working at jobs requiring minimal formal education. Female teachers were earning pay less than or comparable to that earned by women performing mill work. And in making gender comparisons in the teaching profession, Vermont's female teachers generally were earning significantly smaller salaries than their male counterparts.

Note: *Identifying and describing the reasons for these disparities in pay are beyond the scope of this book. However, for those who are interested, Margaret Nelson's article, "Vermont Female Schoolteachers in the Nineteenth Century," offers an in-depth analysis of the social and economic conditions that caused them. It can be found on the Internet.*

CHAPTER 5

The School Calendar

When I was a state representative (1987-1997), I served for four years as vice-chair of the House education committee. At one point during those years, my committee chair and I introduced a bill to extend the school year in Vermont from 175 to 210 ten days.

We doubted the bill would ever pass, nor did we use our committee positions to promote its consideration. But we did believe that a school year that was based on a 19th century agrarian calendar needed to be re-evaluated. However, what I did not know at the time was that Vermont's then- and still-current school year of 175 days was already far longer than what the actual 19th century agrarian calendar had once been.

IN THE 19TH CENTURY

In 1866, according to author George Gary Bush, Vermont's school year lasted 23-24 weeks. By the mid-1880s, the school year in Vermont was somewhat longer. It's important to note that before the turn of the century (19th to 20th), the so-called school "year" was divided into multi-week terms often coinciding with the seasons of the farming calendar, a district's student population, or how long a session a district could afford. Note: *A reminder: into the early 20th century, towns often had several if not many small, neighborhood districts, each with its own school. At one time, Wilmington had 16. School terms among these schools often varied in length.*

However, whether the school year consisted of consecutive weeks or multi-week terms, Bush cautions that "the average number of days' attendance for each scholar was only 88; that is, 48 days were lost by irregular attendance." Bush offers no explanations for this 64 percent attendance rate. However, factors such as farm or home chores, child employment, illness, transportation issues, and parental indifference to education often contributed to truancy.

Note: *In her article, "When Children Were Property," in the May 18, 2024 edition of the Rutland Herald, Joanna Tebbs Young offers one explanation for sporadic school attendance. It came down to simple economics and child labor. "Most families during the 18th, 19th, and even into the 20th century, couldn't afford to raise children who didn't contribute to the household. As a result, rural families often kept their older children, especially their boys, away from school to work on the farm."*

Young continues: "In Vermont, most children worked on the farms, either their own family's or, if a family was too poor to own their own land, on a neighboring farm." In the latter situation, according to Young, "Fathers had a right to claim whatever money their children made." And, according to Young, in some of Vermont's population centers more than 40 percent of New England mill workers were children. Even as recently as 1910, "hundreds of children, many younger than 12, were still working in Vermont's mills."

In Wilmington, it appears that seasonal terms were very much the norm when it came to the length of the school calendar. In the May/June, 1934 issue of the *Mirror*, WHS senior, Virginia Howe, wrote an article entitled, "The Growth of Education in Wilmington." Describing when schools were in session in the mid-to-late 1800s, she wrote, "The school year consisted of a winter term and a summer term...This varied every year according to financial conditions."

Margaret Greene and Rita Staib, in their article "Wilmington's Rural or District Schools," elaborated on the 19th century two-term school year: "School was held at a time when it was most convenient for families to get along without the help of their children with farm work. For instance, the fall term would begin after the outside fall work had been completed, such as digging the potatoes, picking and storing the apples and other fruit, etc. A spring term would end before the children were needed at home for spring planting or haying. Winter terms had to be short enough so that children did not have to walk to school in the coldest of the winter weather."

As the 19th century came to an end, discussion of the school calendar focused less on season-based school terms and more on the number of weeks in a school year. In 1898, Wilmington superintendent of schools Earnest Maynard in his annual report recommended that, "The school year ought to be lengthened to thirty-six weeks." This was prior to the construction of the Central School when the school year was approximately 24 weeks in length. Note: *I found no evidence that Mr. Maynard's recommendation materialized until the mid-20th century.*

IN THE EARLY 20TH CENTURY

The issue of school year length re-emerged in 1901. Wilmington Central School teacher and principal, James Lobban, offered his second annual report to the Wilmington school directors. Within the previous few years, the school year had been extended, but he was advocating for an even longer one. He wrote, "The addition of four weeks has given a far better opportunity to do a year's work in a year's time. The year should be made four weeks longer yet, if the Wilmington schools are to be brought up to the highest standard of work. We must not expect a child's mind to be completely equipped for lifework by about 900 hours of school work per year for nine or ten years any more than we expect a man's body to be completely developed at fifteen."

In order to address the school calendar issue, the warning for Wilmington's 1901 town meeting included the following article: "To see if the town will sustain more than 28 weeks of school during the ensuing year." If Mr. Lobban had his way, the school year would soon be 32 weeks long, just three weeks shy of Vermont's current 175 day- or 35-week minimum school year.

Concurrent with Mr. Lobban's advocacy for a longer school year was the passage by Vermont's legislature in 1902 of an act making 33 weeks the minimum length of the school year for a Vermont high school. In 1903, Wilmington's school superintendent, John Stetson, pushed for an even longer school year recommending in his annual report that "...for the coming year the High School be in session thirty-four weeks, and that after next year all the schools in the town be given a similar length."

IN THE MID-20TH CENTURY

In 1932, Wilmington school directors Dora Hubbard, Leslie Adams, and Porter Fitch contemplated lengthening the school year, especially since they were carrying forward a fund balance into the next fiscal year and perhaps could afford to do so. But this was 1932, the height of the Great Depression. Adding days or weeks to the Wilmington school year would have to wait.

To that end, the directors wrote to the voters in their annual report, "Although we agree that two weeks more of school would be of value to every pupil, in view of the continuance of 'hard times' we believe a decrease of 5c (cents) in the school tax would be a benefit to more and would be a great assistance to some other department of our town. Therefore we recommend that the town maintain 34 weeks of school in the grades, and 36 weeks in the high school for the coming year, as required by law."

By 1947, according to the school directors' report, Wilmington's schools were in session for the minimum state-required length of 36 weeks for the high school and 35 weeks for the elementary grades. In 1951, according to superintendent of schools, James Gunn, the Vermont legislature passed a law requiring a minimum of 170 days for elementary school students and 175 days for those in high school.

IN THE 21ST CENTURY

Today, and for all grades K-12, the length of the school year in Vermont remains at a minimum of 175 days. If a district wishes to have a longer school year, the voters of that district are free to do so as part of a negotiated contract with their school faculty and staff.

CHAPTER 6

Teaching in the Early 1900s: A Personal Story

In 1916, my Grandmother Larsen graduated from high school in Schuylerville, NY, a small town 45 miles north of Albany. She was 18 years old. That summer she enrolled at the Oneonta Normal School in Oneonta, New York. "And then, after six weeks," she once recalled with some amusement and self-deprecation, "I was a teacher."

She continued, "The teaching certificate I earned permitted me to teach for three years before I'd have to return to school for additional training at summer school or a regular teachers school."

By 1916, teacher pay, working conditions, and living conditions were improving from those in the 19th century. But, of course, these improvements were in comparison to the less than desirable pay and conditions of that century. Note: *As you read about my grandmother's teaching experiences in her late teens and early twenties, you'll notice some similarities to teaching in the 19th century described in the previous chapters of this book.*

My grandmother's first teaching job was in East Postenkill, New York, 50 miles southwest of Wilmington, VT. She lived with the trustee of the school, who was elected (perhaps comparable to today's school board chair), his wife and her mother, and, as Grandma described it, "their little kid who was a pest. The boy's grandmother and his mother just fussed over him all the time." Grandma Larsen earned $10.00 per week and paid $3.50 each week to her host family for room, meals, and laundry.

My grandmother Larsen in 1940, outside the one room school in rural New York where she first taught in 1916.

Grandma described the location of this small school: "It was way up. Oh, talk about rural. But I had a lot of fun up there too," she said with a laugh. "And there were boys (students) who were bigger than I was."

Grandma recalled that there were times during her first year of teaching that she would take her knitting or crochet work to do between classes. But, she recalled, as a teacher she also had a lot of work to do. "As an 18 year-old teacher," she said to me, "I didn't know much more than the kids."

During that year, she attended square dances in the area. "Gosh, and they used to invite me to go to dances, you know. And I'd go, and afterwards I'd walk all the way home (to where she was boarding), alone, several miles, in the dark. And there wasn't a soul on the road. And it would be midnight. I wouldn't say I wasn't afraid, but I did it because it (attending the dances) was so much fun. Oh, dear..."

Before living in East Postenkill, Grandma recalled, she had never square danced because, she said with gentle self-effacing sarcasm, "We were too modern in Schuylerville."

Although she liked her job and the people in East Postenkill, Grandma was eager to find a job closer to her family home. So she took a teaching job in Greenwich, NY, close enough so she could go home on weekends. She said, "I wouldn't return (to her home in the school district) on Sunday night. If I went Sunday night, one of the young men over there would have met me with a horse and buggy and taken me from the end of the trolley line. But, no, I had to wait until Monday morning because I might miss some fun at home on Sunday night."

On those Monday mornings she would take the first trolley at 6 a.m. Even on those cold winter mornings, she would walk the final four miles to her school; the same four miles she'd walk on Friday afternoons to catch the trolley as she went home to Schuylerville.

There were a few times, as family lore tells it, when it was so cold walking to or from the trolley, Grandma would wrap newspapers around herself underneath her coat for insulation.

Within a year or two, as Grandma described it, she "got into a big school, with three teachers. And it was a brick school. I think I had third, fourth, and fifth grades. I liked that." This school was close enough for Grandma to live at home. It was, Grandma said, only a couple of miles each way. She taught there for a year. "But by that time I decided," she paused with a chuckle, "the kids didn't sit still enough, and I couldn't stand it, and I decided I didn't want to teach anymore." Courtship with my grandfather and marriage would soon follow.

While the experiences of individual teachers in the early 20th century were affected by many factors, my grandmother's experiences likely provide some insight into the lives of teachers in those days, including those in Wilmington, VT.

Part II

Wilmington's Schools:
Building for the Future

CHAPTER 7

The Consolidation of Wilmington's Schools

The Dix School, a district school located at the corner of Jacksonville Rd. and Ward's Beach Rd.

PRESENT-DAY SCHOOL DISTRICT CONSOLIDATION: ACT 46

On July 1, 2015, Vermont's governor, Peter Shumlin, signed into law what became known as Act 46. The stated intent of the law was to encourage and facilitate (some would say *force*) small school districts to consolidate with other small districts to form larger districts and thereby increase efficiencies, course offerings, and opportunities for students. Many school districts resented the law, some opposed it, and still others defied it.

Due to the foresight of Wilmington's and Whitingham's school directors and citizens, Act 46 had a minimal impact on their schools. In November, 2003, twelve years before Act 46, the voters of each town approved the creation of the Twin Valley unified school district. And in September, 2004, Wilmington and Whitingham middle and high school students began learning together. By the time Act 46 was signed into law in 2015, the two towns had already merged their elementary, middle, and high schools into one K-12 district.

The Wilmington-Whitingham merger was never proposed in anticipation of Act 46 or anything like it. When the voters of each town approved the merger in 2003, those who voted in favor of it did so believing it would provide improved and increased course offerings as well as other opportunities for their students. It would also create a more favorable economy of scale making purchases of products and services more efficient and less costly. In addition, supporters of the merger believed that combining the student populations would generate a more robust academic, social, and extra-curricular environment for all students.

Facilities were also an issue. When the merger was approved by the voters, the newest section of Wilmington High School was already 21 years old. The oldest section of the building was 104 years old. A Wilmington/Whitingham merger would eventually allow the new district to use two buildings (Wilmington's Deerfield Valley Elementary School and Whitingham's K-12 school) instead of the then-current three. Under the consolidation, Wilmington High School as a building would remain. However, as an educational institution that had existed for 105 years, it would close.

The motives and stated advantages behind Act 46 were not new. The benefits of school consolidation were touted in the early 1960s by then newly-elected Democratic Governor Phil Hoff and again in the early 1980s by newly-elected Democratic governor, Madeleine Kunin. However, both governors faced stiff opposition from school boards and citizens in general, especially those in smaller towns where local control was more than a political maxim; it was an established way of life.

EARLIER SCHOOL DISTRICT CONSOLIDATION: THE VICIOUS ACT OF '92

But let's go back even further than the early 2000s, the 1980s, or even the 1960s. More than 100 years before either the Twin Valley merger vote or Act 46, Wilmington's school directors had to decide whether to comply with a school consolidation mandate from Montpelier. In 1892, the Vermont legislature enacted a law that required school consolidation. Until then and even after, there were many one-room and two-room neighborhood schoolhouses in Vermont, also known as district schools, that were dispersed throughout their respective towns and located near clusters of families.

Their scattered distribution was due to a lack of transportation for many of their students. Traveling several miles from outlying farms to a single centralized school and back again by walking or by wagon was simply impractical. In addition, and as soon as possible after the end of the school day, children often needed to return to their family farms or homes to do essential chores.

Certainly the image of the small, white clapboarded or brick one-room schoolhouse represents what was good about education in 19th and early 20th century education. In the Vermont Historical Society's audio recording, "School Consolidation: Farewell to the One-room Schoolhouse," the narrator describes the appeal and the benefits of many of Vermont's one-room schoolhouses: "Many former students and teachers agree that the attributes of the one-room school - close, family-like relationships, multi-age learning situations, and a strong sense of community spirit - often offset the drawbacks of cold drafty buildings, inadequate teaching materials, substandard outhouse facilities and a lack of professional support. And whatever gains are credited to school consolidation, in many communities, the loss of the one-room school has removed a social center not easily replaced."

Consistent with this perspective is a statement in "Schools in Wilmington," written by Marilyn Howe and presented by her at Wilmington's sesquicentennial town meeting in 1941. She wrote, "The district (one-room) school was the center of business and social functions. It was the place where town meetings were held...Each district school was the center of one distinct neighborhood or area of the town."

Understandably, the school consolidation law in 1892 was not well received in many of Vermont's smaller towns, especially those in which district schools were both the focal point of civic activity and a traditional and respected setting for educating the town's children.

The 1892 law had a major impact on Vermont's district schools. To say that it significantly reduced their number is an understatement. According to authors Samuel Hand, Anthony Marro, and Stephen Terry in their book, *Philip Hoff: How Red Turned Blue in the Green Mountain State*, "Way back in 1892 the legislature had forced consolidation of the multiple tiny school districts - neighborhood schools for the most part - within most towns into a single town district. That had reduced Vermont's 2,214 school districts by almost 90 percent. For years afterward, the law was referred to by advocates of local schools as 'the Vicious Act of '92.'"

WILMINGTON'S EARLY DISTRICT SCHOOLS

For many current Vermonters, the one-room school house experience is an abstraction, something we read about in history books. But for others it is a collection of fond memories. In an undated paper written before she died in 2000, Wilmington resident Evelyn Fitch Keefe described her education in the early twentieth century: "I'm so glad I attended a rural school. It was small, it had all kinds of variety and down-to-earth every day-ish studies."

Her paper includes excerpts from the 1881-1882 annual report written by her great uncle and then-superintendent of schools Erastus Fitch. In his report, Superintendent Fitch described in detail for each of Wilmington's 13 district schools the effectiveness of its teacher and its curriculum.

Mr. Fitch's commentary and evaluations of the district schools' teachers and programs are overwhelmingly positive. However, almost twenty years before the construction of Wilmington's Central School, and ten years before the "Vicious Act of '92, he offered his strong support for consolidation: "In conclusion, allow me to say several obstacles in the way of success in our common (district) schools are purely incident to the system now in use. Many of them would be entirely removed by abolishing the present District system and adopting the Town system, which would give uniformity in operation and expense, place the schools on a much higher plane of usefulness, and give new impulse to the cause of education."

According to Marilyn Howe's essay, prior to 1882, some of the Wilmington neighborhoods where district schools were located included the current location of Pettee Memorial Library; near the current location of the Averill Stand at the intersection of Vermont routes 9 and 100; on the eastern shore of Lake Raponda; and in Medburyville. In 1882, two of the 16 districts were "annexed to the town of Dover" and another district was "dissolved" into two other districts. During this time, according to Marilyn Howe, "Throughout the schools the total attendance was 265 pupils and there were twenty-seven teachers employed."

In the 2009 newsletter of the Historical Society of Wilmington, Leland Cross described life as a young student in the Coldbrook District School: "We all took our lunch pails and often built a fire behind the school or down by the brook and toasted our sandwiches. The 9th or 8th grade students would take turns as janitor which required going early to sweep the floor and build a fire in the wood stove heater. We often walked a mile or so to school. The school was on a dirt road which we used as a baseball field."

George Davis wrote in the same newsletter, "In the winter the mothers would take turns and bring something hot for us to eat for lunch."

Another district school was the one-room Castle School. It is featured in a video entitled, "Little White Schoolhouse on the Lake - A Hoot Toot and Whistle for Vermont's Lost Valley." The video was produced by Martin Kasindorf in 2011. The parents of his wife, Irma Hawkins, once owned the schoolhouse located on the shore of Harriman Reservoir (aka Lake Whitingham). They converted it for use as a lakeside cottage. It, along with the privy, still stands and can be found close to the road on the southern side of Castle Hill.

Mary Buffum Maynard (1899-1980) was a student at Castle School from 1905 until 1912. She is interviewed in Martin Kasindorf's video: "When Mountain Mills was flourishing, they had between 30 and 35 children down here at Castle School. And then, eventually, they built a two-room schoolhouse at Mountain Mills." Mountain Mills was a small town positioned just west of Wilmington on the road to Bennington. Note: *More on Mountain Mills appears at the end of this chapter.*

She continues, "It was just simply the basic three Rs, and also history and geography; and we did have penmanship. I remember that we had a wood stove...and I used to stand right close to the stove, and every one of us that had these wool skirts or dresses, at some time or other, it burned holes in their wool garments because it did heat up terrifically.

"And they used to spank the little ones, just the same as the mothers would; and then they had this ruler - that was called a 'ferrule' - and they used to hit it pretty hard on the hands." Note: *Small town Vermont continues to reveal many interesting and surprising connections and relationships. During my research, I saw a photograph of Mary Buffum Maynard in her later years, and she looked familiar. It turns out that I had met her. I knew her daughter, Jackie, and taught four of Jackie's children - Mary's grandchildren. In addition, I taught at WHS with the husband of one of Mary's granddaughters. Several years later, Mary's son, Reggie, was my opponent in 1990 for our district's seat in the Vermont House of Representatives.*

According to Kasindorf, the Castle School was established sometime between 1840 and 1845. Thirty-six children were educated there in 1849 during an 18-week session. Marilyn Howe reported that in most or perhaps all local district schools, "The school terms were comparatively short - six weeks in the summer and six weeks in the winter."

Most district schools opened and closed intermittently. If there were enough students in a specific district (or neighborhood area) to warrant a district school, the school was open. If, as defined by state law, there were too few district students in a given year, the school was closed for that year, and the students were transported to a nearby district school. In the next year if the student population increased in that school's district, it would reopen.

Sometimes, however, a school would remain open simply as a matter of convenience for those families residing in the area. Wilmington's 1932 Auditors' Report (aka the Town Report) stated that, "Raponda and Cold Brook schools have been closed this year, and we think that for still another year it would be best to transport the children from these districts to the village (central) school." But the report also highlighted the occasional need to keep a district school open even if the enrollment was small: "Fitch school has a small enrollment, but due to difficulty of transportation in a severe winter we felt it would be wise to keep it open."

In some cases, Wilmington's school directors appear to have been especially responsive to the needs of even a few parents and students. In the February 1, 1935 Auditors' Report the school directors wrote that, "Schools opened in September with only one new teacher. Mrs. Earlene Fitch at Dix (school). Because of unsettled conditions it seemed best to have a teacher for Dix on a weekly contract, but with the entrance of three new pupils in November it was decided to keep it open for the year, and the parents wished us to retain Mrs. Fitch." For her 19 weeks of teaching Mrs. Fitch was paid $380. Note: *After retiring from teach-*

ing, Mrs. Fitch became Wilmington's town clerk and was still serving in that capacity when I arrived in Wilmington in 1972.

CONCLUSION

By 1899, the citizens of Wilmington determined that the time had come to consolidate and centralize their schools. This could have been due to specific or general dissatisfaction with the small and widely dispersed district schools. It could have been a response to the Vicious Act of '92, the legislative mandate to school districts to close or consolidate their small schools. Or, of course, it could have been a combination of these and other factors.

Regardless, the decision to consolidate resulted in the 1899 construction of a new school centrally located in the village of Wilmington. That new school would serve Wilmington's students as the Central School and later as Wilmington High School for more than 100 years until its closing in 2004.

ADDENDUM: THE MOUNTAIN MILLS SCHOOL

Note: *As its own community with its own identity and facilities, Mountain Mills had its own school. Accordingly, it deserves mention in this chapter.*

In the early 1890s, the Hoosac Tunnel and Wilmington railroad was completed. It connected Wilmington with Mountain Mills, a small but flourishing logging and mill community to the west and located at the northern end of what would eventually become Harriman Reservoir. The railroad also connected Wilmington and Mountain Mills with Jacksonville, Whitingham, Readsboro, and a connector line in Massachusetts. The purpose of the railroad, according to Martin Kasindorf in his "Little White Schoolhouse" video, was to "fetch the lumber and pulp produced in the Deerfield Valley for mills down (the Deerfield) river."

As the 19th century came to an end, and due at least in part to the railroad and the commerce it generated, the Wilmington area was growing. In 1894, the company town of Mountain Mills was planned and then built where the two branches of the Deerfield River merge (on the south side of Route 9). According to Kasindorf, a boarding house for single men and row houses for mill workers and their families were built, along with a water tower, a general store, an office building, a post office, and a six-bed hospital.

Although Wilmington had a relatively new Central school, built in 1899 (more on that in the next chapter), in 1917 and 1918, a schoolhouse was built in Mountain Mills. According to the February 1, 1918 school directors report, the plan was to close the Medbury District school and send its students to the new Mountain Mills school. However, according to the report, "the question of getting them there caused great annoyance because of the fact that transportation would have to be provided going around\over the Castle bridge, as the School Board were not willing to assume any responsibility by reason of the children crossing the dyke over the dam..."

The Castle District school was also closed around this time. Its students were sent to either the Mountain Mills school or the Central School in Wilmington's village. According to Kasindorf, the third (uppermost) floor of the Central School was used to accommodate the Mountain Mills children while their schoolhouse was being constructed."

In the late 1970s, in a paper they wrote for their local history class, Wilmington High School students Myrna Green and Marcia Green described Mountain Mills' new school: "A school was built in 1917 to 1918. It cost $5,087 to build...It had two rooms and enrolled fifty to sixty students. There were two teachers...Mr. Van Wyck taught grades one through four. The school went from grade one to grade eight. The students who wished to continue their 'book learning' went to Wilmington High School."

Note: *According to the Greens, the original budgeted cost for the school was $4500. The plan was to have no basement and to heat the building with one or more wood stoves. However, the Vermont State Board of Health and its sanitary engineer required the building to have a basement as well as a "heating apparatus," perhaps an early 20th century version of central heating. Regardless, the building was still heated with wood.*

Mountain Mills' population continued to grow, and the school's size soon became inadequate. In his article, "What Lies Beneath the Lost Town of Mountain Mills" (sentinelsource.com - the Keene Sentinel, 8/6/2019), Eric Stanway wrote regarding the growth in Mountain Mills, "There was only a bit of a hiccup when it was discovered that the town school was inadequate to accommodate the town's 52 students, and some of them had to be shipped over to neighboring Wilmington."

In spite of this growth, the brief lifespan of Mountain Mills was coming to an end, and the community would soon be submerged. In 1909, Henry Harriman and Malcolm Chase, described by Martin Kasindorf as "two Boston industrialists," formed the New England Power Company (NEPCO) and began the purchase of river rights in the Deerfield River watershed. They also purchased 400 local farms and the company town of Mountain Mills. Central New England was hungry for electric power, and NEPCO was formed to feed that hunger.

A dam (reportedly the world's largest earthen dam at the time) was built upstream in Somerset to harness the power of the river. It was completed in 1912. Another dam, this one located in Whitingham at the southern end of what is now Harriman Reservoir, was completed several years later.

According to Martin Kasindorf, in February, 1924, the spring runoff in the Deerfield watershed began to fill the newly created reservoir, and Mountain Mills would soon disappear: "Mountain Mills was closed after 30 years. Its machines sold off, its schoolhouse burned to the ground...And so the spring runoff came, and it ran up against the waiting dam. The Deerfield (River) backed up into the valley, inundating farms, mills, and the small settlement of Sage City...2184 acres drowned

- a treasured place with them. Three cemeteries were moved; 14 miles of roads were abandoned."

By May, 1924, what remained of Mountain Mills had disappeared beneath the waters of Harriman Reservoir.

CHAPTER 8

Wilmington's New Central School

Wilmington Central School, ca.1900

CONSOLIDATION AND EARLY PROGRAMS FOR HIGH SCHOOL-AGE STUDENTS

Following the consolidation act passed by the Vermont legislature in 1892, Wilmington began to consolidate its small neighborhood district schools into a larger unified system. The 1900 reunion edition of the *Deerfield Valley Times* appears to have supported the notion of school consolidation: "The town system of schools superseded the old district system in 1893, and whatever may have been the advantages of the well known 'deestrict schools,' (district schools) there is no doubt that a central control and a uniform plan of work for all the schools gives far greater satisfaction in every particular."

Marilyn Howe in her 1941 essay, "Schools in Wilmington," wrote that in 1893, a year after passage of the so-called Vicious Act of '92 and six years before the construction of the new Central School building, at least some centralization of Wilmington's education programs was already under way: "A short time before the building of the new high (Central) school, the town system of public schools replaced the old system of district schools. A carefully planned system was introduced into all the schools providing for nine grades (K-8) under the high school. The trend began towards consolidation of the many schools into fewer and larger schools, each operating on a similar plan with similar textbooks."

Decades before the construction of the Central School in 1899, and in an apparent attempt to better serve Wilmington's older students, two "select schools" were established. The select schools were actually programs that offered advanced courses for students. Marjorie White (WHS '24) wrote a lengthy article in the March, 1924 issue of the school's literary magazine, the *Mirror,* entitled, "The History of Wilmington High School." Miss White wrote that there were no records of exactly when these select school programs originated. However, she did state that by 1856, "they were being held each fall, and had been for some time."

She described how the mid-19th century select school arrangement worked: "The little district schools kept two terms, a summer and a winter term of twelve weeks each. During the fall, some enterprising young college graduate would rent the village school and charge tuition to all the students who enrolled to take advanced subjects not taught in the 'little red school house.'"

Miss White continued by citing "one of the students of the old-time school" who told her that, "the tuition for a simple (select school) course in English grammar cost three dollars, and the pupil was charged extra if he took mathematics or any of the languages."

Miss White quoted a former select school student, Clark Chandler, who said that a variety of classes were offered including English, Latin, French, Greek, arithmetic, algebra, and geometry: "When I asked whether chemistry or any science was given," she wrote, "my informant remarked that some of his classmates had made water burn and caused some excitement by letting things blow up, so he guessed they did have something of a sort. Evidently, our grandfathers had as much fun doing chemistry experiments as some of their grandchildren do."

In the May/June, 1934 issue of the *Mirror*, WHS senior Virginia Howe indicated that later on the select schools were located in specific locations in town. She described them in an article entitled, "The Growth of Education in Wilmington." She wrote, "One of these schools was in the upper part of the fire house (close to where the Pettee Memorial Library is currently located); the other, in the vestry of the Congregational church. The two schools were rivals. The persons going to the school held over the fire house were called 'goats,' while the ones from the rival school were nicknamed 'sheep'... Pupils came in from other towns and boarded themselves in homes in the village. We find that the curriculum included the advanced subjects of bookkeeping and algebra, besides the ordinary grammar school courses."

Virginia Howe described in her article how in Wilmington the high school concept grew: "After several years passed (perhaps in the early 1890s), a regular high school was started in the upper part of the fire house. There were fourteen pupils ready to begin high school subjects. At first the whole school was taught by one teacher. Rhetoric and zoology were among the subjects taught. There was one session of school each day from about 8:30 until 12:00."

According to Virginia Howe, by 1897, two additional classrooms were in use. One was in the parlor of the Universalist church, which according to Marjorie White, "was a rude affair, for the room was badly lighted and there were no desks, only long benches." The other was in a room "over the (local) bank," according to Miss Howe.

Virginia Howe did not cite any published sources for her article in the *Mirror*. However, it's possible or even likely that in 1934 she was able to interview former students who in the latter 19th century had attended the select schools or high school programs she was describing.

While these select schools might have been adequate for some of Wilmington's students, in his 1898 annual report, Wilmington superintendent of schools Earnest A. Maynard offered a strong argument for a new, centralized school building: "The greatest need of your schools is consolidation. By bringing the pupils from all parts of the town to the center, the work which now requires twelve teachers could be done by six…The schools could be graded better; better teachers could be hired and the children could be given a much better education than now, while the expense would be no greater."

PLANNING THE NEW CENTRAL SCHOOL

Whether it was in response to Superintendent Maynard's urging, the Vicious Act of '92, the work of locally-elected education leaders, or a combination of these and other factors, by the late 1890s planning for the new centralized school building was under way.

According to the plan for the new school, it would be constructed on the Wilmington fairground, and the majority of Wilmington's students would attend there. But according to Marilyn Howe, even when the Central School was being planned, there were still "four rural schools, namely Cold Brook, Cutting, Fitch, and Dix." But as if to assure her audience that all of Wilmington's students, including those in the small district schools, were receiving an equal education, she wrote, "These schools are operated on the same principles as the central school, and the system of education is uniform throughout the town."

With plans for the new Central School proceeding, the February 17, 1899 edition of the *Deerfield Valley Times* included an article entitled,

"What it Will Look Like When Finished - Floor Plans as Drawn by the Architect."

According to the *Times* article, the new school building "will be located on the fair ground at or near the height of land in the rear of the place formerly owned by E.A. Willard, Jr. It will front toward East Main St."

The building was described as being two stories in height. And, "Each story will finish 11 ft. clear. The first floor will contain three class rooms of ample size to accommodate 40 pupils each. The second floor will have two class rooms; one for the Grammar, one for the High school with a large recitation room (classroom) in connection. The class rooms are all lighted from one side and one end as to bring the light to the rear and left of pupils. The windows are 7 ft. 1 inch in height and 3 ft. 8 inches in width; six windows in each room so arranged as to perfectly light all parts of the room. Each room will have a closet for books and supplies."

Note: *I was curious about the statement regarding bringing "the light to the rear and left of pupils." Was this lighting electric or was it sunlight? If it was sunlight, were the building and its windows oriented to favor the 88-90 percent of students who were right-handed? The website* https://www.heritageall.org/wp-content/uploads/2013/03/Americas-One-Room-Schools-of-the-1890s.pdf *may provide a general answer below but one that is not Central School-specific.*

Windows on one side were favored by those who thought that light coming from two directions (cross-lighting) could harm the eyes. Therefore, some schools in the 1890s were directed to put in windows on the side where light could fall over the left shoulder. It was a great idea for right-handed pupils, however, no thought was given to the left-handed pupil as the left arm blocked out the light. When possible, the windows were placed on the north side of the building to provide even, year-round light. Windows were the primary source of light during the day. Kerosene lamps were used for special evening events. Half- curtains, usually made by the teacher, were used to cover the windows in order to let light in, but to discourage daydreaming out the window.

Note: *One might conclude that if a teacher wanted to orient the student desks to better illuminate them, she could have simply rotated them. On the other hand, each desk's wrought iron feet were sometimes fastened to the classroom floor. Some 60 years later, lighting was still a problem in some classrooms, in this case in the Central School's newly constructed brick addition (1956). In their 1961 annual report the school directors wrote, "Light reflection on the chalkboards in the new building has always been a problem, so in the fall the board had spotlights put over those boards. They have greatly helped the condition."*

The 1899 *Deerfield Valley Times* article continued its description of the new school building: "Corridors are commodious and well lighted and will contain coat and hat rooms sufficient to accommodate the schools. There will be a basement under the whole building nine feet in height which will contain the furnaces, playrooms, and sanitary appliances. The girl's play-room (is) in the southern end and is 24 ft.x 45 ft. The boys' play-room is in the opposite end, and is of nearly the same dimensions. Both rooms are reached by a separate flight of stairs, and there is also an entrance to each from the rear.

"Room for furnaces is in the center with ample space for fuel. The building will be heated throughout by two latest improved 'Thatcher Tubular' warm air furnaces set in battery; or so arranged that one can be used to warm the building in the spring and fall when but little heat is needed. Note: *The Thatcher tubular furnaces were manufactured in Newark, NJ. They burned coal and were quite advanced for their time. Further information on them can be found on the Internet.*

"Each room will have an improved system of ventilation, so arranged that the warming and ventilating is under perfect control of the teacher.

"The plastering will be of hard mortar, a new process for mortar that is hard as stone. The finish or trimming will be spruce, painted. On account of the size of the building and the appropriation, all the trim, both exterior and interior, will be plain but substantial. The roof will be covered with No. 1 slate.

"There will be no belfry.

"The latest thing in bells is an electronic gong 12 to 14 inches in diameter, placed on the outside of the building and connected with the principal's desk.

"As there has been no provision made for a bell (a traditional large school bell in a belfry), here is a chance for someone with public spirit to make the new schoolhouse a donation.

"There will be an article in the warning for town meeting asking the voters to appropriate a sum of money for the purpose of cementing the floor of the basement; also to back plaster the building."

THE COMPLETED NEW CENTRAL SCHOOL

In mid-August, 1900, Wilmington held its decennial Old Home Week. Being celebrated for only the second time, this Old Home Week was special because it ushered in a new century. But on a more local and possibly more meaningful level, it marked the beginning of a new era in public education in Wilmington. The construction of the new Central School building was complete, and it would house the vast majority of Wilmington's elementary and high school students. According to "One Hundred and Ninety Years of Progress," written by Barbara Haskins in 1941, "On the first floor were the first six grades and on the second floor were the high school rooms and the assembly room."

To commemorate Wilmington's 1900 Old Home Week, J. H. Walbridge compiled, and the *Deerfield Valley Times* published, an impressive compendium that celebrated Wilmington's attributes. Included in this is a congratulatory reference to a more centralized approach to education in the town: "With reference to the moral status, the social gifts and the harmony of good fellowship and public spirit, Wilmington outranks almost any other small New England town.

"The four churches (Baptist, Congregationalist, Methodist, and Universalist) representing different phases of religious belief, unite in conserving public morals; the social and literary institutions unify and crystalize public sentiment, while the new High School, more thoroughly graded and in closer touch with the other public schools of the town, is, under the present able management, laying broad and deep, the foundations of future intelligent and conscientious citizenship."

Described by the *Times* as both "substantial and convenient," the new school had four "compartments: primary, intermediate, grammar, and high." However, the *Times* added, "A kindergarten is greatly desired and needed." Construction of the new school building resulted in establishing "nine grades under the high school," all in the same building. And, the *Times* also added, "The tendency of the schools of the town is toward consolidation. During the past year, two of the outlying schools have been discontinued, one being merged with the village school (the new Central School), by the transportation of scholars (students)."

However, in spite of the tendency toward consolidation, not all students were educated in the new Central School building. The *Times* wrote, "Consolidation has the effect of giving the interest that comes from larger classes. At present there are seven schools in operation in addition to that in the village, the total attendance being around 250."

According to the *Times*, the course of study at the new school, "provides for as liberal an education as can be obtained in any school outside of large towns and cities; it gives a thorough preparation for active life-work."

Included in this course of study were, "Systematic practice in drawing and singing" which "rounded out the more prosaic work." In addition, the curriculum included "the study of nature in the forms of natural scenery, birds and plants."

Upon its completion, and as one might expect, the new Central School was clearly a symbol of local pride. According to the *Deerfield Valley Times*, it was located "on the site of the old fair ground, giving plenty of play room for the scholars...The building is imposing and commodious, containing four recitation rooms, a large assembly hall, and roomy entrance halls. The basement, which also contains the furnaces, has been fitted up into two large play rooms for the boys and girls. The system for heating and ventilation is perfect."

The primary, intermediate, and grammar classrooms were located on the first floor. The high school classrooms along with the assembly hall, were located on the second floor. There is no mention in the *Times* of the school's third floor, or attic.

THE FACULTY

The *Deerfield Valley Times Reunion Edition* suggested that only one teacher was responsible for each section or group of what would have been two- or three-grade groupings for first grade through eighth grade. The *Reunion Edition* proudly described the teachers: "The primary grade teacher (most likely grades 1-3), Miss Linda Douglas, is an experienced and trained teacher (who) has been doing very successful work...Mrs. Geo. Barber, a teacher of long and competent experience, is in charge of the intermediate room (most likely grades 4-6). The grammar school teacher (most likely grades 7 and 8), Miss Emma Clahane, a graduate of the Bridgewater (Mass.) Normal School, has met with great success in her work."

Even though the new Central School building had been completed only a year earlier, a high school program, according to the *Times*, was now in its fourth year, possibly in coordination with some or all of the district schools or select school programs. The Central School's principal and superintendent of all of Wilmington's town district schools was James A. Lobban. A native of Scotland, he came to the United States at the age of seven and lived in Milton, Massachusetts. He graduated from Middlebury College in 1898 and spent a year at Harvard studying English and earning an A.M. degree (Master of Arts). Note: *Wilmington High School's final principal (1988-2004), Frank Spencer, like Mr. Lobban, grew up in eastern Massachusetts and was Harvard educated. After the creation of Twin Valley High School in 2004, Mr. Spencer continued as its principal until his retirement in 2011.*

As with its descriptions of teachers Douglas, Barber, and Clahane, the *Deerfield Valley Times* spared no praise when it came to describing the professional performance of Mr. Lobban: "Mr. Lobban is doing earnest and thorough work in grading the schools of the town, with the view of the ultimate reception of the more advanced students into the high school. He possesses the unreserved esteem and confidence of directors, teachers, and pupils. Wilmington may very well be gratified with the present efficacy of her schools which is in a great measure due to the ability and enthusiasm that Mr. Lobban brings to his work."

Note: *The above quote refers to "the ultimate reception of the more advanced students into the high school." This suggests that students were required to apply for admission to the high school. This is supported in the August 20, 1909 edition of the Deerfield Valley Times: "An examination will be held at the Wilmington High school building August 26 and 27 for all those who have not taken the state examination that wish to enter the high school this fall. The examination will begin at 9 o'clock." However, passing the state's examination was optional. According to the school's 1910-1911 handbook, a prospective student did not have to pass or even take the examination, provided he could "give some assurance to the Principal that he can do the work of the school.*

It's unclear whether Principal Lobban was the sole educator in grades 9-12. As well educated as he was, especially for the early 20th century, the comprehensive nature of the high school curriculum might have made that a challenge. On the other hand, according to Marjorie White's article in the *Mirror* (March, 1924), he may very well have been up to that challenge. She wrote about Principal Lobban, "The subjects Mr. Lobban offered were English, including work in rhetoric, Latin, French, civil government, zoology, botany, physical geography, physics, astronomy, English history, ancient, mediaeval and modern history, algebra, geometry, business arithmetic, and bookkeeping."

And then, as if anticipating the obvious question of whether Mr. Lobban could have taught all of these subjects on his own, Miss White wrote, "It is a puzzle to me how Principal Lobban managed to teach all of these subjects, for if he had any assistants, I can find no mention of any."

THE HIGH SCHOOL CURRICULUM

In Wilmington the curriculum of the high school was impressive by early 20th century standards. The *Deerfield Valley Times* wrote, "The high school (program) is now in its fourth year. This year (1900) a definite course of study has been instituted under the capable direction of the present teacher, Mr. Lobban, leading to graduation in three years, with opportunity for a fourth year of advanced work. There are two courses, Latin-English, giving preparation for college, and English-Scientific."

The 1910 annual report of Reverend A.N. Blackford, Wilmington's school superintendent at the time, described in greater detail the two courses of study being offered at the high school. The college preparatory course consisted of four years each of English and Latin; two years of history (general and ancient); three years of math (algebra, geometry, review of algebra and geometry); two years of French; and one year of chemistry/physics. English classes met three times each week. All other classes met five times per week.

The general course or track consisted of four years of English; two years of history (general and ancient); two years of French; two years of math (algebra and commercial); and one year each of physical geography and physiology, commercial law and commercial geography, American history and civics, correspondence and bookkeeping, soils and animal husbandry, chemistry and physics. All classes met five times each week. English, however, met only three times per week. There is no information in Rev. Blackford's report that explains the differences between the number of recitations (classes) in a subject each week.

According to Marjorie White, within ten-to-fifteen years after the 1899 dedication of the Central School, improvements to the building were occurring. Large rooms were partitioned, a science laboratory was created, the heating and ventilation system was improved, a cement sidewalk was built, new blackboards were installed, and new books were purchased.

And, according to Miss White, "In 1915 a room was finished off in the attic for a domestic science (home economics) kitchen, but it was not immediately used for that purpose. The Teacher Training class used it for a classroom in 1917, and some time passed before domestic science work was taken up there."

MOVING FORWARD

With its emphasis on improving education and the facility that offered it, the town of Wilmington was very much in sync with 19th-century national trends in education. By the end of that century, the United States was becoming a more urban and industrialized society. In 1870, 25 percent of the US population was considered to be living in urban areas. By 1920, that percentage had doubled to 50 percent or more.

According to Encyclopedia.com, "The American high school was born in the nineteenth century, and although there were high schools as early as the 1820s and 1830s, these schools existed primarily for a small segment of the population. At the end of the (19th) century, adolescents and their families faced the unsettling consequences of the early commercial and industrial revolution, urban growth, and immigration — all of which rendered familiar strategies for personal mobility obsolete.

"In response, political activists and school reformers redefined the educational experiences of high school students, investing more money and reshaping existing secondary schools to confront the dilemmas of this new age. By the 1880s, especially in the Northeast, the free public high school was no longer an anomaly. Social reformers had eliminated most alternative forms of secondary instruction, such as tuition academies, seminaries, and other private institutions. Without a national ministry of education to dictate policy and implement reform, Americans built high schools through local initiative."

As rural and seemingly isolated as Wilmington might have been in the 1890s, its leaders and its citizens understood the importance of progressing with the times. Clearly, Wilmington was part of the national trend when it came to establishing a local, centralized school that included a robust high school program.

It might appear that the *Deerfield Valley Times* was guilty of hyperbole when describing the positive qualities of Wilmington's new Central School building and the educational benefits it offered. However, there can be no doubt that Wilmington's 1900 Old Home Week provided the perfect opportunity to celebrate the building and the institution it housed - an institution that would proudly serve its children, its citizens, and the community for the next 105 years.

But then, just two years later in 1902, Wilmington's superintendent of schools, John Stetson, urged the good citizens of Wilmington not to rest on their laurels. As superintendent, it was his responsibility to visit each district school and assess the teaching and learning occurring therein.

To drive home the benefits of further centralization, he wrote in his annual report contrasting the smaller district schools with the Central School, "During the past two terms I have spent fourteen afternoons in visiting schools...The outside (district) schools are doing fair work. Some of them, however, are too small. No teacher can obtain the best results in a school of five or six pupils of varying ages...." He stated that, "In general the schools of Wilmington are doing good work." But, he added, "A greater degree of centralization will lead to better results."

CONCLUSION

For several generations, Wilmington's 16 one-room district schools had provided for many of its children what was considered by most to

be an appropriately personalized and perfectly adequate educational experience. But times were changing and would continue to do so. School
centralization would continue in some form well into the 21st century,
and in Wilmington the Central School and the programs it housed
would continue to evolve with the times.

CHAPTER 9

The 1930 Addition

Wilmington Central School after the 1930 addition.

PLANNING FOR THE FUTURE

WHS principal Arthur L. Welcome in his 1929 report described the curricular offerings in Wilmington High School: "...four years of English, four years of Latin, four years of French, three years of mathematics, three years of Science, three years of History, one year of Community Civics, four years of Home Economics, and two years of Vocational Agriculture."

As impressive as these offerings might have been, in that same year Wilmington's superintendent of schools F.E. Sawyer advocated for an even broader selection of learning opportunities for Wilmington's high school students. He urged the citizens of Wilmington to think about the future when it came to their high school. He predicted that Wilmington, like other small Vermont towns, would soon be expected to offer educational opportunities similar to those provided for students in Vermont's larger towns.

Mr. Sawyer recommended offerings in "manual training" which would require added space for "shop work." He touted the benefits of adding a "special classroom" for "commercial" and bookkeeping courses - with "typewriters and other paraphernalia." He stressed the importance of "physical training and health instruction" as integral elements of student health, all of it being a "prime necessity for the boys and girls who have to contend with the strenuous demands of the times." Finally, Mr. Sawyer stressed the importance of drawing and art. He stated that these subjects were being taught by classroom teachers who, one can assume, were doing their best. However, he suggested there was room for improvement, writing that the teaching of art at WHS was being done in a "desultory fashion of the non-professional."

In addition to improving the curriculum, the Central School's administrators and the town's school directors were taking steps to make the building safer. In the summer of 1928, a tubular fire escape, as it was referred to in the 1929 School Directors' Report, was attached to the east side of the school. According to their report, this was done at least in part with the goal of the school receiving a "standard, if not a superior plate on the building."

Note: *During my years at WHS, I recall seeing in the main office a green metal sign or plaque, about the size of a license plate, mounted on a piece of wood. The January 25, 1939 issue of the "Brattleboro Reformer" includes a photo of WHS principal Newton Baker and school directors Merrill Haynes, Juliet Adams, and Claude Maher watching as Wilmington Superintendent of Schools Edward Boak affixes to the exterior of the*

Central School a metal "honor plate" declaring that the "high and central school" had been designated a "Superior School." The photo is in the files of the Historical Society of Wilmington, Vermont. The whereabouts of the plaque are currently unknown.

The tube fire escape from the second floor.

The tubular fire escape ran from the top (second) floor of the school to the ground. In the late 1940s, it was accessible through a small latched double door in the high school homeroom/classroom. This room ran the entire depth (north and south) of the school on its eastern side. Note: *When I was hired in 1972, the room served as the school's library but only for the next few years until the art room was located there and the library was moved to classroom spaces on the first floor of what was the 1899 building.*

The entrance to the tube was approximately three feet above the classroom floor and a foot or two below the windows. As 1948 WHS graduate Bill Cimonetti described it, "You entered the tube feet first, facing east (towards Brattleboro). You immediately did a lefthand turn as you started down. The tube then ran along the side of the building angled towards the north, or the front side of the school house, and exited at the northeast corner of the building."

The tube was used only by high school and junior high students whose classes were held on the second floor. Sliding down the tube was like an amusement ride, and the students enjoyed it. In the 1930s and '40s, fire drills were held perhaps once or twice a year. As one former student told me, "We wished they had been held more frequently."

The tube also served as a piece of de facto playground equipment. In the 2009 Historical Society of Wilmington, Vermont newsletter Eleanor Dix Day remembered that "when school was closed we enjoyed climbing inside it (the tube from the bottom). It was quite a feat to make it to the top without losing your grip and sliding down before you were ready to." She was not alone in her enjoyment of the tube. John Boyd (WHS '66) wrote to me, "I remember good times with others climbing up the fire escape tube and sliding down."

Bill Cimonetti had similar memories. He wrote, "The exciting thing about the unique fire escape was that it was a metal tube, no windows or lights, just an opening and an exit. The escapee was in the dark, on his or her back, feet forward, not able to see the exit until arrival. The exit was perhaps a foot, probably a little less, off the ground. So you didn't arrive running; more often you landed on your butt, sometimes in a mud puddle. We very seldom had an organized fire drill, most of our experiences were attempting to crawl UP the tunnel to slide down, usually taunting others to try."

As much fun as using the fire escape might have been, it was not without its minor disadvantages. WHS graduate Mary Van Wyck Patch wrote, "No one wanted to be the first one out for a fire drill because the tube might be dirty or even rusty, but after the first few went down, it was a big thrill."

In the 1930s and 1940s, both high school girls and boys were allowed to use the tube for fire drills. However, in the early 1950s, girls were no longer permitted to use it. Sharon Adams (WHS '60) wrote to me, "I remember there was a fire escape chute on the (east) side of the wooden building back in the '50s. Unfortunately, back then we girls were not allowed to use it, only the boys! The girls had to use the stairs. Modesty, I guess. Our noses were a little out of joint!!" Note: *Eventually, between 1954 and 1955, the tube was removed. While it was removed at least in part to make room for the addition of the brick wing in 1955, by then Vermont schools were required by the state to have at least two exits from every room. In addition, fire drills were required to be held on a monthly basis. By then, the tube seems to have simply outlived its usefulness.*

CALLS FOR CHANGE CONTINUE - STUDENT SAFETY

In 1930, a year after Wilmington school administrators Sawyer and Welcome advocated for improvements to the school building and its curriculum, newly-arrived school superintendent Benjamin Hamlin called for an addition to the Central School. In his February, 1930 town report he forcefully supported upgrading the 1899 building and the advantages this would offer. Chief among them was student safety. He described the dangers resulting from a potential explosion under the hood in the chemistry room by emphasizing that "there is no fire escape from this floor."

When Mr. Hamlin referred to "this floor" we have to assume he meant the third floor, sometimes called "the attic." A photo taken of the school around 1916 shows a metal fire escape on the west side of the building from only the second floor. Photos of the school taken in the early 1930s, if not earlier, suggest that it had been removed by then. The fire escape tube from the second floor on the east side of the building still existed at this time. However, there was no comparable fire escape on the building's west side.

Later in his report, Superintendent Hamlin clarified that he was, in fact, referring to the third floor - the attic. He described the condition of the building as "endangering life in the event of a fire." He also predicted that panic would result from several structural impediments to students attempting to exit the building in an emergency. Among the impediments were: narrow, poorly lit alleyways (hallways); oddly spaced steps; no fire escape from the third floor; the chemistry hood blocking the main exit; a stairway with no handrail; and exposed floor beams.

Mr. Hamlin also mentioned that on that same floor, cooking classes were held using four oil stoves. In addition, the superintendent pointed out that junior high students under the age of 16 also used these class-rooms on the third floor. Note: *While the door to the attic was always locked, and the attic itself was off limits, I do remember the stairway from the second floor that led to it. It was, of course, all wood, and it was steep and narrow. Having students quickly exit the third floor and then the building during a fire would have been difficult if not impossible. And there was no external fire escape or exit from that floor.*

As if to drive home his point, Mr. Hamlin wrote, "Continued use of this floor for laboratory purposes or for large classes, beyond the time when the town is able to remove these unusual hazards, would seem to be well-nigh criminal."

In his February, 1930 town report, WHS Principal Welcome de-scribed why the proposed addition was "...by far, the most vital project that Wilmington has undertaken, as regards its schools, since 1899, when the present building was erected...The present building is below the standard for a community which seeks to give its boys and girls the best advantages possible."

Mr. Welcome stated that the current building, including its assembly hall, was too small for the student population. He described the fire hazard on the third floor as "grave." The lab facilities for science and Household Arts on the third floor were "inadequate." Wardrobe (closet) space was "insufficient." Toilet arrangements were extremely poor, he wrote, and there was no suitable place for school socials.

Continuing to make his case, Mr. Welcome indicated that "because there is no rest room, there is no suitable place where a pupil may retire in case of sudden illness." Artificial (as opposed to natural) lighting, he said, was "insufficient."

Principal Welcome also pointed out that due to a shortage of recitation rooms (classrooms) and a teacher or two, several times each day teachers were required to supervise a study hall that was occurring in the same large room where they were also teaching a class.

And there was the issue of a gym. As late as 1930, Wilmington High School had no gymnasium. Principal Welcome stated that currently "a physical education program for the entire school is impossible."

But to make matters worse, he continued, Wilmington's basketball team played its home games on the second floor of the town hall. About this situation Mr. Welcome wrote, "Other schools are refusing to play interscholastic contests with the local High School in the cramped quarters of the Town Hall because spectators cannot be accommodated."

CRUNCHING THE NUMBERS

Later in his 1930 report, Superintendent Hamlin shifted the emphasis from student safety to money. With a tone and the use of statistics that bordered on bravado, especially for a newly-hired superintendent, he compared Wilmington's grand list and per pupil expenditures to those of ten other Vermont towns. Whether he intended to shame Wilmington's taxpayers into supporting improvements to their school or was simply presenting the facts as he saw them, Superintendent Hamlin's statistics were revealing.

The 1927-1928 total school expenditures for each of these ten towns with grand lists comparable to that of Wilmington averaged $39,516. In contrast, stated Hamlin, Wilmington's total school expenditures for that period totaled only $24,224, or 39 percent less, even though its grand list was comparable to that of each of the other ten towns.

Stated another way, Mr. Hamlin wrote, "Per dollar of grand list, Wilmington spent 92c (on its schools) as compared to $1.75 expended by the average of these 10 towns, or compared to the $1.79 so spent by the entire state."

He continued, "This would indicate that 10 other Vermont towns, whose grand list averaged only $22,504 as compared to the Wilmington grand list of $26,264, averaged to spend almost twice as much for schools as was spent by this town...If Wilmington were to give the same support to her schools as was given by the average of these towns, the proposed addition to the Central School could be paid for in less than two years." Note: *To those who followed the state aid to education debates in the Vermont legislature and throughout the state during the 1980s and 1990s, these comparisons of grand lists and per per pupil expenditures may sound familiar.*

Having made his point and perhaps wanting to end his report on a relatively less forceful note, Superintendent Hamlin identified the positives of Wilmington's school system: "the well trained corps of teachers who are working in harmony and with good results," a strong Parent Teacher Association, and the state-approved (Standard) ranking given to three of the four district schools.

Finally, and in a most gentle and lyrical manner, Superintendent Hamlin concluded his report by stressing the importance of reading for all students in the primary, intermediate, and high school grades: "And, in after years, if he can sail to the Islands of Adventure on the swift wings of the modern short story, the tire of the day's routine slips away like hoar frost before the warm rays of the mounting sun."

THE REPORT OF THE COMMITTEE ON REMODELING THE SCHOOL BUILDING

As is often the case involving seemingly large, complex expenditures of local public funds, a committee was formed to evaluate how the Central School should be modernized. Committee members were Ralph W. Howe, Merton Barber, Guy C. Hawkins, Leslie H. Adams, and Porter J. Fitch. The committee solicited input on the project from the public, the local PTA, the local school board, and the administration.

In their report, the committee echoed the many safety concerns and recommendations identified by the school's principal and its superintendent. They also recommended that the high school's 4.5 teachers be increased to 5.0 teachers and that a classroom be provided for each of those teachers.

Their report also included remarks from Vermont's commissioner of education, Clarence Dempsey. The commissioner pointed out that the school was originally built for 100 students, and the current student population was 200. However, and more to the point, he wrote that the third floor (attic) science laboratories "...should be condemned and the use of the third floor should be discontinued entirely at the earliest possible date. The importance of promptly remedying this cannot be overemphasized."

Specifically, the department of education's recommendations were as follows:

1. The addition to the school be on the west end.
2. A gym be added to include room for spectators along with dressing (locker) rooms.
3. On the first floor two classrooms with wardrobes (coat closets) and a "teachers' retiring room be provided."
4. On the second floor of the addition that "one large and two smaller class rooms be provided, the large room to be fitted up as a combined science laboratory and recitation room." Note: *This room continued to serve as a science classroom and chemistry room/lab until the 1980-1981 renovation when two new science rooms were added to the eastern end of the lower floor of the brick wing. The former chemistry room/lab and regular classroom on the second floor of the 1930 addition were combined in 1981 and served as a large art room until 2014 when the building was no longer a school.*
5. A home economics room be created.
6. Recitation room (classroom) lighting be improved.

7. Hallways and stairways be improved.

8. "That the front of the completed building be made symmetrical and attractive."

Near the conclusion of their report, but almost as an aside, the committee reminded the voters that the New England Power Company "will have to pay 70% of whatever is appropriated for this project. Your committee has informed the Power Company representatives of its activities and they have given us their very hearty and helpful co-operation." Note: *It's reasonable to conclude that at the time, the property owned by New England Power constituted a significant portion of Wilmington's grand list.*

And finally, as if to add emphasis to the caveats about fire-related emergencies expressed by both the school's principal and superintendent, the committee wrote: "The fact that the lives of our children attending classes on the third floor of this building are put in constant jeopardy is too heavy a risk for any town to assume. It is our opinion that every father and mother and every public spirited citizen of this town will insist upon this condition being remedied at once."

In an effort to involve the students in civic engagement and promoting the improvement of the Central School facility, the March, 1930 issue of the *Mirror* reported that, "Town Meeting was held in the Memorial Hall, March 4th. The Senior High School was given permission to attend. The vital question was on rebuilding the School House."

Whether the students' presence at the meeting made a difference is not clear. However, the voters of Wilmington took to heart the pleas and the rationale offered by school and community leaders to improve the Central School and approved the funds to do so.

According to the *Mirror*, "It was approved by the voters to take the $12,000.00 which the Power Co. has paid the town, also the accrued interest and in addition 65 cents on a dollar of the grand list be raised by taxation for the current year." According to John Taft in his January 31, 1990 newsletter, "A Tale of Two Hill Towns," when the vote at town meeting was taken, the taxpayers approved spending $16,540 for an addition and improvements to the school.

THE BENEFITS OF THE CENTRAL SCHOOL ADDITION AND REMODELING

In their respective reports following the completion of the addition and other improvements to the Central School, the school directors, the principal, and the superintendent were effusive in thanking the voters and in extolling the new benefits of the remodeling project.

According to their reports, among the improvements were:

- The new "well equipped" gym/assembly hall with a new player piano.
- Added classrooms.
- New desks and tables in some classrooms.
- Five new synchronized electric clocks.
- "The girls now have physical training under one of the women teachers. This consists of the usual exercises for the promotion of good posture and grace, with some basketball between groups 'just among themselves.'"
- Students in classes and study hall are now separate.
- Five full-time teachers in the high school.
- Home economics classes have a new electric range and hot plates.
- The PTA is supplying a "one dish hot lunch" for students to supplement their bag lunches from home.
- Use of the new gym for more than physical education (school parties, dancing, assemblies, etc.).

THE NEW GYM

Of all the improvements made to the school in 1930, the new gymnasium was the most intriguing, to be sure. As early as 1925, a gymnasium for the school was a matter of public consideration. In that year, five years before the construction began, a full-page ad sponsored by the Wilmington Athletic Association appeared in the March issue of the *Mirror*. In it the association proclaimed that "the greatest aim of this association is to erect a gymnasium on the High School grounds directly in the rear of our building."

In the ad the association solicited new honorary members whose dues would be used to fund this new building. "In what better way," the ad asked with emphasis, "can the WILMINGTON HIGH SCHOOL be improved and be attractive to outside students than to have a new building." With the completion of the 1930 addition, the Central School had its new gym.

Students lining up in the new gym.

One former student remembered as a young girl watching the construction of the new gym. She described "seeing the hole for the gym dug out with teams of horses."

In the 2009 newsletter of the Historical Society of Wilmington, Eugene "Rummy" Sullivan described his memories of how the gym's construction began. "I remember back in 1929-30 when the gym was added to the school. They were digging a hole to put the gym in. There was a group of farmers that got together. To name a few: Forest Woffenden, Howard Taylor, Ralph Canedy, and Harry Covey.

"After they got done with their chores on the farms, they would meet at the school with their horses and with what they called a scoop to do the digging. The scoop was made of a metal bowl shape with wooden handles on each side for dumping. It held 2-3 bushels of dirt. I'm pretty sure their time was free labor. The gym was smaller than most and was often called a cigar box."

A 2017 publication by the Historical Society of Wilmington included an article, "Recalling Educators from the '50s at WHS," written by WHS graduates Harriet Maynard, Priscilla Lumbra Lackey, and Pat Crawford Morris. The authors wrote about the 1930 gym: "Basketball players recall the tournaments played in bigger gyms, especially the Taconic Tournament in Bennington which Wilmington won. Due to the small gym at WHS called the 'bandbox,' Coach Roberge was a driving force for a better larger gym facility for the WHS students. The original WHS gym measured 27' by 60', it was below level so people took stairs down to the wooden floor."

The three WHS grads continued: "The sideline was one foot deep, cement walls, one balcony and one set of bleachers on the east side. A regular size gym in those days was approximately 40' by 66'."

Despite all its unique features, or perhaps because of them, by the early 1950s the school's 1930 gym was in need of significant improvements especially, it seems, where safety was concerned. In their January, 1951 annual report, the Wilmington school directors and the superintendent of schools described some of the recent improvements made to the gym to make if safer for both student athletes and spectators: "An exit door has been installed near the center of the balcony. The balcony has been extended all of the way around the gym, thereby allowing entrance from either end. Another cable was added to the front of the balcony and a ceiling installed to cover up the open rafters and improve the lighting of the playing surface." Note: *As part of a future expansion in the mid-1950s, the gym was filled in to ground level and the space became the cafeteria. More on the gymnasium appears in the chapter on sports.*

ROOM USAGE

In the mid-to-late 1930s into the 1940s, the Central School continued to serve students in grades 1-12. George Van Wyke was one of those students. His unpublished memoir housed at the Historical Society of Wilmington provides a detailed description of how the building was used during at least part of his time there. "The first and second grades had separate rooms, but the third and fourth grades were in one room with one teacher. These four rooms (and the high school home economics room which doubled as the "hot lunch" room) were on the first floor. Note: *This room, on the ground floor and facing south, continued to be used as the "Home Ec." room until the building closed as a school in 2014.*

Mr. Van Wyke continued: "On the second floor were four more rooms, the high school home room which doubled as the study hall, the junior high home room, which doubled as the math room, and a science lab and a language and English room. The business classroom was carved out of the boiler room in the basement.

"There was a girls rest room on the first and second floor, but the only boys room was in the basement. This also doubled as the boys locker room. It had two showers, two toilets, one sink, and a six-foot urinal - plenty for the whole school."

CONCLUSION

The additions in 1930 of a gymnasium and classroom space, along with general renovations, greatly improved the overall educational experience for students in Wilmington's Central School. Educational opportunities and offerings were increased and student safety was enhanced. And in five years, a purchase of land would improve the grounds of the school, the benefits of which exist to this day.

CHAPTER 10

1935 Land Acquisition

In 1935, according to WHS supervising principal Edward Boak's annual report, the town of Wilmington (not the school district) purchased 6.31 acres of land along Beaver Brook, south of and adjacent to the Central School. The purchase was made possible through the efforts and generosity of Porter Fitch, Trustee of the Haynes fund, and Charles H. Parmelee, who donated a portion of the property.

Principal Boak offered his hope that in addition to the 1935 purchase, "some of the federal funds which at the time are being used extensively throughout the nation, may be obtained to improve the ball field, repair the grandstand (located behind home plate), install a field hockey field and tennis courts, deepen Beaver Brook, and provide walls to hold back the spring freshets (floods)."

Even without these desired improvements, the 1935 purchase of land was seen as a significant benefit to the students, especially those in the high school component of the Central School. Mr. Boak wrote, "No better location for a recreation park is available anywhere in town. The ability of classes in physical education in a single school period to dash from the building onto the playing field and then back into the showers is a privilege the appreciation of which will grow through the years."

Note: *Although still prone to occasional flooding, the land described above continues to be used today as athletic fields for Twin Valley Middle/ High School. Baker Field is used for baseball and Hayford Field is used for soccer. Baker Field is named after former WHS principal, teacher,*

and coach, Newton Baker (1930s and 1940s). Hayford Field is named af-
ter WHS graduate and and longtime WHS/TVHS physical education
teacher and coach, Buddy Hayford (WHS '76).

CONCLUSION

Within 12 years of this land purchase and just 17 years after the
1930 addition and renovations to the Central School, it was time once
again for Wilmington's voters to consider further improvements to the
school.

CHAPTER 11

A Proposed 1947 Addition

NEWTON BAKER: ADVOCATE FOR CHANGE

In 1944, 14 years after the most recent improvements to the Central School building and three years before Wilmington's school directors began seriously contemplating making additional improvements to the building and its academic programs, WHS principal Newton Baker was advocating for change. He urged the people of Wilmington to support funding for an additional building to house a new gymnasium and "a shop which would provide for boys at least one year of wood working, one year of metal working, and one year of automobile mechanics."

To support his advocacy he wrote, "I submit it is well-nigh criminal to send our boys to our schools for twelve years without their once having had, as students, a hammer, saw, screw driver or wrench in their hands...Every single boy going to school would benefit from it, and for more than half the boys a shop would be the most important department."

He continued his advocacy by citing four points. His first point was the importance of attracting tuition students. Mr. Baker informed Wilmington's citizens that, according to Vermont's Department of Education, one-third of the state's high schools would close by 1964 due to regionalization. Although at the time in Wilmington there was no pending bond vote for construction, he urged the town's voters to support future improvements to the school building and its programs. This, he believed, would allow WHS to attract tuition students from neighboring towns. "We are surrounded by towns which need to send their youngsters somewhere. We can do them and ourselves a favor by maintaining a good school."

Point two was that Wilmington's voters could be doing much more to improve their high school. He wrote, "Indeed when we compare this high school with the typical school found in towns similar to ours, there can be no doubt of the numerous points of superiority which we enjoy. However...we should use as a standard, not what others are doing, but how much we can reasonably do of what we ought to do." And here, Principal Baker states emphatically and with no lack of candor, "By that standard, I submit, our school is not so very far from pathetic."

Mr. Baker's third point was that based on its grand list Wilmington could afford to be spending more on educating its students. In his 1944 annual report, he did not hold back. Much as school superintendent Benjamin Hamlin had done fourteen years earlier, Mr. Baker tried to make his point with forcefulness and conviction as he seemed to scold the citizens of Wilmington for being less supportive of their school than their income or property wealth might permit them to be.

Finally, Mr. Baker pointed out that Vermont ranked 26th nationally in per capita income and 27th in per capita wealth. However, he stated, Vermont ranked 35th in money spent on education and 47th (of then 48 states) in "the proportion of money spent on education which goes to teachers' salaries. Would it not be reasonable in view of Vermont's position in respect to per capita wealth and per capita income to expect that it should be 26th or 27th in the other two items also?"

And then, as a harbinger of a debate that would engage Vermont's citizens and lawmakers for more than the next 80 years, he compared Wilmington's grand list to its education budget and declared that the town's taxpayers could afford to pay more for their schools. "For the past decade at least, Wilmington's school tax has consistently been about thirty cents less than the state average...I realize that Wilmington's high grand list means that Wilmington can quite possibly do more with a low tax than most towns can do with their high one. There can be little question, however, but that we could do much more than we are now doing if we wanted to and felt the need for doing so. I submit that the need exists."

Mr. Baker continued this portion of his 1944 annual report by presenting the voters of Wilmington with a choice: "A town which is fortunate enough to have a high grand list can use that advantage to have a better community - better roads, better schools, better planning - than towns not so fortunate. Or it can do, as Wilmington has done to date in respect to its schools, cancel its original advantage with a low school tax rate."

Note: *Until 1997, there were several towns in Vermont that, like the Wilmington Mr. Baker describes, had a large grand list and a relatively small student population. This allowed them to raise a significant amount of money to support their schools with a relatively low school property tax rate. This advantage, however, was nullified in 1997, when the Vermont Supreme Court issued the Brigham decision. This ruling created essentially one grand list for the entire state and radically altered Vermont's formula for state aid to education. As of this writing, however, while the Brigham decision still stands, the Vermont legislature is poised to significantly revise the current formula or create a new one.*

Finally, Principal Baker appealed to the patriotism that perhaps he hoped or even knew that three-and-a-half years of a brutal and exhausting world war had generated: "We adults have contributed to the making of a fine mess in the world. We expect the youngsters to straighten it out for us and for themselves. It is not enough to honor boys with honor rolls, speeches, and memorial services. The only real memorials are deeds. The best deed we can do is to give our youngsters the best education we know how to provide. That would be something few towns anywhere have ever tried to do."

Newton Baker knew that those were difficult times, and he acknowledged as much. He suggested, however, that planning for improvements to the school could begin immediately and then be implemented at the conclusion of the war.

Some who read Mr. Baker's comments in his report might have concluded that he was sanctimonious and being overly and unnecessarily critical of the town, the town where he had lived and led the education community for more than a decade. Perhaps in anticipation of this possibility, he concluded his report with a decidedly different tone: "In conclusion let me say nothing in this report is intended to be critical of anyone unless it is of myself...I am now completing my tenth year as principal of the Wilmington High School. It seems to me that if I had been much of a principal, all, or nearly all, of the above suggestions would have been made nine years ago. As I think of the apologies I owe all the boys I ever had, believe me, this report is humbly and respectfully submitted."

LAYING THE GROUNDWORK

Three years after Newton Baker's passionate plea for improvements to the Central School, and 17 years after the 1930 improvements, Wilmington's school directors decided it was time to act. In their January 1, 1947 annual report, Earlene Fitch, Rodney Foster, and Albert Cole, along with superintendent of schools Edward Boak, wrote, "Another serious problem in our Central School is the necessity for more room. The (elementary) grades are overcrowded and the teachers overtaxed with the work of teaching two grades. We found it necessary to separate the first and second grades this year. To accomplish this we installed a temporary partition in what was the primary room. The partition gives us two rooms but they are small, inadequate, and difficult to heat."

There was also the issue of an increasingly popular hot lunch program and its effects on the home economics classes. The report stated that, "The hot lunch has proved so popular that we are serving over 140 each day, the highest record being 161. Preparation of the meal in the homemaking room requires much work from 8:30 a.m. to 1:30 p.m.

and makes it difficult to teach homemaking classes at the same time. A separate room for the cafeteria is needed."

In that same year, principal George Perry wrote in his report, "There are still a few things that we need badly. The most essential of these, I feel, are a shop for woodworking and metalworking, adequate facilities for homemaking - we had to ask some girls to drop out of homemaking this year for lack of room - , a cafeteria, a gymnasium, more classrooms, and a school office. The fulfillment of even one of these depends upon more space, and this, of course, means a new or an additional building."

A TIME FOR ACTION

On the evening of June 30, 1947, a town meeting was held at Wilmington's Memorial Hall to vote on a proposal made by Wilmington school directors Cole, Fitch, and Foster. The proposal asked the voters in the "Town and Town School District (to) vote to instruct the School Directors to purchase for school purposes the property known as the William A. Brown Estate, make alterations, install vocational courses and raise money therefore or act thereon."

Just five days earlier, on June 25, 1947, the school directors had presented a typed letter to the public. It was entitled, "An Opportunity Now For Practical School Work For Wilmington Boys and to Relieve Overcrowded Conditions in the Wilmington Schools." In it the directors made their case for the purchase of a house, garage, and property across School Street to the immediate north of the Central School known as the William A. Brown property, sometimes referred to as "Victorian Manor." Note: *This building was situated in the approximate area where the M&T Bank is currently located and was torn down in 1969. The property itself appears to have extended westward to Beaver Street.*

The letter pointed out that, "Whitingham School, Leland and Gray Seminary, Brattleboro, and North Bennington have all renovated separate buildings (a barn, a residence, a creamery) for work of this type." It continued, "By act of the last legislature Wilmington will be compelled to pay half-tuition to these towns for any pupil who desires to elect vocational courses not provided here." Note: *The right of high school students who attend a school without a vocational/career program to attend one of Vermont's 14 regional career technical education centers continues to this day.*

The plan was to purchase the garage on the Brown property and use the basement as a workshop "with various power and hand equipment," and the ground-level floor as a "classroom for the course."

As stated in the school directors' letter, the purpose of the proposal was to meet the perceived needs of high school-age boys: "...Wilmington High School has continued largely as a college preparatory school...Homemaking has helped the girls and the Commercial Course has helped both boys and girls but still there has been little for the practical-minded boy to do with his hands."

But the practical, hands-on education of girls was also an important consideration as the school directors contemplated the future of the high school program in the Central School. In addition to purchasing the Victorian Manor, the school directors proposed moving the teaching of homemaking from the Central School building to the first floor of the Manor building. They supported this move by stating, "The teaching of Homemaking is now in serious conflict with the use of the same room for a cafeteria." And then, somewhat understatedly, they pointed out that, "The preparation and serving of meals for 150 pupils daily in the same room in which one is endeavoring to teach naturally provides an interesting distraction for the pupils."

The school directors added a rather novel approach to the teaching of Homemaking. They suggested that the Homemaking teacher could live on the second floor of the Victorian Manor. In addition to a new unit on laundering, a new program could be instituted whereby two girls at a time could live with the teacher for a period of one week, "...planning the meals, buying the food, preparing and serving it and paying the bills. Such work," the school directors continued, "is in line with the best modern teaching and is practiced in the Housatonic Regional High School in Canaan, Connecticut, and in whole or in part in many other high schools."

The directors added that purchasing the Victorian Manor would help alleviate the overcrowding in the district: "As is well known, the High and Central Schools, with 240 pupils, are overcrowded and need more teaching spaces." Note: *The directors are referring here to two separate student sections, elementary grades and high school grades, that were still housed in one building - Wilmington's Central School.*

One final benefit offered by the purchase of the Brown property, according to the school directors, was that it would "...carry the possibility of a splendid entrance from the main street (to the school) and also provide a corner lot adjoining the present school playground which the schools have used for play but have not owned."

The proposal, which included purchasing the property ($11,500), renovation ($7000), rewiring ($1700), new industrial arts equipment ($2500), new homemaking equipment ($2500), and hiring a teacher of industrial arts ($2600), was estimated to cost a total of $27,800.

THE OUTCOME

The timeline for the 1947 addition was tight. The letter from the school directors to the community was dated June 25, 1947. The vote was scheduled for June 30, and the purchase option for the property expired on July 3rd.

Whether it was the brief timeline, perceived excessive costs, an unnecessary expenditure, curricular disagreements, or something else, and in spite of Newton Baker's advocacy for change three years earlier, the request by the school directors was unsuccessful. At the bottom of the typed letter written by the school directors and currently located in one of the binders containing Margaret Greene's documents, someone wrote, "Voted down."

In spite of the defeat, home economics education continued in the high school section of the Central School. In those days, home economics was for girls and consisted mostly of food preparation, sewing, and other domestic skills. During some years, they were taught not by licensed teachers but on a part-time basis by local women.

Note: *Hiring local women to teach home economics may not have been a rare occurrence in Wilmington. In the August 27, 1953 edition of the Brattleboro Reformer there appeared the following notice: "Due to the fact that it is impossible to find a fully certified home economics teacher for Wilmington High School, the school directors are considering the possibility of engaging a local housewife to teach home economics classes. Anyone in the community who would like to be considered for the position should contact any member of the school board or Supt. James Gunn before Aug. 31."*

CONCLUSION

It's likely that the defeat of the 1947 proposal for improvements to the school was a disappointment to its advocates and its supporters. Nevertheless, by the mid-1950s progress beckoned, and significant changes to the Central School were imminent.

CHAPTER 12

The 1954-1956 Additions

The newly-completed brick wing, 1956.

MORE SPACE IS NEEDED

In spite of the 1947 defeat of the proposal to purchase the Victorian Manor, the need to increase and improve the instructional space at the Central School remained. With the 1930-1931 improvements to the school now 20 years old, there was discussion in 1950 of additional school construction and renovation. Three factors drove this.

First, Wilmington's student population continued to increase. The K-12 population in 1945 was approximately 230 students. It was projected to be more than 280 by 1955, an increase of 22 percent.

Second, there was a move to continue having single grade classes with one teacher per class. In their 1950 annual report, school directors R.H. Foster, Harry Morse, and Earlene Fitch reported that, "The arrangement of all pupils in town placed in single grades with one teacher per grade is proving very satisfactory." In their 1952 report they wrote, "As to the lower grades, statistics show that we will be having enough children enter each year so that it will be necessary to remain on the one grade per teacher arrangement."

Third, by 1950, students had been moved from the remaining district schools to the Central School. This exacerbated the overcrowding problem. The school directors urged the voters to sell Wilmington's district schools "as they will in all probability never be used again for school purposes." The directors authorized various title searches to facilitate this process.

The new arrangement of single grades with one teacher per grade required more physical space than the traditional multi-age classes of the past. As a result, in the early 1950s some classes were held in the Victory Grange building on South Main Street, across from what is now Buzzy Towne Park. Grades three and four met in the Grange Hall from 1950 through 1952, and grades four and five met there from 1952 until 1956.

In 1950, Wilmington's voters authorized the formation of a School Exploratory Committee to investigate and evaluate solutions to the school's overcrowding problem. Among the committee's recommendations were the construction of four additional classrooms, a "double gymnasium," and space for a "Shop Course." The committee also recommended that the then-current gymnasium space "be used to improve the facilities of the hot lunch program."

Note: *The 1930 gym area, after undergoing significant changes, would in fact become the school's cafeteria.*

Two years later in their annual report, Wilmington's school directors continued to emphasize the need for more space: "Each year finds us coming closer to the time when the large grade groups will be entering high school. We are already crowded to the point where the scheduling of classes is a real problem...The solution to the problem is obvious and lays in the hands of the parents and other citizens of the community."

In January, 1954, and perhaps resulting from the momentum of the 1950 and 1952 reports, the voters approved funding for construction of a new wing, a new gymnasium, and other improvements to the wooden Central School building.

ACQUIRING THE LAND

Before planning or construction could begin, there was the issue of acquiring the land. Twenty years earlier, in April, 1934, a special town meeting was held to act on Article 3 of the warning: "To see if the town will vote to instruct the selectmen to purchase the property known as the Ball Ground and Brown meadow adjoining, and appropriate a sum of money therefore."

Whether this vote was intended to purchase land for future but as yet unspecified school building expansion is not clear. Regardless, the voters approved by a vote of 71-36 a motion to "appropriate $750 for the purpose of acquiring a deed of the property offered for sale by Clara M. Brown and known as the Ball Ground and land adjoining the School Grounds, to be used by the inhabitants of the town as a play ground and for recreational purposes."

In 1954, and as a result of the 1934 vote, the town (not the school district) now owned the Clara Brown property, and the school directors needed to act. In an April 22, 1954 letter to Fred Thomas, chair of the selectboard, school directors Harold Wheeler, Ruth Streeter, and Henry Meyer wrote that in order for Wilmington to receive state aid for any school construction project, "We must have ownership of the land on which the buildings are to be situated or a long-term lease of this property."

They continued, "Specifically, we are asking the Selectmen to grant a 99-year lease to the School District of the property conveyed by Clara M. Brown and Martin A. Brown by Warranty Deed dated May 12, 1934."

The school directors' letter ended with, "Naturally, we should expect that this lease be subject to the public uses to which this land was devoted by vote on Article 3 of the warning for the Special Town Meeting May 1, 1934." This refers to the 1934 vote that the land be used for "play ground and recreational purposes." However, that the land would now be used for a structure, the 1956 brick wing, appears not to have been an issue.

But there was one final matter that had to be resolved. The directors wrote, "There is some doubt as to the ownership of the property lying immediately around the present school building. In the event that it is found to be possible to include this parcel also, we would like to be able to rent it, along with the other property."

Note: *In my limited research, I found no evidence of such an agreement. However, it's probably safe to assume that this was resolved through a rental or sales agreement.*

PLANNING THE 1954-1956 ADDITIONS

Within months, and having acquired the necessary land, Wilmington school and town leaders were hard at work planning the school improvement project. The new wing would be a brick addition adjoining the eastern side of the original wooden Central School building, and extending to the east. A new gymnasium would adjoin the brick wing to the south.

As with any school construction project, this one required some creativity when it came to finding temporary classroom space. According to a late 1970s report written by Russell Hanson and Ruth Streeter, during the site preparation which began in the spring, 1954, the sixth grade students were temporarily moved to the Cutting (district) School located in the northern part of Wilmington, and the fourth and fifth graders were educated in the Grange building. Note: *Even though school leaders had recommended in 1950 that the remaining district schools be closed, the Cutting School had either remained open since then or was temporarily reopened during the 1954-1956 construction.*

After the completion of the construction, grades 1-5 returned to the new brick wing, and the sixth graders were located in a classroom in the older part of the Central School.

MR. MEYER'S MEMORANDUM

Part of the planning process was a memorandum written by Henry W. Meyer, Jr. On November 1, 1954, Mr. Meyer, a well-respected community leader and school director, wrote a memorandum to a small group known as the Expediting Committee. After having consulted with local leaders Guy Hawkins, David Wheeler, Philip Ware, Russell Hanson, and A.W. House, Mr. Meyer listed several "suggestions," as he called them, for consideration in designing the additions. Most of these suggestions focused on the rooms in the new brick wing and the existing rooms in the wooden Central School building, specifically where they would be located and how they would be used or repurposed.

Regarding the eastern section of the second floor of the wooden building, Mr. Meyer wrote, "Have the fire door from the English (room) and Library open directly to the roof with a fire escape from the roof if necessary." Note: *In 1972, the school library was located on this part of the second floor and would remain there for a few more years. Before that, the area had been a study hall room. The room still had the original wooden floors from 1899. About those floors, Bill and Sharon Adams (WHS '58 & '60) wrote to me, "The wooden floor in the study hall was a little springy, so of course once in a while, and boys will be boys, all the boys in study hall would get their legs and feet going in rhythm and the floor and windows would all be just-a-shaking!"*

At the time of Mr. Meyer's memorandum there were separate faculty rooms for male and female teachers. The faculty room for female teachers was located on the second floor. Mr. Meyer recommended that this be converted into a science storage room. The male faculty room was on the ground floor. Mr. Meyer suggested that it be converted into a storage room for band instruments. He further recommended that there be one teachers' room, relocated to serve both genders.

The teachers' room for female teachers in the original building also served as the nurse's office. Mr. Meyer recommended that the school nurse have her own room "for vision tests, first aid, and examinations." In 1972, the faculty room was located in the west end of the brick addition. It served both female and male teachers and also served as the nurse's office.

There was also the issue of locks. Mr. Meyer wrote in his 1954 memorandum, "A system of locks should be very carefully designed by Mr. Hanson (the principal) for the entire building. There should be one key that will fit all rooms for use of Mr. Hanson and the janitor, and then there should be sub-sections so that no one has to carry a ring around with about forty keys on it as is now necessary." Note: *When I read this, I had to chuckle. During my time as acting principal at WHS (January - June, 1981), I had a key ring like the one Mr. Meyer described. It was four inches in diameter with, yes, approximately 40 keys: keys to the building's front, side, and back doors, keys to the classrooms, offices, storage rooms, supply closets, supply cabinets, the library, the gym, the locker rooms, the boiler room, my office... The list was endless.*

Continuing with his memo, Mr. Meyer addressed the importance of space for the main office. He wrote, "There is no reason to have both a clerk's space and a secretary's space. Increase the area of the principal's office and the guidance room. An office for the principal only 9 X 10 is a ridiculocity [sic]." Note: *After this construction project and until the 1981-1982 construction project, the principal's office was located in the northeastern corner of the wooden Central School building. At the time, it measured approximately 11' by 13'. In 1982, it was relocated to the north-western corner of the brick building and the sizes of both the principal's office and the main office increased significantly. Those offices currently house the Windham Southwest Superintendent of Schools and their staff.*

Finally, as he concluded his memo, Mr. Meyer wrote emphatically, "Above all, remove from the plan all references to the stage in the gym." Note: *The cafeteria that replaced the 1930 gym in the 1954-56 construction was originally referred to as the "cafetorium." At its northern end was an elevated stage as wide as the room, with a curtain. Throughout my time at WHS, the stage remained, and it remains to this day. However, I don't recall it ever being used for any school-wide performances. During lunch periods, the teacher(s) who had cafeteria duty, along with some of their colleagues, would sit there while they ate their lunches.*

Starting in 1956, in addition to serving as the school's cafeteria, the "cafetorium" served at various times as a classroom, a study hall, a banquet hall, a school-wide assembly room, a post-graduation reception room, a community meeting or event room, and a place to celebrate state athletic championships after the victory parades through town.

Although it was never anyone's recommendation or part of the school board's plan, the *Brattleboro Reformer* reported in April, 1956, that the Wilmington Lions Club "added another sprig to its laurel crown with the announcement that it will give an electric scoreboard to the new gym at Wilmington High School. In these days of high scoring games, this is a necessity and it will help the crowds know what's going on. Looks like, with a new gym next year and the new (score)board, the Warriors are on the upgrade." Note: *This scoreboard remained in the gym, mounted on the southern wall, for at least the next 25 years.*

CONSTRUCTION COMPLETED

The Wilmington school directors reported in December, 1954 that the construction had not been completed. However, principal Russell

Hanson and Superintendent A. Weldon House reported no consequential interruptions to the educational programs of either the elementary or secondary students.

Finally, by 1956, with the construction of the new brick wing completed, elementary students could be housed in their own section of the school, and all of Wilmington's students would now be educated in one building, the Wilmington Central School.

With World War Two and the Korean Conflict still fresh in the minds of Wilmington's citizens, principal Russell Hanson wrote in his 1956 annual report that, "the (brick) building has been dedicated as a living memorial to the sons and daughters of the town who served in World War II and the Korean Conflict." Memorial plaques that included the names of over 200 of these local veterans were purchased at a cost of $690 and mounted adjacent to the doors in the middle of the north face of the new brick wing. Note: *After the construction project in 1981-1982 which eliminated that entrance to the brick wing, the plaques were relocated to the newly constructed southwest-facing entrance to the school.*

Praising the benefits of the improvements to the school, Mr. Hanson continued: "The spacious gymnasium, the cafeteria with its stage, the homemaking room and the shop are nightly scenes of school and community activities apart from their daily use in preparing our youngsters. This is as it should be."

In addition, Mr. Hanson described the specific ways in which the addition enhanced the school's operation and educational program:

- "A shop program that serves forty-eight boys from Grades Seven through Twelve in wood-working instruction.
- A more flexible program in commercial subjects by having separate machine and bookkeeping rooms so that typing machines may be used while other business classes are going on.
- Enhanced the expansion of the instrumental music program.
- Increased space for physical education.

- Each grade has its own homeroom for better class spirit and identity.
- Many teachers have their own classrooms.
- The office provides far more efficient record keeping and service.
- Increased space for guidance services."

One former student wrote to me about the excitement among the students when the brick extension was added in 1956 and the desks were new - all of them with metal frames and Formica tops. Previously, the students had used wooden desks from the early 20th century. Note: *It's quite possible that these older wooden desks had been manufactured in Wilmington. The original building on the site of the Old Red Mill Inn, located on the west side of North Main Street just north of the village's main intersection, was constructed in 1828. It burned in 1904 and was rebuilt a year later to manufacture school desks.*

In a nod to the taxpayers of Wilmington, WHS senior, Guy Nido, wrote in the February, 1954 issue of the *Mirror*, "Speaking on behalf of the students of Wilmington High School, we would like to express our appreciation to the townspeople for the proposed addition and improvements to the original school building. You haven't any idea what this means to all of us, from the seniors right on down to the seventh graders. It means that we will have a school that will provide us with all of the essential physical equipment - such as, new large classrooms, more adequate toilet facilities, better hot lunch space, and more space for activities...So once again, THANKS, from the students of W. H. S."

OVERCROWDING CONTINUES

Just eleven years after Guy Nido publicly thanked the people of Wilmington for supporting the construction of the new brick wing and a new gymnasium, overcrowding in the school was once again an issue. By 1965, student enrollment numbers at the Central School were increasing, and Wilmington's school directors publicized the effects of overcrowding in their December, 1965 report: "The last available space has been converted for classroom use, and it now appears that we will be teaching secondary classes in five areas that were not intended for use as a classroom, - the band storage room, the cafeteria, a custodial storage room, the former *Mirror* room, and the gymnasium...additional changes may be needed to accommodate next year's enrollment."

They concluded by stating, "The constant and increasing pressure placed upon secondary school facilities has been a concern of the School Directors for some time. There are in existence definite indications that some action must be taken to resolve this situation."

Principal Russell Hanson echoed this message in his own 1965 report to the town. He stated that the 1966 school year would begin with at least 38 first graders which would necessitate two first grade groups and an additional teacher and classroom for each. Note: *Six years later I would be teaching these students as seventh graders, and there would be 50 of them!*

He pointed out that growth in the elementary section (the 1956 brick wing) of the school would affect classroom availability in the high school section. "A possible solution might be to partition the present study hall to make two smaller classrooms."

Note: *When I first taught at WHS, I had my own classroom in the brick wing for my four junior high classes. However, I taught my high school sociology class in room 110 in the southwest corner of the wooden building. In those days, my classroom was half of the original larger classroom. The other half was an equally small, narrow classroom running east-west along the southwestern edge of the building. In order to get to that classroom, students had to enter through my sociology classroom. By the time we created a middle school section in 1993, I was again teaching in that classroom. However, the partition separating the two smaller classrooms had been removed (probably in the late '70s or early '80s), and room 110 was once again a single, large classroom. Remnants of the partition are still visible on the western wall of the room where the old partition was once attached.*

Principal Hanson in his 1965 report offered possible ways to mitigate the effects of overcrowding: "...convert the cafeteria stage into another small classroom, and use the main cafeteria for a study hall for all but one class period of the school day allowing time for lunches to be served to the elementary children."

Concurrent with the conversations regarding overcrowding was the formation of a study committee consisting of school directors from the towns of Wilmington, Whitingham, Halifax, Readsboro, and Searsburg. Note: *It's unclear why Stamford, a current member of the Windham Southwest Supervisory Union, was not represented on this committee.*

According to the school directors' 1965 report, the group was tasked with studying the future of secondary education in those towns, including "enrollment, transportation, teacher assignments, pupil course selection, minimum standards, and many other items." While it is unclear whether the study committee discussed or recommended that these five towns join to form a union high school, such an idea had surfaced as far back as 55 years before. In his 1910 report to the town's citizens, Wilmington's superintendent of schools, Rev. A.N. Blackford, recommended, "The formation of a union with other towns." He didn't elaborate, and his proposal quickly faded.

Occasional discussions, studies, and proposals promoting town and supervisory union cooperation and mergers continued. However, no appreciable collaboration among schools resulted. But that didn't prevent Wilmington from moving forward.

BUILDING A NEW SCHOOL

In the late 1960s, with crowding and in some cases overcrowding in the Central School building being a problem, Wilmington's voters approved a bond to build a new elementary school north of town on Route 100. Deerfield Valley Elementary School (DVES) opened in September, 1970, on land purchased from Wilmington residents Joseph and Viola Crafts. It welcomed 233 students in kindergarten through sixth grade.

Relocating more than 230 elementary students from the Central School to DVES provided additional space for the remaining 190 junior high and high school students. Still, in his 1970 annual report, principal Russell Hanson predicted continued growth in the Central School's student numbers. Part of this was due to accepting for the first time seventh and eighth grade tuition students from Dover. Note: *High school students from Dover were already being accepted as tuition students to WHS.*

And while Mr. Hanson encouraged this practice, he offered this caveat against accepting too many tuition students: "It would seem wise to allow a definite and limited number of tuition students to attend Grade 7 and 8 classes to assist in defraying the cost of added teaching personnel."

In spite of having completed major construction and renovation projects in 1956 (the Central School building), and again in 1970 (DVES), the growing student population continued to be a challenge for Wilmington's education officials. In addition, the broadening of educational opportunities for students was becoming an increasingly important issue nationwide. In 1968, Wilmington High School was evaluated for accreditation by the New England Association of Schools and Colleges (NEASC). Consistent with local and nationwide trends, one of the association's recommendations was the establishment with nearby communities of a regional high school.

This notion of regionalization was not new. As noted above, school superintendent Rev. A.N. Blackford had recommended it in 1910. And in 1947, Wilmington's school directors and superintendent wrote, "As we look to the future, we cannot help but feel that Wilmington needs larger building accommodations. The most economical way for this and other neighboring towns would be to build a regional high school. This would allow for vocational, practical courses for our boys and girls, would permit more attractive salaries for our teachers and would make room for the consolidation of our rural schools in our Central (elementary/high) School. All of which, we believe, would furnish improved educational opportunities for our Wilmington pupils and we recommend the most careful consideration of this proposition."

Principal Russell Hanson endorsed the 1968 NEASC recommendation writing, "I feel that an area high school is absolutely necessary for the future efficient and more comprehensive education of our students. Our school has some advantages in its small size. It, however, has more disadvantages for efficiency and effectiveness and breadth of program." Note: *Russell Hanson passed away in 1997. And while he never lived to see the actualization of his recommendation, just six years later in 2003, the towns of Wilmington and Whitingham voted to merge their elementary, middle, and high schools.*

CONCLUSION

Both the addition of the brick wing to the Central School in 1956 and the construction of Deerfield Valley Elementary School in 1970 were significant improvements to what Wilmington could offer its students. Concurrent with these improvements was the occasional formal or informal discussion of creating a regional high school or having Wilmington and Whitingham merge their high schools. However, at the time, neither of these ideas ever gained any traction.

In the meantime as the 1970s came to a close, Wilmington's student population continued to grow, and the high school building was aging. It was time once again to look to the future, and Wilmington's school directors moved forward with plans to improve the brick and wooden sections of what had become Wilmington High School.

CHAPTER 13

The 1981-1982 Addition

The newly-extended and renovated brick wing, 1982.

PLANNING AHEAD

During the 1970s as the school's population continued to grow, the subject of merging the high schools of Wilmington and Whitingham was occasionally discussed by school directors and the public. Votes were taken, but the voters in one or both towns rejected the idea.

In 1979, with the possibility of a future merger of the two high schools an unlikely possibility, Wilmington's school directors embarked on a plan to improve the town's high school building. It had been 25 years since the last renovation of the school. The science labs were in need of significant updating, and the Vermont Department of Education was taking note of the school's overall aging facilities. In addition, the school's student population was increasing, and overcrowding was once again becoming an issue.

Without making substantial renovations in the old building and adding space to the brick wing, the high school was in danger of losing its accreditation by the New England Association of Schools and Colleges (NEASC) and, possibly, by the State of Vermont. Precisely what this meant was sometimes open to debate. However, there were enough apparent negatives looming that the school directors decided it was time to act.

In March, 1980, they adopted a proposal costing slightly less than $1.5 million to extend the brick wing and make some additional changes in the wooden building. This was based on a ten-page report submitted by a local committee formed to consider the future of the high school.

A month later in an effort to explore all options, the school directors considered a proposal presented by the school's administration that would purportedly result in some savings by not extending and renovating the brick wing. The administration's report also called for moving the seventh and eighth grades to Deerfield Valley Elementary School. In addition, the report recommended combining some ninth through twelfth-grade programs or courses with Whitingham High School.

Based on a variety of factors, including transportation costs, required changes in faculty and program configurations, wanting to keep the junior high students in the high school, and believing that students' needs could best be met by enhancing the current building, the school directors opted not to accept the administration's less expensive proposal.

Even though the school directors rejected the administration's plan, they were not averse to future consolidation. According to "Wilmington Board Okays School Addition," an article written by Kathy McMasters in the June 3, 1980 edition of the *Brattleboro Reformer*, a report adopted by the school directors advocated "further study of the concept of a union high school with Whitingham...." But for now, the directors' focus was on improving the Wilmington High School facility.

A PROBLEM ARISES

A month after the school directors decided to move forward with a proposal, the voters approved it by a two-thirds margin, 306-181. But there was a problem. The warning for that vote had placed a limit of eight percent on the rate of interest at which a bond would be retired. The early 1980s were an economically volatile time, and interest rates were increasing at an unpredictable rate. Even though the directors had received professional counsel in determining the rate at which interest rates would increase, the eight percent limit turned out to be too low. Therefore, the results of the first vote were no longer valid, and a second vote was scheduled.

In December, 1980, the bond re-vote failed, with 96 voters in support and 98 voters against. Not accepting defeat, the school directors reworked the numbers and scheduled a third vote for early February, 1981. The new warning included a higher interest rate and several hundred thousand dollars of state aid funds. It passed, 248-178. Construction began less than five months later.

PLANNING FOR THE CONSTRUCTION

Planned changes in various parts of the building were:

- Removing or changing several partitions.
- Adding new lighting and heating systems.
- Replacing old windows with new, energy-efficient windows.
- Adding four classrooms (including two new science rooms) to the brick wing.
- Adding locker rooms.
- Adding a library.
- Renovating the gym.
- Replacing insulation.
- Adding an industrial arts classroom and work area.
- Increasing storage for athletic equipment.

- Adding stairways.
- Adding an elevator connecting all three floors (ground floor, 1st floor and 2nd floor).

THEIR SCHOOL'S LOSS WAS OUR SCHOOL'S GAIN

During the first half of 1981, I served as the interim principal of Wilmington High School. One April Saturday in 1981, I drove to Windham College in Putney, Vermont. I was joined there by Chuck Duzinski, our school's chemistry teacher, and Bill Kunz, our guidance counselor, both of whom lived in Brattleboro. Our mission was to save our school district and its taxpayers some money.

Windham College was closed. According to the December 15, 1978 issue of the *New York Times*, it had closed the day before, on December 14th, "...after money for food and heating oil ran out." Whether the college's creditors recovered any of the $6 million they were owed is difficult to determine. However, Wilmington High School was going to do its part in helping to liquidate a few of the college's assets.

Chuck, Bill, and I approached the college's sciences building not knowing quite what to expect. It had been 28 months, including three winters, since the school had closed. I don't recall how we were able to enter. It's possible that Chuck had acquired a key from Security.

To say that Windham College closed abruptly is probably an understatement. Inside the building there was a chill in the air - an eerie atmosphere with all sorts of personal and science-related items strewn about: a half-full coffee mug, student papers piled on a desk - graded but never returned, articles of clothing, pens, microscope slides, test tubes and beakers. A 20th century version of an academic ghost town, suddenly abandoned and deathly still.

As fascinating as it would have been to explore the building and imagine what it must have been like in its heyday, the three of us were there on a mission: to assess the value of the science equipment and furniture that remained, and to determine whether some of it would be suitable for purchase and use in our school's two new science classrooms and labs. As it turned out, much of it was.

Note: *Thirty three years later in 2014, when the Wilmington High School building (by then, Twin Valley High School) closed its doors to students, much of that equipment and furniture (lab tables, an eye wash station, storage cabinets, etc.) was still in use. Some of it, according to Twin Valley Middle/High School science teacher and WHS graduate, Jessica Greene Hammond, then found its way to her classroom in the renovated building in Whitingham that was now Twin Valley Middle/High School.*

Another part of my job as principal that spring was doing what I could to prepare and help others prepare for the construction that would begin as soon as the school year ended in June. Wilmington High School's attic, located on the uppermost level of the wooden building, had been used for storage in recent decades. As part of the renovation it was to be permanently sealed off, so we had to empty it. It was accessible by a set of stairs off the second floor located in the center front of the wooden building. It had been decades since the attic had been used for classes. Its door had been locked, and the area had been off-limits.

Until I was principal, I had never seen the attic. But now, as I entered, I saw outdated ski equipment and display racks from previous Parent Teacher Club-sponsored ski/skate sales. There were large glass jars filled with formaldehyde and a variety of small fish, amphibians, and invertebrates once used in biology classes. These would have to be disposed of in an environmentally responsible manner, the exact details of which I cannot recall. However, science teachers Chuck Duzinski and Russell Hanson took care of it.

The wooden walls of the attic, along with the pine studs and rafters, had been inscribed by decades of students with their names, nicknames, and harmless comments. Exactly how, why, or when students had been in the attic long enough to scribble their names or messages is unclear. Note: *The skis, skates, racks, and glass laboratory jars are long gone. The graffiti, of course, remains.*

THE CONSTRUCTION AND RENOVATION

Logistically, and due to the construction, much of the 1981-1982 school year was a challenge. Note: *My time as acting principal ended on June 30, 1981. By then a new principal, Jurgen Combs, had been hired, and I met with him in early July to facilitate the transition to his new role. Construction crews had been hard at work for two weeks, and parts of the building were in considerable disarray. Noise, dust, equipment, tools, and dozens of workers in hard hats were omnipresent. When Jurgen and I sat down in what was now his office, and referring to the busyness and disruption that surrounded us, he quipped with a smile, "Now I know why the school board interviewed me at night."*

Due to the construction, the entire brick wing, consisting of four classrooms on the second floor and locker rooms and the shop on the ground floor, was closed off for much of the year. Half the gym was used for storing furniture, equipment, materials, and supplies. The other half was used for physical education classes. That space was cramped, and because it was close to the new construction of the library and industrial arts area, the dust in the gym was a constant irritant.

In spite of that, the boys and girls basketball teams practiced in the half of the gym that was available. However, both teams played all of their "home" games at the Vernon elementary school. With those "home" games in Vernon, as well as the regular away games, players and coaches logged a lot of bus time that season. Note: *Even under these conditions, the boys varsity basketball team played well enough to be seeded 6th in the end-of-season state tournament. They lost to number three seed South Royalton, 60-43 in the quarterfinals.*

During the construction, and because space in the high school was at a premium, some classes were held upstairs in the town hall and others were held in the fire house on Beaver Street. Note: *Not wanting to teach my classes in a variety of different classrooms, I was able to take over what had been the reference room of the school's library and use it as my classroom. It was half the size of a regular classroom and was cramped quarters, for sure, but we made it work.*

WELCOME CHANGES

By April, 1982, the brick wing had been expanded and its original classrooms renovated. My new classroom was Room 101, located in the southeast corner of the renovated brick wing. This room and the room across the hall were created by extending the eastern end of the brick wing. Underneath these two new classrooms were two new science classrooms and labs.

All classrooms in the brick wing had new student furniture as well as new desks and chairs for the teachers. The windows were new and much smaller than the original north-facing windows that had been installed 25 years earlier when heating oil was much less expensive.

Speaking of windows, prior to the renovation of the brick wing, there were other windows, as well, and these were a nuisance. For almost the entire length of each of the four classrooms on the upper floor of the brick wing there were large windows, bolstered with steel hex chicken wire embedded in them, that faced the hallway. This made it possible for students who were "in transit" (as in wandering the halls or taking the long route to and from the bathroom) to wave or otherwise distract their friends in the classrooms. Those of us who were teaching in those classrooms quickly determined that well-placed posters were an effective solution to that problem. Mercifully, these windows were now replaced by solid walls.

Carpeting was installed in all of the brick wing classrooms. I was a big fan of classroom and even hallway carpeting. It offered a quieting and almost calming effect as students moved in and out of their classrooms. And when appropriate, it allowed students in my classes to comfortably sit on the floor to work on a project or engage in small group discussions.

The gym had a new wooden floor that was installed on top of the original 1955 tile-on-concrete floor. The old bleachers were removed from the eastern side of the gym and new bleachers were installed on the gym's western side. The old bleachers were relocated to the eastern end of the fairgrounds where they were used either for the Farmers Days horse pulling competition or the demolition derby, and they remain in that general vicinity.

The newly constructed boys and girls locker rooms, including office spaces and storage rooms, were added to the far eastern side of the brick gymnasium, separated from the gym by a hallway.

A new library wing was built along the western side of the gym. The former library had been located on the first floor (not the ground floor) of the original 1899 building. The new library was a large and impressive room with its new furniture, carpeting, and increased shelving and storage capacity. Within a few years, desktop computers mounted on carts or tables would line one wall of the library.

The two industrial arts rooms were moved from the lower (ground) floor on the eastern end of the brick wing into a new area: a classroom adjacent to the southeast corner of the gym and an enlarged shop area that ran along the southern wall of the gym.

Replacing the old locker rooms that faced north on the ground floor of the brick wing was a spacious vocal and instrumental music room with generous storage and practice areas.

On the second (top) floor of the brick wing, the school's main office was relocated from the northeastern corner of the 1899 building to the northwestern corner of the brick wing - the location of my first classroom.

The faculty room was placed where the office used to be, and the guidance office was relocated to where the principal's office was previously located.

The old guidance office adjacent to the classroom in the northwest corner of the wooden building became a boys bathroom that adjoined a custodian's closet.

The hallways and most of the classrooms in the wooden high school building were carpeted, except for the top floor section facing west where the art room in the southwest corner of the building was expanded into the northwest corner where the chemistry room had been.

The biology room across the hall was converted into a special education room.

A photography dark room used in the 1970s was converted into rest rooms.

The chemistry and biology rooms were relocated to the ground floor in the expanded brick wing. To honor his decades of service to Wilmington education, when he retired in 1981, the school directors named this portion of the brick wing the "Russell S. Hanson Science Wing." They also installed a plaque to that effect. It remains to this day. Note: *Russell Hanson served as principal of the Central School for twenty years, and for 11 years after that, beginning in 1971, he taught junior high science and high school biology. He retired at the end of the 1980-1981 school year.*

Finally, the front door to the 1899 building that faced north and was centered there was sealed shut and covered with siding. A new front entrance was created between the 1899 building and the 1956 brick wing.

CONCLUSION

As we review the school's four major construction projects (1899, 1930, 1955-'56, and 1981-'82), a few patterns emerge: (1) although Wilmington's student population fluctuated, its trend was consistently upward; (2) whether it was to accommodate increasing student numbers or to stay current with state and national trends in education, or both, every 25-30 years the building was improved and expanded; (3) Wilmington was consistently blessed with education and community leaders who recognized the need to progress with the times; (4) these leaders planned and advocated for appropriate ways to improve education in Wilmington; and (5) the voters of Wilmington consistently supported these improvements.

CHAPTER 14

Wilmington Middle School

When I arrived in 1972, Wilmington High School (WHS) consisted of grades seven through twelve, and the building was called simply, "the high school," even though it contained both junior high and high school students and programs.

In 1991, our principal, Frank Spencer, and Wilmington's school directors began discussing the feasibility of transforming our junior high program for grades seven and eight into a middle school program for grades six, seven, and eight. The middle school concept, including its underlying philosophy, had gained nationwide momentum and popularity in the 1980s.

Describing the differences between the junior high school philosophy and the middle school philosophy is beyond the scope of this book. However, and essentially, the traditional junior high model views its students as younger versions of high school students and educates them accordingly. The ideal middle school model treats sixth, seventh, and eighth grade students as having unique characteristics, both individually and collectively, as they enter puberty and develop through early adolescence, and it creates a social and academic environment that acknowledges and accommodates those unique characteristics.

A proposal was developed in 1991-1992 by an eleven-person planning committee consisting of Deerfield Valley Elementary School (DVES) and WHS faculty and principals, school board members, and community members. The proposal was formally approved by Wilmington's school directors in early 1992. In September, 1992, the middle school plan took effect.

The creation of a middle school program did not require physical or structural changes in the high school building. However, transitioning from a junior high school model to a middle school model did include some logistical changes. The sixth grade was moved from DVES to the high school building. While middle school students shared facilities with high school students, most of the middle school core classes were taught in the original Central School building; others were taught in the brick wing.

The middle school core faculty consisted of six teachers. The sixth grade team consisted of two teachers: one teaching language arts and social studies, and one teaching math and science. The seventh and eighth grade team consisted of four teachers, one each for language arts, math, science and social studies.

In addition to receiving instruction in their four core classes, all middle school students at different times through the year received instruction in the unified arts: physical education, family and consumer science, art, world languages, industrial arts, and music.

Wilmington's middle school program lasted from the beginning of the 1992-1993 school year until June, 2004. At the beginning of the 2004-2005 school year, Wilmington's middle school program merged with that of Whitingham in the Whitingham school to become Twin Valley Middle School. In 2014, Twin Valley High School moved to join the middle school in the renovated Whitingham school building to form Twin Valley Middle/High School.

CHAPTER 15

OSEC: Connecting the Past to the Future

In 1899, the Wilmington Central School was built. In September, 1970, when newly-built Deerfield Valley Elementary School opened, the Wilmington Central School building became the Wilmington High School building. In September, 2004, it became the Twin Valley High School building. And in June, 2014, the building became vacant. It had served as a school for 115 years, and now its time as such had come to an end.

However, due to the vision and hard work of a group of dedicated volunteers, the building itself was poised to continue serving the public in a different way, this time as the Old School Community Center.

In 2013, in anticipation of the school building being closed, the Old School Enrichment Council was formed. Its purpose was to explore ways in which the building could be preserved, improved, enhanced, and used to serve the public. According to its website, "The Old School Enrichment Council's vision is to inspire enrichment, wellness, social, and economic opportunities in the Deerfield Valley."

In 2024, the Old School Community Center website listed as its tenants several offices and services that met a wide variety of needs and offered various opportunities for the Deerfield Valley community. The longest-term tenant is currently the Windham Southwest Supervisory Union and its offices. The gymnasium is used for youth sports, town recreation commission activities, town meetings, and occasionally for memorial services. Other rooms are regularly used as town polling places and for community meetings.

The Wilmington Central School building no longer serves Wilmington as it was originally intended. However, because of the Old School Enrichment Council and the many volunteers who have donated time, energy, and financial support, the building that was planned and erected at the close of the nineteenth century and then served as the physical, cultural, and educational hub of Wilmington into the twenty-first century, continues to serve the community today.

Aerial View and Timeline
of the School

1899: The original Wilmington Central/High School is constructed.

1930: An extension is added in 1930 to the west side of the 1899 building.

1955-1956: The brick wing and new gymnasium are added. The 1930 below-ground level gym is filled in and it becomes the ground-level cafeteria.

1970: Deerfield Valley Elementary School opens. Wilmington Central/High School becomes Wilmington Jr./Sr. High School.

1981-1982: The 1955-1956 brick wing is extended and renovated. New main and rear entrances are created. The previous main entrance is covered over.

1992: Wilmington Jr./Sr. High School becomes Wilmington Middle/High School.

June, 2004: Wilmington Middle/High School comes to an end. The building becomes Twin Valley High School

September, 2014: The building no longer serves as a school.

Main entrance
1899-1982 1982-2004

Main office
1982

Brick wing
1956

Brick wing
extension
1982

1930

1899

1899

Gym
1930-1956

Rear
Entrance
1982

Library
1982

Gym-1956

Locker rooms
1982

Industrial
Arts 1982

Part III

Student Life at Wilmington's Central/High School

CHAPTER 16

Student Well-being

When I was a boy in the 1950s, I was aware of two major threats to my well-being. And to my young mind, my elementary school offered my classmates and me protection from each.

One threat, the then-Soviet Union's use of what was called the atomic bomb, was mitigated, or so I believed, by being in school. Upon hearing the wail of the air raid siren on our school's roof, my classmates and I would exit dutifully and silently from our classroom into the interior hallway, face the light yellow ceramic tile wall, kneel on the floor, and cover our heads with our hands. I don't recall feeling imminently threatened by the Soviets or their bombs. But I figured if I was in school, I was safe if they ever did decide to attack us.

A more immediate and visible threat was poliomyelitis, also known simply as polio. A neighborhood friend of mine had suffered the disease but had survived. He walked with a slight but noticeable limp, and it concerned me. Even more concerning was seeing newsreel footage as well as photos in *Life* magazine of children wearing leg braces or even worse, being condemned to what I was convinced was a lifetime of confinement in an iron lung. It was frightening. But then came relief.

One day at school in the late 1950s, my classmates and I were marched into the nurse's office. We passed by several dozen pink sugar cubes neatly arranged on an aluminum tray. Each was infused with the Salk vaccine. As instructed by the nurse, I took a sugar cube and let it dissolve in my mouth. That, I was told by my teachers, would prevent me from becoming a polio victim. I could now resume my childhood, free from the nightmare of life in leg braces or in an iron lung.

Whether it has been protecting children from the threat of Soviet missiles, poliomyelitis, or any number of other threats or maladies, including Covid-19, public schools have long been directly or indirectly responsible for the health and general well-being of America's schoolchildren. In Wilmington's schools that was the case for more than 100 years. In some ways, protecting and improving student health meant creating an atmosphere in the school and on school grounds in which students were safe from illness or injury. In other ways, as we'll see, it also meant safeguarding the students' intellectual, mental, and social well-being.

PRE-1900

Prior to the construction of the Central School in 1899, Wilmington had as many as 16 district schools, or one-room schoolhouses. The annual town reports from those pre-1899 years said little or nothing about student health and safety. However, WHS senior Virginia Page in the May/June, 1954 issue of the *Mirror* offered a few insights supplied, perhaps, by her great-grandmother who taught in Wilmington in the latter part of the 19th century. She wrote, "As the six year-old entrance regulation was not then in force, many of the pupils were tiny tots. The teacher asked their mothers to send pillows, and each day the youngest pupils had a school nap...In our schools of today sanitation is a point that is greatly emphasized...However, in the eighteen hundreds, instead of having fountains to quench one's thirst, a privileged pupil went to the school spring, filled a tin pail, and passed the dipper around." This reference to the dipper reminded me of a conversation I once had with my paternal grandfather.

Many years ago I asked my grandfather Larsen to describe what his elementary school was like. He attended a one room schoolhouse near Geneva, New York in the state's Finger Lakes region. His small school was not unlike the district schools in Wilmington. He was born in 1892, so his description would have been from around 1896 to the early 1900s. "We had grades one through eight," he said, "and one teacher. And she'd have 35 or 40 kids. And all of us sat in one great big room, everybody...and they had a little corner, in each corner of the back. That's where you sat at recess and ate your lunch.

"And they had a well out there (in front of the school) and, of course, they had an outside privy. Then, the kids with good behavior, they were allowed to go and get a pail of water now and then. And if you raised two fingers, or maybe one, I can't remember, you had to go to the toilet, and two was you had to get a drink of water or something like that." Mirroring what Virginia Page wrote, my grandfather said, "And they had a pail and one dipper, and everybody drank out of that same dipper." Grandpa then concluded with this observation: "It wasn't too sanitary."

THE IMPORTANCE OF BEING IN SCHOOL

During this time, shared dippers for drinking water and outdoor privies notwithstanding, educators in Wilmington consistently did what they could to enhance the overall well-being of their students. Occasionally, however, there were obstacles to these efforts, obstacles like student truancy.

In 1899, as Wilmington's new Central School was nearing completion, superintendent of schools Charles Hinkley implied in his annual report that the schools could not be held responsible for the general well-being of their students if those same students were frequently absent. Whether chronic truancy in Wilmington was a problem is difficult to ascertain. However, it's certainly possible. Superintendent Hinkley wrote, "The teachers are hindered in their attempts to improve the condition of their schools by the lack of interest in the schools shown by many parents." He went on to explain the negative consequences of truancy and parental disinterest. "Especially is this seen in the irregular attendance of many pupils who are allowed to stay away from school for reasons which do not prevent them from doing as they please during the time they are absent."

In 1903, Wilmington's superintendent of schools, John Stetson, opined on the truancy problem. He wrote in his annual report, "A few families persist in keeping boys under fifteen at home that they may work. Anyone guilty of such a practice should be punished to the full extent of the law."

He continued, "Too many scholars, especially boys, leave school soon after the age of fifteen. No doubt this is sometimes necessary, but many times a grave mistake is made."

A year later, Superintendent Stetson reiterated his call for improved attendance: "The attendance upon the various schools is still too irregular. Whatever may be one's individual opinion as to the proper length of the school year, the State law calls for 28 weeks in the grades and 33 in the high school."

1900-1929

In 1901, James Lobban, the district superintendent and Central School principal, devoted the majority of his annual report to praising the new school and its teachers, and describing the school's current and future curricula. There were no specific references to the physical health or safety of Wilmington's students.

However, Mr. Lobban did include a firm message to parents regarding their role in nurturing their child's behavioral health and supporting school discipline. He wrote, "...moral education must be obtained largely in the home. The attitude of the child toward authority...depends far more on the influence of the parents than on that of the teachers, as the teacher meets the scholar only about nine-hundred hours out of the year...All that a teacher asks, and this the teacher has a right to expect, is that parents will assure themselves of the facts before they allow their children to show any tendency to rebel against the school..."

In his report, Mr. Lobban also addressed the intellectual health of the school's students. He advocated for a longer school year. But, he cautioned, "If the school year is not to be further increased, parents should see that their children's minds are cultivated during vacations. Children should be supplied with good, wholesome literature at all times, and parents should see that the literature is good."

And then, turning it up a notch, he wrote, "It is bad enough to let the mind starve, but it is worse to feed it on cheap and sensational books or story papers."

Mr. Lobban also reminded parents about homework: "...all scholars above the sixth grade and many below have occasion for home-study at night. I say this because it is a generally accepted fact that the children who are allowed to spend their evenings on the street are less apt to prosper in school work than those who are kept under the influences of the home.

"I certainly do not advocate depriving a boy of his play, but I do maintain that the parents should see that play does not occupy all of a boy's time out of school...Home is a far safer place after dark than the street is."

A few years later, convenience and safety for students, staff, and teachers appeared as important concerns. Central School principal, H.H. Rice, described in his annual report two upgrades to the school, lighting and egress: "Electric lights have been put in throughout the village (Central) school building. These are of great use in the fall and winter terms, as days are so short, and teachers, especially in grade work, need to prepare work for the next day on the evening before."

Regarding the other upgrade, Mr. Rice described a "substantial" walkway consisting of wooden planks that had been installed at the front door of the school to facilitate safe and rapid egress in case of a fire.

The State of Vermont by this time had instituted fire safety requirements for schools. Mr. Rice wrote, "Also, a fire escape, required by the state, has been placed on the village side of the building." This fire escape was a traditional structure consisting of a set of iron steps and hand railing extending from the second floor to the ground. However, it appears that Mr. Rice felt the fire escape was unnecessary.

He wrote disparagingly about the state's fire escape requirement and the fire escape itself: "This is likely to be more ornamental than useful. Fire drill is kept up regularly, as required by law, and the building is emptied each time in about a minute and a quarter. It is pretty hard to see how a fire, which must be preceded by smoke enough to give warning, could gain headway enough to obstruct the passage of the pupils in so short a time as that."

A more unique form of emergency egress from the upper floor of the Central School was "the tube." It functioned as a chute from the second floor, but it was essentially a metal tube approximately three feet in diameter. In the earlier part of the twentieth century, similar tubes were commonly used in schools and hospitals.

The school's tube was installed during the 1928-1929 school year. Fortunately, it was never needed to escape the flames, heat, or smoke of a fire. However, it was used during fire drills. Note: *Student memories of the tube and the fun it provided appear in Chapter 9.*

During this time, in at least one instance, Wilmington's school directors actually delayed the construction of a school building until they could be assured that its location would not pose a threat to student health. The controversy occurred in Mountain Mills, a small settlement west of Wilmington. According to their February, 1918 report, Wilmington's school directors, along with Vermont's State Board of Health, were concerned about toxic fumes from one of Mountain Mills' two pulp mills wafting their way into the school. Note: *The Mountain Mills school was included in the Wilmington school district, and therefore it was under the jurisdiction of Wilmington's school directors.*

The source of the fumes was a sulphate paper mill, and according to a 1970s paper written by WHS students Marcia and Myrna Green, the concerns of the school directors were well founded. They wrote, "The sulphate smelled awful, and the townspeople hated that." The authors reported in their paper that several millworkers either died or suffered respiratory issues because of the fumes.

The school directors wrote in their report that there was "some agitation in the air as to the attitude of the Board of Health towards the fumes from the pulp mill." However, according to the report, the dilemma was resolved when "the State Sanitary Engineer finally did arrive ...and gave his consent for the school building to be built." Note: *Although some may exist, I found no evidence that the fumes adversely affected the health of the school's students or teachers.*

1930S - AN EMPHASIS ON PHYSICAL HEALTH

In 1930, Central School principal Arthur Welcome in his annual report renewed the theme of parental responsibility for student welfare espoused by James Lobban 29 years earlier: "It must be remembered that boys and girls spend only one-fourth of their time in school and that the home is responsible for seventy-five percent of the development of character building, social development, and citizenship training."

But in 1931, two years after the onset of the Great Depression, the emphasis on student well-being seemed to shift from parental responsibilities to the actual physical health of Wilmington's students. In his annual report that year, Wilmington superintendent of schools Benjamin Hamlin emphasized the role of the schools in promoting and protecting the health of their students. He wrote, "Health and education are both so essential that neither can be neglected with impunity at any stage in a child's development. Altho directly charged with the responsibility for the child's education, school authorities are coming to realize that they have a very definite duty with regard to the child's health."

Also in 1931, Superintendent Hamlin specifically promoted a "program of medical inspections" of students. He identified the "removal of adenoids and enlarged tonsils, filling badly decayed teeth, and expert diagnosis of defective eyesight" as those maladies most in need of treatment. He also suggested an "annual stethoscope examination of all those taking part in our organized athletics."

Superintendent Hamlin also advocated for other health-related improvements including a full- or part-time school nurse and physical exams for school-age children. He recommended that these physical exams occur in May so parents could arrange to have any medical issues addressed during the summer. He also recommended having the PTA, the school district, and the Red Cross combine their resources to pay for these health-related services.

It's reasonable to conclude that the health of many if not most of Wilmington's children suffered to some extent during the Great Depression. If his report in 1931 is any indication, Superintendent Hamlin made it a priority to convince the town's voters to provide through their schools whatever student health care the district could afford.

A year later, superintendent Hamlin focused on student nutrition. He wrote in his annual report to the town, "I look forward to the time when our Household Arts (home economics) department will be able to offer, on the cafeteria plan, a nourishing but inexpensive lunch. From the 1st of October to the 1st of June, hot lunches are well worthwhile."

Within a year, the Central School was offering a "one dish hot lunch" to its students. Home economics students provided it as a supplement to the lunches brought from home. And soon thereafter, hot lunches were offered at the Cutting District School. Looking ahead, Mr. Hamlin wrote in his report, "There are always a few children who are underweight or with an anemic tendency who benefit greatly from a glass of milk during the morning recess and I hope we may be able to take care of this need in some way in the future."

According to Mary Van Wyck Patch in her paper, "Wilmington Schools," students at the Central School began their school day at 9 a.m. and were dismissed at 4 p.m. They had an hour for lunch. Some students, including Mrs. Patch, would walk home as far as a mile for lunch. Students who brought their lunches ate in their classrooms, while students who received hot lunch ate in the home economics room. Recalling those days she wrote, "A special favorite hot lunch of mine was their meat loaf and mashed potatoes, so if that was on the week's menu, I might ask my folks for the $.15 it cost."

Intellectual health and development and the parents' role in facilitating it emerged as a topic in school superintendent Benjamin Hamlin's 1932 report. He wrote that on average, a high school student should expect between two and two-and-a-half hours of homework five times a week. He reminded parents that, "Father and mother are entitled to their relaxation at the end of their day of work." But, he cautioned, they should do their best to provide a quiet, well-lit place in the home for their children to complete their homework and to minimize outside distractions by "toning down the radio or talking with visiting neighbors as quietly as possible."

On the other hand, Mr. Hamlin recommended a good night's sleep, even at the expense of a completed assignment. If a homework assignment should prove to be too challenging, he wrote that "...it is the father's or mother's duty to send their boy or girl to bed at the proper time, with the assurance that there is probably no occasion for worry, regardless of whether their evening (work) has been completed or not."

By the early 1930s, in addition to offering advice to parents, the Central School was providing dental and medical examinations for Wilmington's students. In 1932, a dental hygienist was hired to clean the teeth of the students in the Central School and in the remaining district schools, and either a nurse or doctor was hired to perform physicals.

Both services were paid for by the Thompson Trust, created in the late 1860s by the last will and testament of Thomas Thompson. According to its website, the trust was designed to "promote health, education or the general social or civic betterment in Windham County, Vermont and Dutchess County, New York."

In their 1932 annual report, school directors Dora Hubbard, Leslie Adams, and Porter Fitch itemized the results of the dental hygienist's work on the 236 students who were examined: "444 cavities in baby teeth; 61 baby teeth were decayed down to the gums; 748 cavities found in secondary or permanent teeth, with 49 decayed down to the gums."

As of February, 1932, the annual physical exams offered to students had yet to be completed. However, at the time of their annual town report, the school directors reported that, "For each 100 pupils, the posture of 33 is good; 47, fair; 20, poor. For nutrition, 80 are good; 16, fair; and 4, poor. For each 100 the throats of 77 are normal; 7 have enlarged tonsils or adenoids needing treatment; and 16 are advised to have an operation. For each 100 pupils, 1 has ear trouble needing treatment; 2 have lung trouble needing treatment; 2 have goitre (goiter) conditions needing treatment, and 90 have teeth needing treatment. Out of each 100 children, 14 have been vaccinated while 86 have not been vaccinated."

The annual school report emphasized that while the school could identify health problems among its students, it was up to the parents to have them treated: "Of course all this work is only preliminary and the results may be measured only by the cooperation of the parents in seeing that these defects in our school children are corrected."

Since Vermont, like all of the US, was in the depths of the Great Depression in 1932, it's difficult to know how many of Wilmington's children in need of dental or medical care received it. However, Superintendent Hamlin did report that, "...through the energetic work on the part of our Parent-Teacher Association and the local Red Cross in cooperation with the Thompson Fund, 12 of our boys and girls who were badly in need of an operation for adenoids and diseased tonsils, were able to secure this at the Memorial Hospital in Brattleboro at the hands of a specialist in this field, but at a price which was less than is usually charged."

In his 1932 annual report, school superintendent Hamlin reported that an epidemic of "persistent cases of grippe," or influenza, in at least one district school had caused it to be closed for some portion of the school year.

There was also an outbreak of measles. About this Mary Van Wyck Patch wrote, "Also in the medical line was a big episode of measles in our family. At that time, if any member of the family had a contagious disease, every one of the family who had not had the disease was put in quarantine. This meant putting a sign on the outside of your house to alert people about the disease. At first it was great to miss school as it also meant that those of us who were quarantined could not go out. With so many brothers and sisters, that entailed a long period of staying home. I was about the last to develop the disease and missed the first six weeks of school, but Mrs. Pratt (first grade teacher) made sure I did not fall behind in the school work."

Showing concern for the students' visual health in one district school, Superintendent Hamlin made a case for improved lighting: "With that low, insufficient lighting coming from both sides, we need to do all that we can to safeguard the eyesight of the pupils at this school."

In another nod to the visual health of Wilmington's students, Superintendent Hamlin described the importance of fresh fruits, vegetables, and raw milk to the development of eye health and strength which, he stated, was not complete until the age of ten. He then offered this opinion which seems to suggest that young readers might suffer eye-related ailments: "We cannot condemn too strongly the practice of teaching children to read at too early an age, as at four or five."

During the 1935 school year, the emphasis on teeth cleaning and dental examinations continued. The vast majority of students in the Central School and the rural district schools received these services. The March 8, 1935 edition of the *Deerfield Valley Times* reported that, "Arrangements are practically completed for a dentist to start work in Wilmington...doing such work as the filling and extracting of teeth of school children as the recently prepared dental charts may show to be necessary." Note: *Dental programs continued into the 1990s when the Beaver Brook Parent/Teacher Club raised funds to pay for a dental clinic that served all children in Wilmington's K-12 system. Later, and for many years, the Deerfield Valley Healthcare Volunteers secured funding for similar dental programs.*

Supervising Principal, Edward Boak, wrote in his annual report that, "Our physical examinations by the local doctors are being conducted as usual...Considerable interest is being aroused to have toxoid treatments for the prevention of diphtheria." According to an article in the March 8, 1935 edition of the *Deerfield Valley Times*, 83 percent of Wilmington's 240 students were immunized against the disease. The toxoid (vaccine) was supplied by the state of Vermont.

In addition to school-wide programs designed to enhance student health and well-being, there were high school courses designed to accomplish the same goals. The February, 1937 issue of the *Mirror* included descriptions of these courses. The WHS sociology course was intended to show how "modern institutions shape an individual and how maladjustments injure an individual's chance to become a normal, happy person...Great care is taken (in the course) to demonstrate that useful and happy living depends on learning to think realistically, without self-deception."

The high school's civics course was designed to "interest students in the problems and duties of citizenship so that they may be intelligent and responsible citizens later on and be in the welfare of the community and country."

Finally, according to the *Mirror*, the object of the boys' home economics course was to "fit the boys to be better members of their family group - present and future."

Note: *I was interested to read that in the 1930s there was a home economics course for boys. The same was true in the early 1950s, in this case a cooking course. There was also a class in foods and nutrition for both boys and girls. By 1972, at least for WHS junior high students, home economics and industrial arts (sometimes called "shop") had become gender based. Girls enrolled in home economics, and boys enrolled in industrial arts. However, by the late 1970s, according to former WHS home economics teacher, Pat Spencer, this began to change. She wrote, "By 1978, there was a three-week switch where the boys took home ec. and girls took shop. Within a few years, home economics became "family and consumer sci-*

*ence," and the junior high courses and high school electives in that disci-
pline were co-ed."*

1940S - CONTINUING THE CARE

During the 1940s, while the annual town and school reports do not specifically describe many of the programs instituted during the 1930s, it is likely that most of them continued in some form.

In 1940, Superintendent Edward Boak reported that while the Wilmington schools were able to afford the services of nurses who were partially funded by the state or federal government, the school district still did not employ one. In advocating for a full-time nurse he wrote, "Cooperation of all authorities in our town is needed as well as the co-operation of neighboring towns. We all try to do health work from time to time but for the best services it needs a paid professional worker on the job every day." Within a few years this situation improved.

By the 1943-1944 school year and until the end of the decade, a public health nurse, while not necessarily on staff, was employed by the Wilmington school district. She arranged for Wilmington's two town doctors to conduct physical examinations for students in pre-school and in grades 1, 4, 8, and 10. It was also the stated hope of the school directors to provide either dental care on site or transportation to a nearby dental office.

And by this time, there was also a relatively robust hot lunch program being offered to Wilmington's students. Superintendent Boak wrote in his report, "One of our best health projects is the school hot lunch...The pupil pays three cents and it is our endeavor to give him seven cents worth of food for his money."

One late-1940s WHS graduate recalled that during his time there was no school nurse. However, the school's secretary was authorized to dispense aspirin. "And," he wrote, "in grade school we were visited perhaps once a year by a dentist from Bennington who would do a hasty oral examination."

1950S - EXPANDING THE MEANING OF STUDENT WELL-BEING

In the early 1950s, James Gunn, Wilmington's superintendent of schools, wrote in his annual report about the hot lunch program: "With some financial assistance from the School District, it has been possible to serve what fulfills at least one third of the daily nutritional requirements and keeps the price of the meal at ten cents." And then, with supportive data, hyperbole, unabashed pride, or all three, he concluded, "This is without a doubt the lowest cost per meal of any school lunch program in Vermont."

With the hot lunch program well established, in 1954, Central School principal Russell Hanson reported that the school had added the Federal Milk Program to its hot lunch program, and 230 half-pints of milk were being consumed each day by its students.

Principal Hanson took additional steps to further insure the health of the Central School's students. The school required anyone who handled food as it was being prepared, to undergo an annual physical at the beginning of the school year.

As part of the focus on student well-being, in the mid-1950s the Central School students and teachers were offered an insurance policy that covered "hospital, nurse and medical expense, loss of life, limbs, and sight resulting from accidental bodily injury...while the insured is on school grounds, participating in supervised activity, or going to and from school."

For an extra 25 cents, a student was insured against injury while participating in interscholastic sports, including the school's newly-instituted supervised skiing program. In his 1955-1956 annual report, A. Weldon House, superintendent of schools, reported that 54% of the school's students purchased this insurance.

With the advent of widespread use of the Salk vaccine to prevent polio, schools around the country began to make it available to their students. Wilmington's Central School served as the location in June, 1956 at which "84 children (44 from Wilmington), ages two months to 19 years, received their first Salk vaccine shots," according to the *Brattleboro Reformer*. The newspaper reported that Milton "Mickey" Wolf was the attending physician and was assisted by several nurses and other women from the area.

In addition to addressing specific health services for area students, the Central School focused on improving physical education. In 1951, physical education was available for boys at WHS but not for girls. First-year WHS Principal Russell Hanson in his annual report attributed this to "limitations of staff." He wrote, "It is hoped that in the near future such a plan can be realized." However, it appears that formalizing any physical education program took a while.

By 1957, a new, full-size gymnasium had been constructed at the Central School. However, in that same year, Mr. Hanson in his annual report highlighted the fact that in spite of having a new gym, the school still had no comprehensive physical education program: "We sorely need a full-time instructor in this area...What we need is a well-organized program in the fundamentals of health and physical activity, graduated to the muscular coordination and physical needs of all pupils in grades 1-12."

Mr. Hanson continued by offering this frank assessment: "Many of our youngsters are pitifully weak, physically. They have acquired unsatisfactory habits of posture and exercise which detract measurably from their physical and mental well-being."

Finally, he pointed to the irony of the situation. "We have provided adequate facilities (a new, full-sized gym) for such a program and have omitted the program itself. Can we afford not to have physical education?"

Two years later in 1959, the school directors advocated for an improved physical education program at the Central School. They placed an article in the warning for town meeting that would approve a "plan to hire a female physical education instructor to work on the physical development of the children in grades VII thru XII." They added that "The usual sports program will continue for boys in grades VII thru

XII." Note: *As noted earlier in this book, in 1930 girls at the Central School did have some sort of "physical training." However, it was under the supervision of one of the female classroom teachers, not a trained physical education teacher.*

The school directors, apparently in agreement with Mr. Hanson, asserted that "a physical education program rightfully begins in grade I in training the minds and bodies of young children in muscular and mental coordination. This should result in better physiques for teen-agers, better general health, better adaptability for sports, and better ability to concentrate on studies."

1960S - ADVOCATING FOR IMPROVEMENTS IN STUDENTS' PHYSICAL AND MENTAL HEALTH

As the 1950s came to a close, Principal Hanson, along with school directors Henry Meyer, Jr., Harold Wheeler, and Ruth Streeter, advocated for the position of guidance counselor. In 1959, the directors placed an article in the town meeting warning requesting funding for a supervisory union-wide guidance program to serve students in Wilmington, Whitingham, Readsboro, Stamford, and Searsburg. The total cost would be $7000 and, according to the report, "To make this a successful venture, both Wilmington and Whitingham will have to appropriate funds since they will supply almost 80%."

To support their request, the directors wrote, "Guidance is more than a scheduling of courses for the individual student so he can get into the college or the training school of his choice. It pertains to problems of an academic, social, personal and vocational nature."

Wilmington's 1959 guidance proposal did not come to fruition. However, Russell Hanson's desire to improve guidance services for the school's students remained. With a few months remaining in the 1960-1961 school year, the district hired Gertrude Watkins, a part-time clinical psychologist and guidance consultant, on a one-day-a-week basis. For the following school year she was hired for two days each week.

Wilmington did not yet have a full- or even part-time guidance counselor. However, under the leadership of Russell Hanson, and with the support of the school directors, the part-time position for which Ms. Watkins was hired began to focus on students' social and personal needs as well as their post-secondary employment or educational futures.

After Russell Hanson opined in 1957 that Wilmington's youth were "pitifully weak" and that they demonstrated "unsatisfactory habits of posture and exercise," in the early 1960s the Central School hired a physical education teacher. Principal Hanson wrote in his 1961 annual report that, "Considerable emphasis has been placed on evaluating the physical condition of our boys and girls as evidenced by physical fitness tests administered by the physical education instructor. These tests will be administered in the Spring to determine the degree of improvement."

In 1967, Mr. Hanson continued advocating for improved physical education. "There is great need for a woman instructor in physical education. Our present program for the girl students is inadequate because of the heavy load of the lone male instructor." Note: *As a result of this request, one might conclude that physical education offerings and opportunities at the Central School during the latter 1960s were greater for boys than for girls. However, Meg Streeter and Bonnie Aubertine Lorimer, both 1965 Wilmington graduates, confirmed that this was not the case. Ms. Streeter wrote, "My recollection is that boys and girls had the same amounts of PE - I loved the activity in PE class, so I think I would have remembered if we girls were shortchanged...I wonder if the school population was increasing then, and this prompted Mr. Hanson's remarks."*

But the physical health of Wilmington's students was not the only concern of Mr. Hanson. He continued to emphasize the need for improved guidance services at the school. Regarding Gertrude Watkins and her guidance services, in 1961 he wrote that "we hope to have her at our school three days one week and two days the following week."

However, just five years after the completion of the 1955-56 brick wing addition, finding space for a guidance office was a challenge. Mr.

Hanson described the solution: "An office for guidance work was set up by rearranging the storage of janitorial supplies and converting a storage room into a reasonably attractive office."

In 1963, guidance services at the school continued to improve as Wilmington and Whitingham began sharing a guidance counselor. Mr. Hanson reported that this arrangement was "working out well." Interestingly, according to Mr. Hanson, this was "the first such type of shared program in Vermont and the results are being watched with keen interest by the (Vermont) Department of Education."

Consistent with evolving trends in guidance, Mr. Hanson wrote that these services included "some group guidance in Grades 7 and 8 and much individual counseling with all pupils in Grades 9-12. A rather complete testing program is administered to all grade levels. Guidance services in the elementary grades are on an individual consultation basis at the teacher's request."

In the 1960s, as the emphasis on guidance continued to increase, so did the emphasis on the students' physical health and well-being. In 1963, the school districts of Wilmington, Whitingham, and Readsboro agreed to jointly hire a school physician. As stated in the superintendent's report, the purpose of "such action was to unify services, secure sequential health examinations, insure sight and hearing testing, obtain school sanitation inspections, and receive advice on public health problems."

EXPANDING THE FOCUS ON MENTAL HEALTH AND COUNSELING SERVICES

During the final three decades of its existence, the physical well-being of students at Wilmington High School continued to be a priority. A registered nurse was either full time at the high school (grades 7-12) or shared with Deerfield Valley Elementary School. Also during this time, the nation's schools, including WHS, increased their focus on the mental health and well-being of their students.

In 1972, Wilmington High School hired its own guidance counselor. Traditionally, and certainly in my experience as a high school student in the early-to-mid 1960s, the primary role of the guidance counselor was to assist students with planning their class schedules and exploring college, career, and occupational post-secondary options.

However, as times changed, the role of guidance counselor began to change with them. Alcohol and substance abuse in society increased in the 1960s, and the effects were felt in schools across the nation. In addition to the traditional responsibilities of the guidance counselor, it often fell upon them to deal with the numerous problems related to substance abuse and related behavioral and social problems. This could take the form of recommending disciplinary measures to the administration, conducting informal counseling sessions with a student, or working with parents and state- or federally-funded social services to assist a student and their family.

Incidents involving drinking or drugs on WHS's school grounds were historically rare, but they did occur, some at the Central School as early as 1960. In his article in the *Mirror* that year, assistant editor Allen Atherton wrote about students being denied entry into a dance after having left the dance earlier. His article included a brief reference to student drinking that indicates it might have occurred now and then. He wrote, "When a student arrives at a dance, he receives either a ticket or is stamped. So his going in and out (of the dance) is protected by evidence of his payment of admission. A constable stationed at the doorway leading into the school could eliminate individuals who have been drinking. Consequently we feel more relaxed regulations about leaving a dance or party should be considered."

As worrisome as drinking at or before high school dances was, substance abuse in general by adolescents in Vermont, even in the 1960s, was not a new issue. Surprisingly, concern among Vermont educators and lawmakers about substance abuse among school-age children and adolescents was evident at least as far back as the 1880s, at which time the Vermont legislature took action and required Vermont's schools to do the same.

In his book, *History of Education in Vermont*, George Gary Bush, Ph.D., explains that during the late 19th century, the Woman's Christian Temperance Union successfully "agitated" for the passage of a law in Vermont "making the study of elementary physiology and hygiene, which should give special prominence to the known effects of stimulants and narcotics upon the human system, a part of the common-school course of instruction." This requirement was based on the legislators' belief that "the most important part of education is to form character by inculcating correct ideas of conduct and formation of good habits."

Bush continues, "The legislature provided that textbooks on the nature of alcoholic drinks and narcotics should be furnished at the expense of the State. The law required that instruction on this subject should be given 'to all pupils in all public schools in the State.'"

A century later in the late 1970s, Vermont lawmakers continued their efforts to require schools to eliminate or at least mitigate substance abuse by children and adolescents. They enacted legislation that required schools to implement drug and alcohol abuse programs. As a result, educators in Vermont, including those in Wilmington, attended mandatory annual in-service sessions designed to make them more aware of substance abuse by students and how to deal with it.

INVOLVING THE STUDENTS AND THE COMMUNITY

In subsequent efforts to address student mental and physical health, various student-led and faculty-advised organizations were established at Wilmington High School. Their purpose was to help students avoid or address a variety of substance or emotionally-related challenges they or their classmates might be experiencing.

In the mid-1980s, Wilmington High School students along with a faculty advisor formed a chapter of SADD, Students Against Driving

Drunk. In 1997, the national group changed its name to Students Against Destructive Decisions.

In the late 1980s, the Windham Southwest Supervisory Union received federal Drug Free Schools and Communities (DFSC) funds. In 1988, according to former DVES physical education teacher Cindy Hayford, schools in the supervisory union (Halifax, Readsboro, Stamford, Whitingham, and Wilmington) created a Drug Free Schools and Communities Advisory Board consisting of parents and teachers. The Advisory Board oversaw the DFSC funds and awarded grants to schools that applied for specific projects and activities.

In 1992, another group was created. According to former WHS teacher and group facilitator Karen Molina, "The Leadership Project was a collaboration of students, parents, and teacher-advisors from Whitingham and Wilmington High Schools with the purpose of reducing student use of alcohol and other substances, including tobacco."

In 1994, according to Cindy Hayford, "Some members the Drug Free Schools and Communities Advisory Board wrote a Community Partnership Expansion Grant and received $30,000 for three years. The group evolved into a coalition focused on preventing youth substance use and was named the Deerfield Valley Community Prevention Partnership (DVCPP)."

In 2000, DVCPP merged with other local groups to become the Deerfield Valley Community Partnership (DVCP). As of this writing, the DVCP, with Cindy Hayford as its coordinator, continues to work closely with schools and students in the Deerfield Valley.

Another school-related program was the D.A.R.E. program (Drug Abuse Resistance Education), a national program that began in 1983. According to its current website, D.A.R.E. "is a police officer-led series of classroom lessons that teaches children from kindergarten through 12th grade how to resist peer pressure and live productive drug and violence-free lives." In Wilmington it usually occurred in fifth grade classrooms at DVES. However, the program also had an occasional presence at the middle school level.

Concurrent with the establishment of these organizations was the emergence of school and community efforts to address the causes, effects, and temptations of substance abuse among students. One such effort was the creation in the 1980s of Project Graduation, a post-graduation event organized and supervised by parents and teachers of Wilmington High School students. Students and adults involved with the Leadership Project also contributed to this event.

Project Graduation was held at various venues in the Deerfield Valley and was designed to provide a substance-free environment for the year's graduates and underclassmen. Festivities began in the evening following the afternoon graduation ceremony and ended in the early morning hours the next day. Activities at Project Graduation included raffles for prizes provided by local businesses, a hypnotist, games, contests, competitions, music, dancing, food, and many other features or activities that appealed to high school students. The event was held until 2019.

Near the end of the twentieth century, the mental and physical health of students received increasingly more attention at WHS. The school contracted with Health Care and Rehabilitation Services (HCRS), located in Brattleboro. This allowed the school to have an additional counselor on site and bill Medicaid for their services.

According to former WHS guidance counselor Bill Kunz, around the year 2000, Wilmington High School strengthened its mental and physical health services by establishing a student support team consisting of the school nurse, a special education teacher, the assistant principal, the HCRS counselor, and the WHS guidance counselor. The team met on a weekly basis to discuss any students who were in need of support in order to function effectively both in and out of school.

STUDENT SMOKING

Certainly, the use of alcohol or drugs by students has never been condoned in or by America's schools, including Wilmington High School. Tobacco, on the other hand, has been different, and its acceptance in schools or on school grounds has vacillated. Note: *None of the annual reports written by Wilmington's principals, superintendents, or school directors that I reviewed mentioned tobacco use by students. Interestingly, however, there is in the December, 1925 issue of the Mirror a casual reference to the fact that on "Farmers' Day, the Senior Class sold ice cream, soda, candy, dolls, **cigars and cigarettes.** "* (Bold font added by this author for emphasis)

Given today's societal attitudes toward the health dangers of tobacco use and the laws in Vermont that resulted from them, it seems unimaginable that allowing older students to smoke in their schools was in the not too distant past a permitted practice.

In the 1960s, there is some indication that older students at Wilmington's Central School did, in fact, smoke, even with the expectation that they could do it on school grounds at school-sponsored events. And although this was not something mentioned in principals' or superintendents' annual reports, at least one issue of the *Mirror* provides some insight into how student smoking was being handled by teachers and administrators.

In the fall, 1960 issue of the *Mirror,* assistant editor and high school junior, Allen Atherton, wrote an editorial in which he made a passing reference to smoking in school. He objected to the rule in the student handbook that stated that there would be "no leaving dances or parties more than once." He wrote, "There of course is a good reason for this rule, but there are a few points against it also. For example, many school students smoke; at dances they would like to have a couple of cigarettes during the time they are there. A receptacle with sand is placed in the hall for the sole use of smokers. But if a student is seen smoking in the hall, he receives condemning looks and, in one case, was asked to leave. If they were allowed to go outside (to smoke), then this sort of incident would be eliminated."

The Vermont high school (grades 7-12) in which I student taught in the spring, 1972, permitted in-school smoking by older students. It also permitted younger students to hang out in the designated smoking room with older student smokers.

When I arrived at Wilmington High School in the fall, 1972, older students were permitted to smoke in what was called, the "smoking lounge." It was a small room located on the ground floor near the cafeteria. Later, the student smoking area was relocated to an outdoor space between the wooden and brick sections of the school.

Smoking cigarettes on school grounds at WHS was still permitted into the 1980s. There was a specified area outside where older students, with written parental permission, could smoke. The rationale for this is beyond the scope of this book. However, suffice it to say that since schools are reflections of their communities and community values, the decision to permit this practice was not done without at least tacit community understanding and tolerance.

Eventually, laws passed by the Vermont legislature in the late 1980s outlawed the use of tobacco products by anyone, including adults, in schools, on school grounds, or at any school-sponsored event.

FINAL THOUGHTS

Childhood and the subsequent journey through adolescence to adulthood can be challenging. Accordingly, Vermont communities have historically depended on their local schools, at least in part, to assist, guide, and care for their students on that journey.

Sharing drinking water "dippers" in the 1890s and allowing student smoking notwithstanding, the Wilmington community has consistently demonstrated a strong commitment to student health and well-being.

Whether it was reminding parents to supply pillows for student naps, urging parents to provide proper educational guidance to their children and teens, maintaining a safe school building, recommending a diet of fresh fruits, vegetables, and milk, providing medical and dental examinations, dispensing nutritious meals, offering guidance or counseling services, or promoting a healthy lifestyle, the adults who worked within the walls of Wilmington's schools - staff, administration, and faculty - as well as the school directors and community at large, have always made the mental and physical health of Wilmington's students a high priority.

Wilmington Central School ca. 1910. This is the fire escape that was described by principal, H.H. Rice as being "more ornamental than useful."

CHAPTER 17

Traditions

High schools, like many U.S. institutions, have traditions. Some high school traditions are informal, but nevertheless they are practices respected and followed by a school's students. Bill Cimonetti (WHS '48) recalled a couple of examples from his time at the Central School. He wrote to me, "I remember that in the 1930s and 1940s the Wilmington Central School was grades 1 thru 12, with 1 thru 6 downstairs and 7-12 upstairs. So there were two entrances, as 'little kids' we came and went thru the back door, and never ventured to the front of the building at recess. It was a big deal when you moved up literally to junior high. Upstairs the seniors reigned, and tradition granted seniors the back seats in the large home room. On opening day of school in your senior year you rushed upstairs to claim your back row seat."

Mr. Cimonetti described another past practice: "This was not a real tradition but more a hard fact: The Spring Vacation was always listed in the school year calendar without dates. That school vacation was declared when the sap was starting to run. This was most practical, for every school age kid would be expected to work full time sugaring."

More formal high school traditions are based on or celebrate the value of education. A school's graduation ceremony and the events associated with it are probably the most important traditions at any high school.

Because I was not physically present at Wilmington High School from 1899 to 1971, either as a student or as a teacher, I have no firsthand knowledge of the graduation-related or other traditions at WHS during those years. As far as graduation is concerned, a casual perusal of early *Mirrors* reveals that much like today, seniors delivered valedictory and salutatory addresses at their graduation ceremonies, and graduating seniors gave the school a class gift.

In the 1920s, the gift might have been a class photo or flowers presented to an admired teacher. In the 1930s, various classes gave the school a radio, a piano lamp, money to be used toward the purchase of a piano, and a badminton set and three table tennis sets. Gifts from subsequent classes in the 1940s included a trophy case and a filmstrip projector. During my time, class gifts included a sign for the school, a painting of the school, and cash raised by the seniors for the purchase of a specific item.

Starting in the mid-1920s, senior class group photos were published in the June commencement issues of the *Mirror*. These issues also included class histories, wills, polls, prophesies, individual nicknames, personal profiles, and a dedication to a teacher or other adult. By the 1940s, individual photos and thumbnail sketches of the seniors were published in the *Mirror*. In the middle of the 20th century and before, items such as the class song, the school song, a class motto, the class flower, and the class colors were prominent features of each commencement issue of the *Mirror*. However, all of these have long since faded into the past.

The following traditions, unless otherwise indicated, are some of those that existed during all or part of my 32 years at Wilmington High School.

SENIOR TRADITIONS

Class Night

As far back as 1963 and perhaps earlier, Class Night for seniors at Wilmington High School consisted of several student achievement-related presentations: athletic letters, student council and class officer certificates, the *Mirror* Award, the forestry essay certificate, and an honor certificate. All of these were presented by members of the faculty. Less formal student presentations included the class history, class poem, class prophecy, class poll, and class will.

In June, 1973, the end of my first year at WHS, and perhaps before, Class Night was held in the gymnasium on the Thursday night before graduation, a tradition that continued into the 1980s. The seniors, their parents and relatives, other students, a few townspeople, and some members of the faculty attended. By this time, athletic and other awards, along with various certificates of achievement, were no longer part of class night. Most of the evening's program was now more informal and lighthearted with the seniors reading the class will, the class prophecy, the class poll, the class history, and the class poem.

Occasionally, seniors presented a goofy award or a humorous acknowledgement to a faculty member. And every now and then a few faculty members would do the same to one or more seniors.

An example of the latter presentation was in June, 1979. Four years earlier, local teacher, Bruce Cole, my wife, Kathy, and I took a group of eighth graders (this year's seniors) on a six-day trip to Washington, DC. It was the first of several such trips. We stayed in a cottage that accommodated 20 people. The cottage was located in a compound of six such cottages.

On the morning of the sixth day before heading home, Bruce, Kathy, and I conducted a quick check of our cottage and inspected each of the rooms. We probably found an odd sock, a forgotten souvenir, a hairbrush, or something else that had been left behind. In one of the girls' rooms I reached under the bed to retrieve what I thought was simply a piece of scrap paper. However, it was a note. It read: "Knock twice and bring some friends."

Because there were six cottages, there were usually other groups of students present. While we never had any problems with them, I was always watchful. I didn't mind innocent interactions with other groups, and I trusted our kids to use good judgment. Still, these were young adolescents, and we were away from home. Vigilance was the order of the day.

Sometimes, whether it's as a chaperone, a teacher, or even a parent, it's best not to know everything that occurs in the lives of the young people for whom we're responsible. As I read the note, I wondered if this was one of those times. Our cottage was small (it had only one entrance), and coughs, sneezes, and giggles could be heard throughout. Since I had never heard any indication of mischief, I concluded that this invitation, while it might have been extended to boys in another group, for example, was probably never accepted.

I placed the note in my wallet, and when I got home, I put it in a file folder marked, "Class of '79." Four years later at Class Night, it was time to share what I had found.

I summoned onto the stage the four girls who had occupied the bedroom where I found the note. They had no idea what was up, and I suppose it's possible they had no memory of writing it. I shared with their classmates and the audience of parents and teachers what I had found, and where, when, and how I had found it. I then read the note aloud. All four girls took it in stride with smiles and maybe a modicum of blushing and embarrassment. I never asked, and they never offered, if or how the invitation had ever been extended - or accepted.

Most of the senior presentations (class will, class poem, etc.) were humorous, entertaining, and appropriate. However, and in spite of the best efforts of the senior class advisors and the administration to censor or at least manage what was presented at Class Night, occasionally some seniors offered up material that was of questionable taste. Eventually, sometime in the mid-1980s and for a variety of reasons, Class Night came to a quiet end.

Presentation of Awards

Scholarships and other awards (and there were many) to deserving seniors were presented at graduation. As a result, the ceremony, depending on the number of graduates and awards, could get exceedingly long, sometimes by 30 minutes or more. The high school gym, especially in June and with 500 people in attendance, could get stiflingly hot. In the early 2000s, the high School administration decided to hold a separate awards night during the week before graduation.

Graduation Activities

In the 1930s and 1940s, and possibly before, each class chose a class theme. Examples of these themes are, "Changes Within Our Lifetime ('38), "This is Worth Fighting For ('44), and "One World" ('46). This tradition appears to have ended in 1947.

In the 1950s, and probably before, the Wilmington High School graduation celebration occurred during what was called "Commencement Week." It included several elements that by the time I arrived in 1972 had been eliminated. They included: holding the ceremony in the evening and at Memorial Hall, an alumni banquet held at Childs Tavern (Crafts Inn), the junior prom, the senior theatre party, the baccalaureate, the class banquet, and the "last assembly," the nature of which I was unable to determine. Note: *The junior prom continued. However, it was held in May, several weeks before graduation.*

Other elements of the graduation ceremony and program that had been eliminated by 1972 included: requesting that the audience remain seated during the processional, presenting the class history, the class poem, the class prophecy, the class will, and class memories, presenting a pageant, playing of the National Anthem, indicating which graduating seniors had a "four-year average above the college certificate grade of 85%", and publishing in the graduation program the class motto, the class flower, and the class colors.

The Stage and Seating

Most, if not all, of Wilmington High School's graduation ceremonies were held at Memorial Hall or in the school itself. For the first 26 years of my time at WHS and some years thereafter, graduation was held indoors in the gym.

The stage was positioned at the southern end of the gym, underneath the basketball backboard. The backboard itself was usually covered with a sign indicating the year, and adorned with white and blue paper flowers and crepe paper streamers.

The wooden stage was the centerpiece of the high school graduation ceremony. Usually a week before graduation, WHS industrial arts teacher, Bob Filler, our custodians, Mert Learnard and Wayland Hall, and a few seniors would pull pieces of the stage from storage and assemble the plywood and two-by-fours with a variety of nails and screws. If necessary, parts of it would be rebuilt or repainted either blue or white. The stage was adequate, but putting it together was like assembling a large three-dimensional jigsaw puzzle. And it had certainly seen better days. If Bob, Mert, and Waylie hadn't been around, I don't know what we would have done.

In the first half of 1981, I was serving as the acting principal of WHS. In February, Mert Learnard, who was a WHS grad, came to me with a brochure he'd received in his school mailbox. It pictured a heavy-duty but portable platform consisting of several four-by-eight-foot sections. When the sections were attached to each other they formed a stage approximately three feet high and large enough to accommodate our senior class with room to spare.

It included two sets of stairs and several sections of blue skirts or curtains that attached to the stage's front and sides. It came on a large cart for easy storage and transport. By itself, the stage wasn't particularly attractive, but that didn't concern me. It was easily stored and moved, and it could be assembled in a fraction of the time it would take to nail and screw together the old stage. The cost was $4100. But money was tight and, of course, we hadn't budgeted for a new stage. I wondered where and how would we get the money to purchase one. The answer soon came to me: revenue sharing!

Revenue sharing was a federal program in the 1970s and 1980s whereby states and local governments received money to do with as they pleased. If there were certain criteria for local revenue sharing eligibility, I was hopeful that a new stage for the high school would meet them. I presented my request to the school board, and they approved. The next steps were the local selectboard and budget committee, and they also approved. At town meeting I presented my request to the voters, and it was granted.

Several weeks later, the stage arrived. I couldn't have been happier. For me, having to plan and successfully execute a graduation ceremony for the first time was complicated enough. Thanks to Merton Learnard and Wilmington's town meeting voters, having a new stage greatly simplified at least one crucial aspect of that.

As stark and functional as the new stage was that year, a few members of the Class of '81 did an impressive job of decorating it with vases of fresh lupines from a class member's field, as well as blue and white crepe paper streamers and flowers. It looked great, and it continued to serve the seniors of WHS for many years. Note: *As recently as 2020, almost 40 years after its purchase, the stage was used by Twin Valley High School for their Covid-era outdoor graduation ceremony on Hayford Field in Wilmington.*

Starting in 1998, and for several years thereafter, the weather forecast for the afternoon of graduation Saturday determined whether the ceremony would be held outdoors or in the gym. If the ceremony was held outdoors, the seniors were usually seated in the tiered area at the northwest corner of what is now Hayford (soccer) Field.

Beginning in the 1990s, whenever graduation was held in the gym, seats near the front and closest to the stage were reserved for the parents, grandparents, and siblings of the graduates. Until then it was first come - first served. Other relatives, friends, students, and townspeople filled in behind in chairs or in the bleachers. School directors, faculty, and staff had their own section in the first few rows to the right or left of the graduates' families.

The Ceremony

The graduation ceremony itself remained essentially unchanged throughout my 32 years at WHS. Each graduate and senior class advisor wore a white or blue carnation. Marshalls and ushers were siblings of the graduates and were selected by them. For the processional and the recessional the seniors marched, girls first, wearing their traditional white graduation gowns and mortarboards. The boys followed, wearing gowns and mortarboards of blue. Each group was organized by height, probably so those in the back rows on the stage could be seen by the audience.

The president of the graduating class gave opening remarks and later in the ceremony presented a class gift to the school. The class valedictorian and salutatorian offered brief speeches, and the class president introduced the guest speaker (chosen by the graduates with guidance from their advisors and the administration). Diplomas were presented by the principal and the chair of the school board. Into the 1980s, the ceremony began with a member of the local clergy offering an invocation and at the conclusion, a benediction. In 1992, however, prayers at public high school graduation ceremonies were declared unconstitutional by the US Supreme Court. At WHS they were replaced with an opening welcome from the class president and the principal, and concluding remarks by the principal.

For all of my 32 years at WHS, the graduation ceremony was celebratory but appropriately dignified. However, after marching out of the gym into the hallway at the conclusion of the ceremony, the graduates would traditionally let out a raucous cheer or chant. As much of a tradition as this was, the end of the 1981 graduation ceremony was decidedly different from all the others.

The 1981 graduation ceremony itself was celebratory. Like previous graduations, it marked the end of the graduates' time together in a local institution that had mentored and educated them for what everyone hoped would be a successful future. It also marked the end of Russell Hanson's 31-year career at Wilmington High School, as a highly respected principal and later as a teacher.

The school board announced the dedication of the new soon-to-be-constructed science wing to Mr. Hanson and unveiled a bronze plaque to acknowledge it. Former WHS teacher and principal, Forrest Murdock, was the guest speaker, chosen by the graduates. Note: *Mr. Murdock had taken over as principal in the fall of 1971 when the then-principal suddenly resigned. He served capably in that capacity until June, 1980.*

In addition to the celebratory aspects of the 1981 ceremony, other portions were poignant and somewhat subdued because in January of that year we had lost our 48 year-old principal, Paul Caouette, to a massive heart attack. Mr. Caouette's widow attended graduation and presented the first Paul Caouette scholarship.

As acting principal, appointed following Mr. Caouette's death, I thanked the school board, the faculty, the seniors, and the community for their support during the previous six months. The seniors gave me a public "thank you" and presented me with a gift of appreciation: a handheld Casio HR-10 printing calculator. We'd been through a lot together, and their gesture is one I appreciate to this day. Note: *After more than four decades of use, the calculator finally gave out in 2024.*

As the official ceremony ended and the seniors marched slowly from the gym into the back hallway, I expected to hear the traditional celebratory hoots and hollers. But as principal, I also hoped that in keeping with the dignified yet bittersweet tone of their just-concluded graduation ceremony it would be nothing more.

As the last senior exited the gym, I waited, But, in fact, I heard nothing. No hoots. No hollers. No celebratory chant. Nothing. Just silence

as the ceremony came to a close. It was a respectful and appropriate way
to end the afternoon.

The Receiving Line

A tradition that occurred immediately after each graduation ceremony was the receiving line. All of the graduates lined up in no particular order to shake hands and exchange pleasantries with well-wishers.
It was always a personally satisfying way for people to congratulate the
graduates. It also afforded the opportunity for the graduates to thank
those who had supported them through the years. Note: *At school I was
always called "Mr. Larsen." However, while going through the receiving
line, and with the ink on their diplomas barely dry, there was often a
graduate or two, always a boy, who responded to my offer of congratulations and best wishes by saying with a mischievous smile, "Thanks, Dave."
And I made sure to respond with a "You're welcome," and a similar smile.*

The Reception

Immediately following the conclusion of the graduation ceremony
and the receiving line, a reception was held in the school cafeteria. It was
organized by the families of WHS juniors. There was always a large bowl
of fruit punch and an assortment of baked goods, including a sheet cake
frosted with white icing and blue trim, the latter of which would often
result in blue-colored teeth and lips among the celebrants.

SCHOOLWIDE TRADITIONS

School-wide traditions such as holidays can be formal and institu-
tionalized, some by law, or they can be more a function of a school's history and past practice. During my 32 years at Wilmington High School
we had some of each.

Memorial Day and Veterans Day

Memorial Day was always a holiday for Wilmington's schools. Veterans Day became one in the 1980s. Many students and their families participated in the Memorial Day events. Elementary students took part in the parade by riding their bicycles decorated red, white, and blue or by marching with their scout troops. High school students who were in the band marched or performed while riding on a flatbed truck. One or two band members who played the trumpet performed "Taps" at a ceremony on the bridge at the intersection of routes 9 and 100. Starting in the 1940s, and perhaps before, a high school boy recited Lincoln's "Gettysburg Address," and a girl recited his "Tribute to Loyal Women." This tradition continued into the mid-1990s but ended shortly thereafter.

During my time at WHS, both Memorial Day and Veterans Day were acknowledged at the school. For each, students gathered for an assembly in the gym. Some years a teacher, students, or the principal recited a relevant speech, essay, or poem and offered personal reflections on the meaning and importance of the day. Some years local veterans attended to be recognized. An especially poignant program was one year when a local World War Two veteran who had once served as a WHS teacher and later as a board member told of his experience in liberating one of Nazi Germany's concentration camps. He was moved to tears as he described what he had experienced some 50 years earlier. The student reaction was one of attentive and respectful silence.

Halloween

There was no official Halloween celebration at WHS. However, acts of mischief or vandalism were a regular and unfortunate part of Halloween night. Accordingly, it was always with some trepidation that I would walk or drive to school on the morning of November first and approach the school grounds.

What I often observed were some trees adorned with streams of toilet paper, the occasional pumpkin smashed in the road, and a few car windows stained with soap, eggs, or shaving cream. The town and school weren't a disaster area, but it was disappointing to see. And, as the students arrived at school, I would sometimes hear them enthusiastically describing how they had "egged" each other, the school or a local business, or covered each other in shaving cream.

But for me, at least one post-Halloween morning had a rather innocent and humorous outcome. In the mid-1970s, Kathy and I lived on the eastern edge of Wilmington village. We rented a small house with no garage. Many of the students knew where we lived. On Halloween night, the best I could do to protect our little green Volkswagen Beetle was lock its doors. We had several trick-or-treaters that evening, but calmness seemed to prevail.

The next morning, however, and anticipating the worst, I anxiously peered out our kitchen window and saw that someone, probably one or two of my students, had soaped our car with a few streaks on each window. It wasn't destructive, just more of a nuisance.

A few minutes before the start of school that morning, as I sat in my classroom doing some paperwork, two of my eighth grade boys approached me for a brief visit. With impish smiles they said, "Hi, Mr. Larsen."

"Hi guys. How're you doing?"

"Oh, we're fine, Mr. Larsen. How are you?"

Sensing that something was a little abnormal, I responded cautiously, "Oh, I'm fine, thanks."

"Did you have a nice Halloween?" they asked, with a hint of a giggle.

By now it was clear to me that these two boys were probably responsible for soaping my car windows. However, I was not about to give them the satisfaction of guessing correctly or playing their little game. Not yet, at least. "Well, yes," I said. "I had a very nice Halloween. Did you?"

"Oh, yeah," they answered with noticeable emphasis and glee.

After another 30 seconds of idle chit-chat back and forth, they simply couldn't contain themselves any longer. "Did you notice anything about your car this morning?" they inquired.

"Gee, I didn't. Why do you ask?" *Okay*, I figured, *it was time to help them out.* "Hey, wait a minute," I said. "I did notice something. Are you the guys who soaped my car windows last night?" I complained with feigned displeasure.

"Yes!" they giggled with no sense of guilt and no small amount of enthusiasm. And they then proceeded to give me a stroke-by-stroke description of their transgression.

I still chuckle as I recall this exchange. The vast majority of our students were good kids. Like any community, we had a small number of occasional bad actors. But even on Halloween, the majority of our kids, even when they were a little naughty, were careful not to cross the line.

Even though student behavior on Halloween was obviously not school-sanctioned, in the mid-1980s our principal, Frank Spencer, decided it was time to find an alternative to what had become the unacceptable Halloween activities of making a mess of things. A few days before Halloween, he held an assembly for the entire school. He didn't scold or criticize the students. However, he did point out that when the school was defaced or damaged, it was our always-popular custodians who ultimately were tasked with cleaning up or repairing the Halloween mess. He also impressed upon them how wasteful it was to use eggs as weapons. In addition, he stressed the harmful consequences to local residents or business owners when their property was defaced.

As an alternative, he instituted a food drive for a local charity. If a student brought in a food item and also signed a pledge not to participate in any destructive or wasteful Halloween activity, their name was entered in a drawing for various gift cards or gift certificates. In a matter of just a few years, there was a noticeable reduction in negative Halloween activities that, I believe, continues to this day.

In addition, for several years the student council sponsored Halloween costume contests during the school day. Students and teachers arrived at school in a wide variety of creative costumes. At break time halfway through the morning, everyone assembled in the gym for judging and the awarding of prizes.

Senior Citizens Luncheons

In the early 1990s, with the creation of the middle school and the advisories (similar to homerooms) that accompanied it, Frank Spencer instituted luncheons for senior citizens who lived in Wilmington and neighboring towns. Each month the kitchen staff prepared a special meal. Individual advisories hosted the senior citizens in the school cafeteria during middle school lunch period. They welcomed our guests, served them, and cleared the tables at the end of the meal. Rather than have the senior guests sit together at their own large tables, they sat two, three, or four to a table and the students joined them. It was a wonderful opportunity for our young adolescents to converse and show an interest in some of the area's older folks, and vice-versa.

Pep Rallies

Wilmington's varsity athletic teams had frequent successes. Whenever one of our teams made it to the finals of a state tournament, usually held on a Saturday, it was preceded by a Friday afternoon pep rally. Some years WHS had cheerleaders who led the students in various cheers. Absent that, we'd often have students or even the mothers of players volunteer to serve as ad hoc cheerleaders.

I clearly remember the aftermath of one pep rally in the mid-1980s. Following the rally, the students returned to their respective classes. My class at the time consisted of juniors and seniors, and many of them were athletes. A brief conversation revealed how much they appreciated having their teachers attend their games. "You mean you know when a teacher is there watching your game?" I asked with some skepticism.

"Oh, yeah," came the reply. "We can hear you guys cheering and encouraging us. We know who's there."

Many teachers, even those who did not live close to school, often did their best to attend games or portions of them, and it always seemed to make a difference to the students.

Victory Parades

During my time at Wilmington High School, the boys and girls teams won several state championships, most of them in girls and boys soccer and two each in girls basketball and softball. All finals were held in central or northern Vermont. The team bus, usually after stopping for a meal along the way, was welcomed back into town by cheering fans standing along East and West Main Streets and accompanied by police cars and fire engines. In more recent times, the teams rode through town on a flatbed truck supplied by WHS graduate John Greene, owner of Greene's Servicenter in Wilmington.

When the parade ended, the celebration would continue in the school's cafeteria which was adorned with balloons and posters. Soda and pizza were served, speeches were made, and trophies and medals were held aloft.

Recognition Assemblies

Starting in the 1990s, principal Frank Spencer instituted recognition assemblies. These assemblies were usually held at or near the end of each trimester and were an opportunity for students and faculty to be recognized for particular accomplishments.

Those students who made the honor roll for the trimester were asked to stand and be recognized. Some did so reluctantly, not wanting to appear to be boasting. But it was an opportunity for their efforts to be recognized in front of their peers and their teachers. After all, schools are first and foremost academic institutions.

Besides the honor roll, other accomplishments were also recognized. For example, members of a Scholars Bowl, Mock Trial, or Spelling Bee team might be asked to step forward to receive a small memento and hear their coach sing their praises.

Occasionally, a student would be recognized for something they accomplished outside of school, attaining the rank of Eagle Scout or serving as a student member of the local fire department, for example. A faculty member might be recognized for receiving their master's degree.

I liked these assemblies and believe they had value. They were an opportunity to demonstrate to our students that there are many ways to excel. We were acknowledging academic accomplishments, and we were affirming that being a good citizen contributed to the greater good and was achievable in many ways.

A FINAL THOUGHT

Throughout its 105 years, Wilmington High School created many traditions. They provided for the school's students, and often for the community at large, a sense of continuity that defined and preserved what was valued by everyone.

CHAPTER 18

Transportation

My grandfather Larsen, ca. 1899, bottom row seated, third from right, hat on knees - no shoes

"Well, you have it easy. When I was your age, we had to walk to school—over a mile!" When we were young, we might have heard this comment from one of our elders, especially if we were complaining about a long school bus ride and the early morning wait in the cold and wind that preceded it.

Born in 1892, my Grandpa Larsen was quite the storyteller. One of four children of Danish immigrants, he was raised on a small subsistence farm in the Finger Lakes region of New York State. While not immersed in hardscrabble poverty, the family was notably frugal through necessity.

One day in 1977 when he was 85 years old, he was in one of his storytelling modes. He described walking several miles to school in the 1890s. Together, we examined a photograph of him as a young boy taken along with the 30 other students sitting in front of his one-room school house. "You see, Dave," he said pointing to himself in the photograph, "I was barefooted. And in those days nobody wore shoes. In fact," he said with a slight smile, "I didn't know there were such things as shoes until I was 18 years old!"

Although I always enjoyed my grandfather's stories, especially those about his childhood, I learned early on that he occasionally employed hyperbole. However, in this case his point was a valid one. Until the mid-twentieth century, students nationwide, including those in Wilmington, often walked more than a mile to and from school. Some with shoes, and some without.

CONSOLIDATION AND TRANSPORTATION

One of the reasons a town like Wilmington had several (as many as 16) small district schools in the 19th century was that farms and the families who lived on them were widely dispersed throughout the area. Until the mass production and availability of affordable vehicles became the norm, it simply was not feasible for most towns to transport students several miles to and from one centralized school.

However, it appears that even as early as the first years of the 20th century, the Wilmington school district may have provided some sort of transportation for its students. In the 1900 *Deerfield Valley Times Reunion Edition*, J.H. Walbridge wrote about Wilmington's several district schools with a brief reference to transportation: "The tendency of the schools of the town is toward consolidation. During the past year, two of the outlying schools have been discontinued, one being merged with the village school, the other by the transportation of scholars."

In 1932, Wilmington's school directors were still wrestling with which district schools to keep open and which to close, and transportation was a factor. The directors wrote that year in their annual report, "Raponda and Cold Brook schools have been closed this year, and we think that for still another year it would be best to transport the children from these districts to the village (Central) school. Fitch school has a small enrollment, but due to difficulty of transportation in a severe winter we felt it would be wise to keep it open."

WAGONS, SLEIGHS, DRAYS…AND A HEARSE

Before the development and common use of automobiles and trucks, students in Wilmington were occasionally transported by wagons or sleighs. For example, one former Wilmington student remembered the mid-1930s: "We lived on a farm on Ray Hill. My family did not have a car. I walked to school, rain or shine. However, on particularly cold wintry days, my father would take me to school on a horse-drawn dray (a truck or cart for delivering heavy loads, especially a low one without sides) - not a sleigh. Sometimes the village kids would hop on board for a special treat."

In their book, "Images of America: WILMINGTON," authors Julie Moore and her son, Nathan, write, "In some cases, an older student might take a horse and buggy to school while stopping to pick up classmates along the way."

But as motor vehicles became more available and more affordable, wagons, sleighs, and drays fell out of favor. It was not unusual then for some Vermont school districts to hire local townspeople to provide student transportation using their personal trucks or automobiles.

Bill Cimonetti, a 1948 graduate of Wilmington High School, remembers that one family in the late 1930s provided student transportation in a 1930s wood-paneled station wagon: "Our transporter was Mrs.

Schultz of the family next in line (farthest out from the school), and she had a state-of-the-art 1930's Ford 'woody.' In the fall of '38 came the 1938 New England Hurricane, which took out the bridge right near today's Nutmeg Inn (on Route 9 west of the village). For a few weeks Mrs. Schultz drove us to the site of the missing bridge. From there we crossed on foot and hiked to school. Sometime we got a lift from Harry Rice whose Green Mountain Power truck was on the village side of the brook."

In one of the more intriguing approaches to student transportation, Mr. Cimonetti also remembers a resourceful Wilmington resident who provided transportation to some of Wilmington's students in an old hearse: "By the mid-to-late '40s, the school's transportation had advanced to where there were actual routes and contract drivers. Maybe the school district even had a bus or two by then, but not one for the few of us west of town (near the Wilmington-Searsburg town line). The school contracted with Ray Shippee to bus our cohort. I think perhaps Ray started using a sedan, but when there were 3 Cimonettis, 2 Morses, 2 Bickfords, and some others, he needed more seats. That's when he acquired the hearse and outfitted it with plank benches."

Mr. Cimonetti's sister, Ellen Jane Cimonetti McGinnis, in the the Historical Society of Wilmington 1975-2016 Newsletter recalls her rides in that particular vehicle: "The hearse was filled to capacity; Kendall Morse and I (the youngest scholars) had special seats! Mr. Shippee purchased two milk crates and the two of us rode (rear facing) behind the front seat for our three-mile journey to school.

"As we matured, Kendall and I noticed the black curtains on the windows of our 'bus.'...We thought it great fun to draw the curtains as we traveled down Route 9 on the way home to Medburyville!...Mom always watched from the kitchen window to greet me. As I hopped out of the bus on those drawn curtain occasions I could see her bright blue eyes moist and dim. One day I asked her why she looked so sad when we pulled down the black curtains. She lovingly explained to me what our bus was designed to be."

STUDENT TRANSPORTATION IMPROVES

According to WHS principal Newton Baker in his 1944 annual report, since the early 1900s Vermont law had required towns to furnish transportation for students, but only up to and including the eighth grade. Mr. Newton was concerned that this was having an adverse effect on high school students by discouraging them from attending school: "A high school education is considered as essential today - and probably more so - than was an eighth-grade education forty years ago."

Principal Baker advocated strongly for improved transportation services for Wilmington's students. He began by focusing on a child's right to an education: "We like to say in the United States and in Vermont that democracy means an equal opportunity for every youngster. I submit that in Wilmington, a youngster's opportunities for a high school education vary inversely with the distance he lives from the school and then are dependent upon the prosperity of his parents."

He continued in his report using specific examples of how the lack of publicly-funded transportation could interfere with or even deny a child the right to an education. He pointed out that, "the cost to families for transportation for one student through high school varies from one hundred forty-four dollars, for those about two miles out, to four hundred thirty-two dollars for those as far out as the Fitch District. Obviously the latter case is so expensive so as to be almost prohibitive." And then to drive home his point he wrote, "Only one youngster from the Fitch District has graduated from high school in approximately the last twenty years."

The Fitch School, according to a 1941 paper written by Marilyn Howe entitled, "Schools in Wilmington," served school district number 11 which was "the area on the west side of Higley Hill." Why the Fitch school may have produced only one high school graduate in 20 years is unclear. However, there is no doubt that Principal Baker was a strong advocate for transportation services that would facilitate equal educational opportunity for all of Wilmington's students.

By 1947, the voters in the Wilmington School District had approved a motion to require the district to transport not only younger students to the Central School, but high school students, as well. According to principal George Perry in his report that year, "This (requirement) caused an especially heavy burden" regarding student transportation.

In order to address this burden, the district purchased a 24-passenger Ford school bus for $2500. According to the school directors' 1947 annual report, having a bus "operating on Route 9 to bring in pupils from the east and west would be extremely advantageous and would relieve the strain now felt by private owners whose cars are wearing out."

The bus was, according to Principal Perry, "a complete success, traveling an average of about 33.3 miles each day in transporting twenty-one pupils (17 high school students and 4 elementary students) in safe, uncrowded conditions" to the Central School. And, according to Mr. Perry, the bus was also used for "transporting students to the Fitch district school, transporting the Cutting school teacher, trips of athletic teams, and for one trip in connection with classroom work."

Whether by bus or private vehicles, the district was now providing or arranging transportation for its students, including those high school students who lived more than a mile from the Central school. This gave these older students the opportunity to attend high school, an opportunity they otherwise might not have had.

While allowing school districts in Vermont to hire local residents to provide various modes of transportation might have been preferable to having students walk to school, this informal and unregulated approach to student transportation did present some safety concerns.

Children and the 1948 Wilmington school bus

To address this, in 1951, a Vermont lawmaker introduced a bill to regulate the transportation of school children. Authors Hand, Marro, and Terry write in their book, *Philip Hoff: How Red Turned Blue in the Green Mountain State,* that "this touched off a bitter legislative battle when the bill's sponsor introduced a bill setting safety standards for school buses. At the time, many towns hired farmers to transport children to school, and some of them were hauling children in the backs of open cattle trucks." This bill, if enacted, certainly would have prohibited this practice.

The authors continue, quoting the sponsor and obvious supporter of the bill several years later: "It was outrageous. They were hauling those children like cattle in below-zero weather in trucks that had manure on the floor."

During consideration of the bill, its sponsor arranged to have photographs taken and published in the *Rutland Daily Herald.* The photos showed children being transported in one such cattle truck - in winter - with the rather pointed caption, "The rigors of education in old Vermont." The photo was picked up by the Associated Press and published throughout the country. While there are no reports of Wilmington's children being subjected to such conditions, the bill's sponsor certainly made his point, and the bill to enact student transportation safety standards in Vermont was eventually passed into law.

Note: *Continuing the theme of school bus safety, when I was in the Vermont legislature (1987-1997), state law, to some degree, already regulated school busses. However, during that time a bill was introduced to require seat belts on school buses. The major argument in favor of the bill was the same as it was for personal automobiles: seat belts were a tried-and-true method of preventing death or at least minimizing injuries in case of a collision. Opponents of the bill believed that requiring seat belts would create unnecessary costs for the taxpayers and do little to prevent death or injuries. They also saw the bill as one of many examples of state government intruding in the affairs of small businesses and school districts. Finally, a rather graphic argument against the bill was that if a school bus were to be in an accident and overturn, the belted children would be left dangling upside down in mid-air, still attached to their seats. The bill never made it out of committee.*

Of course, many of the Central School's students walked to school instead of riding in a vehicle. Bill Cimonetti (WHS '48) wrote, "There was a reasonable amount of foot traffic to and from school, even in the late 1930's and early 1940's. The concept of paid crossing guards would have been impossible then, but there was concern about elementary grade students leaving school walking to the village, particularly at the intersection of East Main Street and Beaver Street.

"So senior high school girls formed a Crossing Patrol and manned that intersection. I think that becoming a crossing patroller and wearing a signifying white badged harness was an honor. I have a rather vague recollection of being guided along by a pretty high school girl when I was perhaps in 2nd or 3rd grade. I think I've seen a picture of high school girls wearing the crossing guard attire."

Wilmington High School student safety patrol, ca. 1940

INTO THE SIXTIES

By 1960, Wilmington's late-1940s Ford school bus was in need of significant repair or replacement, and the district purchased a new 60-passenger Chevrolet bus for $5900.

Later that decade, the Vermont legislature passed enabling legislation to at least partially address the issue of student transportation but not require it. Vermont Title 16, Vermont's education statutes, states that, "Each legal pupil...may be furnished with total or partial transportation to school...as in the opinion of the school board is reasonable and necessary to enable the student to attend school." The law further states that school boards must adopt policies that address student transportation. As of this writing, school districts in most cases are not required by law to provide transportation. However, Wilmington, in one way or another, always has.

In 1968, Halifax residents Barry and Laura Gerdes established the Gerdes Transportation Company. According to Mr. Gerdes' 2014 obituary in the *Greenfield* (MA) *Recorder*, "Over the years they grew the business and were responsible for transporting thousands of children to and from school each day throughout the Deerfield Valley. The pupils they cared for spanned three generations." I will add that for over 40 years Mr. and Mrs. Gerdes and the drivers they employed also transported countless students on field trips and to and from athletic events.

FINAL THOUGHTS

As we look back on the history of Wilmington's district schools, its Central School, and its high school and elementary schools, transportation was always a priority. Whether it was providing student crossing guards or transporting students in a sleigh, a wagon, a truck, a car, a retrofitted hearse, or a state-regulated school bus, the people of Wilmington did their best to make sure that their children were safely delivered to and from their respective schools.

Note: *During my 32 years at Wilmington High School, and having ridden many hours on school busses as both a coach and field trip chaperone, I have nothing but the deepest appreciation for our school bus drivers. I always welcomed their assistance and sound judgment, both as drivers and as disciplinarians. Through the years, I believe I became fairly good at managing each class and the 25 young learners in front of me. But could I ever have managed those same 25 students placed behind me, all while driving 15,000 pounds of metal, glass, rubber, and steel? Not a chance. So to all of the drivers who through the years safely transported our students, Thank You.*

CHAPTER 19

Sports

N ote: *Because I've divided this chapter into decades, it's inevitable that I've omitted information from specific years. However, what I've tried to present is an overall description of sports at Wilmington's Central School and high school from its early years until its closing, with special emphasis on unique or noteworthy events during that time.*

1899-1919

According to "History of Wilmington High School," an article written by Marjorie White (WHS 1924) that appears in the March, 1924 issue of the *Mirror*, "The first attempt at Wilmington High School to organize athletics of any sort was in 1916, when basketball teams were formed."

1920S

In her February, 1920 annual report, WHS principal Hazel Whitney reported that, "Two basketball teams have been organized and are coached by Miss Goldie Courtemanche."

The first issue of the *Mirror* was published in January, 1921. It reported that in the fall boys football practices were organized, although no schedule of games was published. Starting in December, there were two girls basketball teams and one boys team. On January 14, 1921, according to the *Mirror*, a "special train was procured" to provide transportation for WHS students and teachers, along with townspeople, wishing to attend a basketball game in Readsboro between its team and Wilmington's team. Wilmington won that game, 14-7.

At around this time, the Wilmington High School Athletic Association was formed. According to the *Mirror*, its purpose was to use some of the proceeds collected at various WHS athletic events to "buy all necessary supplies needed by the various teams." It was also at this time that the association selected blue and white as Wilmington High School's official colors. The colors remained unchanged until 2004 when WHS as an institution came to an end. However, I can recall one WHS veteran educator commenting to me that the shades of blue used by the school - navy, royal and light - seemed to vary through the years.

During the 1920s, the WHS girls and boys basketball teams often played against "the Town girls and boys." These were groups of local young men or women who were no longer in school and some of whom played on organized town teams. The WHS teams also played games against their current teachers, WHS graduates, and teams from Leland and Gray Seminary in Townshend and Charlemont School (MA). Once during this time, the boys team played a team from Bliss Business College of North Adams, losing 83-18.

WHS organized a baseball team in 1921. Because the third and final issue of the *Mirror* was published each June and focused on graduation, most of these issues do not include much information about baseball or other spring sports. However, it appears that baseball continued through the 1920s with WHS playing teams from Mountain Mills, the town of Wilmington, Readsboro, and probably other locales. In the mid-1920s, both girls and boys had their own baseball teams.

1930S

Sports in American culture have long been viewed as a way to build character in boys and young men and, more recently, in girls and young women. However, the January, 1933 issue of the *Mirror* offered an interesting viewpoint on the purpose and value of sports, in this case, for boys. Whether the author of the article intended to be critical of the school's male athletes is unclear, but it seems possible.

"From the school's perspective," wrote the student reporter, "the ultimate aim of the whole (sports) program of the boys is sound character and good citizenship, with health as a by-product. However," claimed the writer with a somewhat critical tone, "the aim on the part of the boys is fun and more fun."

The writer continued: "The sports program aims to train the boys to explore new fields of sport, new fields of cooperative effort, and new interests in themselves." The author then concluded with an element of disapproval: "The boys, of course, are untroubled by *any* philosophy."

The same issue of the *Mirror* described the arrival of indoor baseball because, according to the article and perhaps as a nod to the economic challenges of the Depression, it was easier to finance: "Only two gloves at most are needed for a team and the balls and bats are cheaper. The distance between the pitcher's box and home plate is shortened. Stealing bases is not allowed and pitched balls must be thrown underhand."

Finally, the article, looking forward to spring, stated that, "Everything is now ready except the weather, so when spring comes "barnyard golf" (horseshoes) will be added to the list of sports. School and class tournaments will be held for those interested."

In the fall of 1934, WHS organized a field hockey team. It was coached by Mrs. Corkins and Miss Manson. According to the November, 1934 issue of the *Mirror*, the team's equipment had been purchased for them by the local athletic association. The material for their uniforms was also purchased by the association. The uniforms were made by girls in the home economics class.

Note: *Having the school's home economics classes make uniforms for girls teams, while focusing on frugality, was not without unintended consequences. There was one mildly scandalous occasion in the late 1940s described by a former WHS student in which the girls in the home economics class were sewing pinnies (pinafores) as uniforms for some of the girls in the school. In an apparent oversight, the measurements of the girls were posted on the classroom bulletin board, much to the delight of any boys who happened to pass by.*

Unfortunately, the field hockey team was able to schedule only one game that year. It was against Windsor High School and played at WHS. According to the *Mirror*, "The game was well attended by the entire school, as well as some of the parents...Wilmington fought a gallant battle to the end...The final score was 3-0 in favor of the visitors."

As was often the case with sports-related articles in the *Mirror*, this one ended on a positive note: "The girls feel that they learned more from that one game than from any number of regular practice games." After the game, "a light lunch consisting of cocoa and sandwiches was served in the Home Economics laboratory by two of the senior girls."

Finally, the reporter for the *Mirror* wrote, "Before the Windsor girls left, we gave them what they thought was a real treat - a little practice in sliding down the fire escape," referring to the large metal tube attached to the side of the school.

In the 1935-1936 basketball season, the girls played Taconic League games against Wallingford, Arms Academy in Shelburne Falls, and North Bennington. They also participated in a "play day," as described in the *Mirror* by WHS student, Eleanor Cutting, '37: "On March 7, eight girls and Miss Manson went to North Bennington to join in a play day with Chester, Manchester, and Wallingford High School girls...The five schools were divided into four groups and...relay races, volley-ball, and basketball were played." Acknowledging North Bennington's hospitality and referring to what have might have been traditional post-game fare, Miss Cutting wrote, "After this everyone went upstairs for refreshments of cocoa and sandwiches."

Miss Cutting also wrote about an interesting end to their basketball season. "To wind up the basketball season an exhibition game was put on by the boys and girls (teams). The boys played one handed. The final score was 21-2 in favor of the boys."

During the 1930s, the boys basketball team played games against Sanderson Academy (Ashfield, MA), St. Michael's (Brattleboro), Bellows Falls, Brattleboro, Wallingford, Arlington, North Bennington, Leland and Gray, Berlin (NY) high school, and the Orange High School "seconds," probably referring to the Orange High School junior varsity team.

During some seasons, in addition to the boys varsity basketball program, there were successful intramural programs, some including six teams that played a total of 16 games.

In 1937, the boys baseball team played three games against Whitingham, winning two and losing one. The girls were practicing field hockey and participating in a horseshoe tournament.

Cheerleaders in the 1930s could be heard leading the school's fans in cheers such as, "Strawberry shortcake - - - Huckleberry pie - - - V-I-C-T-O-R-Y. Are we in it? - - - Well I guess - - - Wilmington High School - - - Yes! Yes! Yes!"

1940S

During the 1940s, both boys and girls at Wilmington High School participated in a range of athletic activities and interscholastic sports. In the fall and spring, boys played touch football and baseball against nearby schools or in intramural games. In the fall, girls played field hockey, in some years against other schools and other years in intramural games. Both girls and boys played basketball throughout the winter and provided entertainment that was enjoyed by many of the townspeople. At varying times throughout the decade, cheerleading, first aid, and square dancing were additional activities available to girls during the winter months.

During World War II, interscholastic sports were impacted due to the lack of available transportation. WHS graduate Mary Van Wyck Patch, in her paper, "Wilmington Schools," wrote about her senior year in 1942: "Gasoline was rationed which curtailed any sports programs in the high school." In the March, 1943 edition of the *Mirror*, students Gary Hall and Jacquelyn Maynard wrote regarding boys basketball: "Whether WHS will have any basketball games remains to be seen. Many schools have dropped basketball until after the war because of the transportation problem."

During the later 1940s, intramural basketball was available to the younger students in the school.

Baseball in Wilmington was especially popular. Because the field was often not playable until late spring, baseball was a fall sport as well as a spring sport. A grandstand adjacent to the field was built in 1915. Note: *The grandstand was located approximately 80 feet behind home plate at WHS's Baker Field, named after WHS teacher, coach, and principal, Newton Baker. In 1938, the grandstand was seriously damaged due to the flood but was rebuilt. It was finally dismantled in 1970. The baseball field was originally an all grass field. However, in 1947 or 1948, dirt replaced grass between first, second, and third bases to make the field more like the infields of today. Baker Field is still in use by Twin Valley High School baseball teams.*

In a 2007 letter to the Historical Society of Wilmington, WHS graduate Charlie Dunn wrote, "The old grandstand had a window where they used to sell hot dogs, hamburgers, and soda at the (community) ball games, which at the time was about the only entertainment for Sunday after church. It used to draw a large crowd from town and neighboring towns."

Girls field hockey was played to the east of the baseball field. Note: *It was played at WHS when I arrived in 1972 and continued until 1987, when it was replaced by girls soccer. This is described in detail later in this chapter.*

During the 1940s, Wilmington's basketball teams played against North Bennington High School, Arlington, Burr and Burton, Leland and Gray, St. Michaels in Brattleboro, St. Joseph's (North Adams), and Arms Academy in Shelburne, MA.

In general, the lack of easily accessible personal or family transportation to and from school made it difficult if not impossible for some students to participate in school sports. Betty Adams, a WHS graduate from the 1940s who lived on a farm commented, "My future husband also lived on a family farm. He wanted to play basketball in high school. His father said, 'Fine, but you'll have to walk home from practice.' Well, his first practice was his last. By the time he got home, it was too late to help with the chores."

During this time there were no school busses for transportation for away basketball games. Instead, players traveled in cars driven by the coach and parents. Bill Cimonetti (WHS '48) remembers traveling as a sixth grader with the boys varsity basketball team in the early 1940s. In a way, he said, he was like a mascot or the team's "water boy." He was present at the home games and traveled with the boys team to away games. He wrote, "On the days of an out-of-town game I was reluctantly excused early from class by the 5th & 6th Grade teacher Mrs. Folsom, who was vocally NOT a fan of basketball. But I traveled with the team, usually in the coach's car, and at every time-out break in the game I would jump down from the team bench and deliver to each player what was called 'goat milk,' a mix of cold water, milk, and oatmeal. Kind of like a 1940s Gatorade."

"The coach," he continued, "was Newton Baker, the school principal, then still a young, unmarried man and exempt from military service by his occupation."

At times during the 1940s, participation on a team could substitute for any physical education requirements at the school. Based on principal George Perry's 1947 report, it appears that a student participating on a team could be excused from physical education classes: "Those (students) not engaged in competitive athletics have been enrolled in physical education classes." This policy varied during the next few decades. Note: *During much of my time at WHS this policy was in effect, and as of this writing, it is in effect at Twin Valley High School.*

THE "BANDBOX"

Within a year or two of arriving at WHS in 1972, I heard stories about the "old gym" lying beneath the floor of the school's cafeteria. I was incredulous. It was hard to imagine, but it was true. The gym that was constructed as part of the 1930 addition was located on the west end of the original building. The basketball court was literally below ground level.

Playing basketball in this "bandbox," as one former player described it, was a challenge. The court was small, and according to that same player, "Visiting teams hated to play there."

The length of the court ran north and south. There was virtually no out of bounds area. The sidelines and baselines of the court were literally inches from the wall. Bob Boyd (WHS '60) remembered playing basketball in the gym as a younger student: "I played basketball, and the wall of the gym was the out-of-bounds line, so I had to put my foot on the wall before throwing the ball in bounds. I also remember that the (mid-court and foul line) circles on the floor were so close they all intersected."

The walls surrounding the court were concrete and lined with cork laminate several feet up from the floor to act as a cushion for any player colliding with the wall. However, injuries still occurred. One former student, Bill Adams (WHS '58), remembered, "At one time there was a cork cushion-type material in 4'x 4' sheets on the wall. To hold it against the wall there was 3-inch strapping on it at the joints of the cork. The strapping was screwed on with lag screws. The head of the lag screw stuck out a little bit. One day I was playing basketball, and I tripped on something and hit my head on one of the lag screws. It knocked me out. I still have a lump on my head from it after all these years."

The baskets and backboards were attached to the wall. Because there was virtually no space between the backboard and the wall, it made layups especially difficult. And because the ceiling was so low, mid-court shots with any kind of an arc were virtually impossible to make.

There was also a balcony or catwalk above the periphery of the court that wrapped around its northern and western sides. In order to access the benches in the balcony, spectators had to bend over to avoid bumping their heads on the ceiling. While the balcony may have accommodated the spectators, it did occasionally make playing more difficult. John Boyd (WHS '66) wrote to me, "I remember when the (current) cafeteria was the gym. You could not take a corner shot because you'd hit the balcony above."

Despite its disadvantages for some of the players, the balcony appears to have generated some excitement at the beginning of the high school's 1935-1936 basketball season. According to an article in the November 1, 1935 edition of the *Deerfield Valley Times*, "the new balcony in the (WHS) gym is coming along and so are some basketball seasons tickets - $1.50 for eight games and good for a ninth if we have one, as was the case last year. If you want a ticket, just mention it to any boy or girl in the upper six grades, and they'll do the rest."

George Van Wyck, a 1946 WHS graduate, played on the school's basketball team. In his unpublished handwritten memoir housed at the Historical Society of Wilmington entitled, "I remember...or The First Eighteen Years," he wrote about shooting a basketball in another school's gym, this one at Deerfield Academy in Massachusetts: "The school had many basketball courts in one big room...We probably played against their third or fourth team...It was a competitive game, but I lost all sense of distance. At home (in Wilmington's gym) I shot from the corner easily, or I shot from the second balcony support or from the edge of the center circle. I had the distances down pat. But my first shot from the corner at Deerfield ended up about halfway to the basket."

Mr. Van Wyck continued describing the WHS gym: "There were walls all around the gym, only about three feet high on the seating (east) side so the only 'out of bounds' occurred when the ball, not the player, touched the wall. The gym was not conducive to fast breaks so you had to stop fast after driving for a layup. That wall was hard!

"One side and one end of the gym had a balcony so you had to remember to shoot or throw the ball lower. The gym was so short the 'ten second line' which we used was the foul line of the back court, and many of the 'outside' shots came from center court or further out."

He continued, "Of course, on the long shots, the ceiling would easily come into play because the gym wasn't too high. All the lights, which were un-recessed regular fixtures, had wire 'cages' around them which were often hit. When you made a 'throw-in' from out-of-bounds, you had to keep both heels and your back touching the wall, and opponents had to keep at least three feet away. It took quite a while to tell opposing teams all the 'ground rules' the first time they played there."

In one game at least, the confines of the gym seemed not to preclude a decisive WHS victory against Leland and Gray. A December 3, 2022 feature in the *Brattleboro Reformer* entitled, "Looking Back," described a home game that was played in 1946: "Coach Fred Streeter's 1946 Wilmington High boys basketball team coasted to a 49-35 victory over Leland & Gray Seminary of Townshend for its 11th consecutive win...Leading 11-4, Wilmington outscored its foes 20-5 in the second period in order to pull away."

By 1949, the small and rather unique configuration of the WHS gymnasium had become problematic. The school directors and superintendent Edward Boak wrote, "The school gymnasium has been another source of maintaining high morale in the school...In basketball, particularly, our teams have been noted the state over for excellence and clean playing. The gymnasium has been so successful that it has outgrown itself. It is no longer suitable for ten large boys to charge around at the at the top speed of modern basketball, to say nothing of adequate space for audiences. A new, full-sized gymnasium is needed." Note: *A new, full-size gymnasium would eventually be constructed in 1955-1956.*

1950S

In the mid-1950s, the Central School building was undergoing major changes. A brick elementary wing was added to the east side of the original wooden building. The hole that was once the gymnasium was filled in and a cafeteria constructed in its place. While a new gym was under construction during the 1955-56 basketball season, the high school's teams returned to the upper floor of the town hall for their practice sessions. Note: *This town hall is the current Wilmington town hall at the intersection of Routes 9 and 100.*

Barbara Sage, WHS '56, wrote in that year's winter issue of the *Mirror*, "The floor (in the town hall) was much smaller than the floors we'd be playing on. But we planned to make the best of it. Having no gym, all of our games have been played away."

During the 1950s, according to Principal Russell Hanson's annual report, the high school boys and girls had a "full program of interscholastic competition" which included soccer, basketball, and baseball for the boys, and field hockey, basketball, and softball for the girls. According to Mr. Hanson's report, Wilmington High School was classified as a Class C school based on the number of boys enrolled. Wilmington often played larger schools in Classes B and A, but according to Mr Hanson, its teams "were seldom ousted."

Wilmington's girls teams played a variety of schools including North Bennington, Bennington, Leland and Gray, Arlington, Charlemont (MA), and Thayer (NH). Boys teams routinely played Deerfield JVs, Mount Hermon, North Bennington, Leland and Gray, Winchester (NH), Smith's School of Northampton, Putney, Sanderson Academy, Charlemont (MA), and Bennington.

In 1957, according to an article in the *Mirror*, the Molly Stark Softball League was formed. It included teams from WHS, Whitingham, Leland and Gray, North Bennington, Bennington Catholic, and Arlington. The WHS baseball team played in a similar league.

In September, 1957, 21 boys signed up to play soccer. A brief article by WHS students Sam Brissette ('59) and Donald Snow ('61) described how the season began: "The turnout for the soccer squad was good this year. Enough boys went out for the sport to make it possible to scrimmage during practice sessions."

The student reporters continued by describing the normal pre- and post-scrimmage routines: "First, everyone must do at least ten push-ups, at least ten squat-jumps, the same number of sit-ups, toe-touches, and then one lap around the field. Then the team is split up into two teams for a scrimmage. After the scrimmage there is one more lap around the field."

Occasionally, in spite of the fact that WHS had no formal track team, an ad hoc team was formed. The June, 1959 issue of the *Mirror* describes one such time that had surprising results: "On May 9, Wilmington participated in a six school track meet at Arlington. A miracle in athletic events occurred when the Wilmington team, inexperienced and unpracticed, won the meet, collecting 31 points." According to the article, Wilmington placed first or second in all six events: high jump, discus throw, javelin throw, 880 yard relay, 220 yard dash, and the 440 yard dash.

There was one sport that at this time did not exist at Wilmington High School, either on a team or individual level: alpine skiing. However, that did not stop a local ski entrepreneur from touting its potential.

As is the case with virtually all high school yearbooks, advertisements and notes of congratulations appeared in the back pages of each *Mirror* publication. In the Fall, 1956 issue of the *Mirror*, just two years after the opening of Mount Snow ski area, there was a full-page note from its founder, president, and unabashed visionary Walt Schoenknecht. It read:

"We PREDICT- - - Wilmington High School, in the 'Heart of Eastern Skiing,' will develop a ski team threatening the University of Colorado and Dartmouth. We have four years until the next winter Olympics, to be held for the first time in the United States at Squaw Valley, California. We hope W.H.S. is represented at the Junior tryouts during the winter of '59-'60. This takes good sportsmanship, hard training, and top notch instruction. Let's see how far we can go this winter."

Wilmington High School never produced any Olympic skiers. However, in future decades, a substantial number of its students went on to distinguish themselves on skis or snowboards as individuals or members of a school team or teams affiliated with Mount Snow or other entities.

1960S

During the 1960s, Wilmington High School's male and female students continued to enjoy a variety of athletic opportunities. In 1961, boys and girls basketball teams played a full schedule including games against Leland and Gray, Charlemont, Whitingham, Saint Michaels (Brattleboro), Deerfield Academy, Clarke School for the Deaf (MA), North Bennington, Arlington, and Turners Falls (MA). Cheerleading, soccer, field hockey, cross-country, softball, baseball, and a strong intramural program rounded out available athletic opportunities for WHS students.

There was also co-ed gymnastics. The June, 1965 issue of the *Mirror* described the program as including, "tumbling, vaulting, balancing, cartwheels, hand walking, back extensions, and 'monkey shines.'"

During the 1960s, girls softball teams were formed, but it may have been on an inconsistent basis. In the June, 1963 issue of the *Mirror,* Barbara Murray ('64) and Linda Brooks ('65) wrote, "This year the girls at Wilmington High School are a very disappointed group. Why? Last year the girls had a softball team for the first time in many years. The girls played hard and enjoyed themselves tremendously. For the first year they did quite well by winning three out of eight games."

And then, with an air of mystery, they wrote, "This year the girls had exactly the same team and much enthusiasm, but unfortunately something came up. What, for sure, isn't really known or understood. But there isn't a team, causing many, who love the game of softball, to be very unhappy."

And finally, with a sense of both resignation and optimism, Miss Murray and Miss Brooks wrote, "Well, there's nothing that can be done now, but all the girls are looking to next year, with big hopes for a team. I hope the girls get up a team, for I'm sure they will be a successful team - - - well, at least a very happy team."

The situation for girls sports soon improved. Just two years later in the fall of 1965, the field hockey team consisted of 28 girls. The team was coached by high school principal, Russell Hanson. One of their games was against a Marlboro College team. Wilmington won, 4-0.

WHS: AN EARLY TRENDSETTER

It is significant that during the 1960s and even during the 1950s, Wilmington High School (the 1963 softball season notwithstanding) offered three varsity sports for its female students. In this regard, WHS was not necessarily unique, but the school was certainly ahead of its time. In many schools throughout the country, during this time and certainly before, girls had few opportunities when it came to high school interscholastic sports.

Betsey Stevenson in her paper, *Title IX and the Evolution of High School Sports*, writes that in the U.S., "While millions of high school boys played sports, organized high school sports for girls was a relatively obscure activity with fewer than 300,000 girls participating the year that Title IX was passed (1972)."

Stevenson also reports that in the 1970-71 school year approximately 3.5 percent of high school girls nationwide participated in interscholastic sports as opposed to 47.5 percent of high school boys.

Meg Streeter (WHS '65) wrote to me with her perspective on this: "I am grateful that Wilmington High School had girls sports while I was there. This was a great opportunity to play three sports each school year. So many women I know of my generation went to large schools that didn't offer women's sports, even in the 1960's!"

When examining the national data that Stevenson presents, it's unclear whether these disparities were due to the non-existence of sports for girls or to girls simply choosing not to participate in existing programs, or both. What is clear, however, is that in the 1960s and before, Wilmington High School was ahead of its time by offering athletic opportunities to its female students that were comparable to those offered to its male students.

A 1960S HIGHLIGHT

The 1966 baseball team began its season with five straight losses and finished with a record of four wins and seven losses. However, the 1967 season baseball was markedly different. Prior to 1967, Wilmington athletic teams had won various league championships but never a state championship. That was about to change.

On Saturday, June 3, 1967, the Wilmington Warriors played in the Class S championship baseball game. After defeating McIndoes Academy in the semi-finals, they defeated Cabot High School, 15-10, to win the state championship. Cliff Duncan (WHS '67), a member of the championship squad, remembered the game: "It was a slugfest. The game started at 9 a.m. and lasted four hours. And it was hot! By ten o'clock it must have been 85 or 90 degrees."

The game was played in Windsor, Vermont, and Mr. Duncan recalled some particularly interested spectators: "The field was located right next to the state prison. Some of the inmates were waving what looked like pillow cases from their cell windows as they too cheered the game on."

Many years later, Cliff Duncan returned to the field to relive those memories. While standing on the mound where he pitched that day, Mr. Duncan was approached by a man who struck up a conversation with him. It turned out that the man had been in attendance at that state championship game - in person, not from a cell in the state prison.

Unlike today and for the past several decades where state championship games ended a team's season, that was not the case in 1967. There was another championship to be won, that of the Molly Stark League. In order to determine the champion of that league, the Warriors played additional games which had been postponed due to weather. WHS defeated St. Michael's High School, thanks to a dramatic game-ending triple play, and then went on to defeat Arlington High School, thereby winning the Molly Stark League championship.

The Warriors' final game that year, a loss to Leland and Gray, was inconsequential in the standings. However, it did evoke a fond memory for Mr. Duncan: "Unfortunately, we lost our final game at home against Leland and Gray, 11 to 7. But in that game, coach Mike Dymon had some fun moving players around, including some players pitching that hadn't pitched all season."

1972 - 2005

In 1972 at WHS, girls and boys sports were on a par with each other: field hockey and soccer in the fall, basketball for girls and boys and co-ed gymnastics in the winter, and softball and baseball in the spring.

Note: *The website,* vermontsportshistory.com, *provides a record of Vermont high school tournament games along with data on high school championship teams, games, and in some cases scores, from as far back as the 1950s. It is a fascinating collection of individual, team, and game statistics and information for Vermont high school sports. It served as a source for some of the information that follows.*

GIRLS SPORTS AND TOURNAMENT PLAY IN THE 1970S

By 1972, the Wilmington High School field hockey team had established itself as a powerhouse in what was then Class L, defeating larger high schools like Stowe, Vergennes, and Woodstock - and much larger high schools like Mount Anthony Union, Middlebury Union, and Champlain Valley Union, all in state tournament play. In spite of its small female student population, WHS had petitioned the Vermont Headmasters' Association (now the Vermont Principals' Association) to play in Class L, the state's largest athletic division. The petition was granted, and the WHS girls performed exceedingly well.

In late fall, 1973, after three years of regularly making it to the state tournament semi-finals, the WHS field hockey team was declared co-champion of their division, the result of a 1-1 overtime tie. Their opponent and the other co-champion was Mt. Anthony Union High School in Bennington, one of the largest high schools in the state.

According to an article in the November 5, 1973 *Brattleboro Reformer*, in "preliminary tournament games in the case of a tie, the winner is the team with most penalty corners in the contest. However, in the final game, only goals are counted." The *Reformer* reported that Wilmington "outplayed the Bennington team for most of the contest and had 12 penalty corners to only two for Mt. Anthony."

The *Reformer* also reported that because of the overtime tie, "A flip of a coin decided that Mt. Anthony would get the championship trophy while the Wilmington Warriors would get the medals awarded to individual members of the championship squad."

In 1974, the Warriors were seeded number one and Middlebury, number two. Wilmington's field hockey team won the Class L championship outright that year, defeating Middlebury 2-0 and finishing with an impressive overall record of 14-0-0.

The *Rutland Daily Herald* commented about the Warriors that unlike the previous year, "This year they share the large school title with no one," and then quoting a "knowledgeable observer," the *Herald* reported that it was, "Excellent field hockey - even better than the Wilmington-Essex (semi-final) game," a 0-0 tie that Wilmington had won based on corners.

The *Deerfield Valley News* reported that week that, "Wilmington and Brattleboro girls have been invited to the Philadelphia area to play field hockey with the following schools: Radnor Senior High, Springfield Senior High, and Agnes Irwin School...because of the excellent skill they have displayed while playing field hockey."

The newspaper also looked to the future by reporting that, "With 8 sophomores returning next year it should be more of the same for the Wilmington team." WHS continued to compete in Division L for the remainder of the decade but, unfortunately, failed to make it to the tournament finals.

In basketball during the 1970s, there were only three classes or divisions of competition. As a result, the WHS girls teams often played larger schools. They were consistently competitive, but made it to the Barre Auditorium ("The Aud.") only in 1977 where they defeated Northfield, 47-45 in the semi-finals and lost to Twinfield in the championship game, 63-42.

In softball during the same decade the Wilmington girls performed exceedingly well. They made it to the finals three times, winning state championships twice, defeating Thetford in 1974 and Proctor in 1976.

Throughout the 1970s, the girls were coached in all three sports by the same adults. Carol Abar, a physical education teacher at the school, served as head coach. She was assisted by WHS parent and community member Jim Kershaw.

There is little doubt that these Wilmington High School female athletes, their coaches, their parents, their fans, and the school's administration had an impact on athletic programs for girls at WHS. They created and sustained a bridge from the 1950s and 1960s, when Wilmington High School was at the forefront of advancing girls sports, through the 1970s and beyond when equality of athletic and other education-related opportunities was required by federal law, also known as Title IX.

BOYS SPORTS AND TOURNAMENT PLAY IN THE 1970S

Wilmington High School boys sports in the 1970s were competitive, with relatively successful regular season records. Unlike the field hockey teams, however, the Wilmington boys always competed against schools of comparable size. Some of these schools, like Whitingham, Austine School for the Deaf (Brattleboro), and Arlington, were nearby. Others, like Cabot and Canaan, were close to the Canadian border. Schools like Chelsea, South Royalton, West Rutland, and Whitcomb (Bethel) were somewhere in between.

During the 1970s, when it came to boys sports at Wilmington High School, at least in terms of state tournament victories, times were lean. The varsity basketball teams lost in the quarterfinals once and in the playdowns four times. Wilmington's baseball teams lost twice in the tournament playdowns and three times in the quarterfinals. However, when it came to soccer, there was one exception in November, 1977.

Today, Vermont's high school sports are divided by the Vermont Principals' Association into four categories based on student population and signified by Roman Numerals: Divisions I (the largest), II, III, and IV. However, from 1973 to 1979, there were only three categories: Classes M, I, and L. In 1977, Wilmington was in Class M, along with schools like Arlington, Chelsea, Proctor, Stowe, Thetford, Whitingham, Black River (Ludlow), South Royalton, Twinfield (Plainfield & Marshfield), and Danville.

At the conclusion of the 1977 regular soccer season, Wilmington's Warriors were seeded sixth in Class M. Coached by WHS English teacher, Mark Fitzpatrick, and social studies teacher and future WHS principal, Frank Spencer, the Warriors had begun their season with more losses than wins. However, they finished strong and had momentum as they entered the tournament. WHS easily defeated Twinfield, 5-0, in the playdowns. They defeated a favored number three seed Danville team in the quarter-finals and number two seed, Thetford, in the semi-finals.

The Thetford game was especially exciting. At the end of regulation, the teams were tied at one goal each. They played two five-minute over-times with neither team scoring. Three five-minute sudden death peri-ods followed, with Wilmington finally winning the game in the fourth sudden death period. In those days, if the score had been tied after the fourth sudden death period, the game would have been won by the team with the edge in corner kicks. Wilmington had 15 to Thetford's 5.

The 1977 finals were played at UVM's Centennial Field where until the late 1960s, the Catamounts had played football and where they cur-rently played soccer.

The Warriors' opponent that day was fourth-seeded Proctor, a team that was gunning for its third consecutive soccer championship. But the day belonged to Wilmington. As the final horn sounded and the game ended, Wilmington had defeated Proctor, 4-0. WHS had its first boys championship in 10 years and its first ever soccer championship.

WAIT. WHAT?!

Throughout my teaching career at Wilmington High School there was an exceptionally strong commitment among the adults in the build-ing to supporting one another. We were always volunteering to assist our colleagues. It was almost always an enjoyable and positive experi-ence. But there was one time that was, at least for me, a tad stressful.

It was the 1975-1976 basketball season. By this time, Frank Spencer, my social studies colleague, had become the boys varsity basketball coach. For most of his games I volunteered to either keep the official scorebook or operate the game clock.

One night I was keeping the scorebook. It was a home game, and we were locked in a close game with the team from Marlborough, New Hampshire. It had been competitive throughout. The gym was packed, and tensions were running high. While not an arch-rival, Marlborough was a physically rough team from what we Wilmington folks viewed as a rough school. And this was a rough game, one we desperately wanted to win. With 15 seconds remaining, the game was tied. Wilmington had possession of the ball and called a timeout.

As the teams huddled and planned their final strategy, Curly, one of the officials, marched over to the scorer's table and said to me, "Okay now, this could be close. Keep your eye on the ball and your ear on the buzzer." The implication was that I could end up being the one to decide whether a potential game-winning basket would count. In other words, I could be the final arbiter of this very important pressure-packed game.

Before I could ask any clarifying questions or declare unequivocally that as an unpaid volunteer this was far above my pay grade, Curly pivoted and jogged back to his position on the court next to Bill, his officiating partner that evening. Bill and Curly were veteran and well-regarded officials. But all I could think was, *What the heck are you talking about! There are two of you, you're certified officials, and you're getting paid! And you want me to make the call? Why can't you guys make the call?*

I knew enough about the rules of basketball to know that if the ball left the shooter's hand before time expired, the resulting basket would count. However, if it left the shooter's hand after the buzzer sounded, the basket would not count. Simple enough. Well, maybe.

The timeout ended, and Wilmington brought the ball down court. The noise of the crowd was reverberating off the gym walls. The atmosphere was tense.

In those days there was no thin ribbon of red light mounted around the periphery of the backboard, as there is today, to signal the end of a period or a game. In addition, the game clock mounted on the gym wall had been there for more than 20 years. It displayed only the imprecision of seconds, not tenths of seconds. And, of course, there was no video replay, official or unofficial, for officials to study if the precise end of a game was in question. Officials could only listen above the din of the crowd for the buzzer that sounded when the game clock reached

"00:00," and simultaneously watch ten players and one basketball to determine when and how a game had ended.

With only five seconds remaining, one of our players shot - and missed. Our 6' 4" center was in the lane and well-positioned for a rebound. He jumped, grabbed the errant shot, and with both hands released the ball into the air for the apparent winning basket. Game over! Our fans rushed onto the court to congratulate their victorious Warriors. Joyful fans creating joyous chaos. But there was a problem.

I immediately looked to the two officials and couldn't believe what I was seeing. Curly was signaling that the basket was good. But Bill was wildly waving his arms indicating that the basket was void; it had left the shooter's hands after time had expired. *Oh, jeez,* I thought. *Really?*

Both officials raced over the scorer's table, each one asking me, "How did *you* see it?"

Fortunately, I had been paying attention - close attention. I confidently informed them that the ball had left the player's hands *after* I heard the sound of the buzzer. Bill then marched confidently to center court and declared with more certainty than either official had shown just seconds before, "Okay," he said once again waving his arms. "The basket's no good. Scorer says so. We go into overtime."

Wilmington went on to lose the game by two points. Coach Spencer, although he said he disagreed with my call, was gracious. We were friends before the game, and that never changed. At the end-of-the-year athletic banquet, he presented me with a large, handmade cardboard clock, cleverly designed to allow for several long seconds before reaching the end of the game. While this episode is certainly not a consequential event in the annals of WHS basketball, it is one I recall with a smile.

GIRLS SPORTS AND TOURNAMENT PLAY IN THE 1980S

The success of Wilmington High School sports during the 1980s was varied when measured in tournament victories. Most of the teams had acceptable records and usually placed well in the Molly Stark League which by then consisted of Vermont and New Hampshire schools in and near the Connecticut River Valley. However, the 1980s also marked the end of an era in girls field hockey.

From 1980 to 1986, Wilmington's field hockey teams failed to make it to the state tournament semi-finals. However, in 1987, that changed. The 1987 season was bittersweet because it marked two important events in Wilmington field hockey history.

The "sweet" was significant. Coached by WHS graduate and member of the 1974 championship field hockey team, Vicki (Raymo) Capitani, the Warriors won their first state field hockey championship in 13 years, in a 0-0 tie with Proctor. Unlike in the past, this tie was not settled in overtime or by penalty strokes. Instead, it ended with Wilmington and Proctor high schools being declared co-champions. Coach Capitani recalled, "As I remember, we won the second half - we outplayed them - but we just couldn't put the ball in the net."

The "bitter" of the 1987 field hockey season was also significant. This state championship marked the end of field hockey at Wilmington High School. Beginning in 1934, field hockey at Wilmington High School had had a long and successful history of 53 years. But times were changing.

By the 1980s, soccer in the United States was gaining in popularity for both boys and girls. Co-ed summer soccer programs and weekend leagues for younger students in Wilmington and beyond were attracting increasingly more student participation and parental support. And while there was still a field hockey program at Wilmington's high school level, there was no opportunity at the school for junior high girls to continue using and developing the soccer skills they had acquired during their younger years.

And so in 1987, while the WHS varsity field hockey team was working hard to successfully realize their dream of a championship season, a girls junior varsity soccer team was formed. The 13 members of this new soccer team were coached by WHS parent and community member, Ken Lady. The team consisted of freshmen, sophomores, and juniors. In addition, at the junior high level, there were now two co-ed soccer teams.

A year later in 1988, a girls varsity soccer program replaced field hockey altogether. In their first year of varsity competition, the WHS girls soccer team had a full contingent of 18 players, some of whom had played field hockey the year before and others of whom had played on the JV soccer team. They were coached by WHS parent and community member Ken Nieters and posted a record of 3-10. A year later as the 1980s came to an end, their record improved significantly to 8-6.

During the 1980s, the girls basketball teams made it to the semi-finals in 1980 and 1983, losing both times to Twinfield High School.

In 1980, the girls softball team made it to the finals. However, it was not without controversy. The softball championship game was to be held at Enosburg Falls High School, almost four hours north of Wilmington and just a few miles south of the Canadian border. Enosburg Falls was the higher seed, and because of that the game would be played on their field. But there was a problem. The championship game was scheduled for the same day and time as Wilmington's graduation.

Would the senior members of the team be allowed to skip graduation and play in the game? Could the game be rescheduled for another day? Could graduation be rescheduled for another day? Could the game be played at an early hour and graduation moved to a later hour?

At the center of this dilemma was our principal, Forrest Murdock. After dealing with what was likely a very stressful situation, he ruled that graduation would proceed as planned. The team would make the trip to Enosburg Falls, but the seniors on the team would not make the trip. They would attend their graduation. The softball team lost to Enosburg Falls, 18-1. Since then, but probably not necessarily because of this specific circumstance, the Vermont Principals' Association and Vermont's high schools have succeeded overall in avoiding similar conflicts.

In 1983 and again in 1988, the girls softball teams competed in the state semi-finals, losing to Arlington and Stowe respectively.

BOYS SPORTS AND TOURNAMENT PLAY IN THE 1980S

Boys sports in the 1980s were improving in terms of tournament appearances. In 1986, the baseball team made it to the semi-finals but lost to Concord, 2-1. In 1983 and 1984 the basketball teams, coached by WHS teacher Frank Spencer, experienced tournament success by making successive visits to the Barre Auditorium. However, in 1983 the Warriors lost to Sacred Heart (Newport) in the semis, 74-61, and in 1984, they lost in the finals to Danville, 66-50.

The 1980s also marked the emergence of one of the more successful high school soccer programs in the state. Following the 1977 state championship, Wilmington High School made it to the semi-finals of the state tournament in 1978 and 1979, but lost each time. The same was true in 1984 and 1985, both times losing to Proctor. However, in 1986, two-year substitute P.E. teacher and coach, Phil Meade, and his team defeated Black River High School (Ludlow), 2-0, for Wilmington's first state soccer championship in nine years. WHS lost in the finals a year later and in the semis in 1989.

GIRLS SPORTS AND TOURNAMENT PLAY IN THE 1990S

In the 1990s, the Wilmington girls teams made several tournament appearances. In a most impressive stretch, the girls soccer teams won three state championships. In 1994, coached by Ken Nieters and just six years after their inaugural season, the WHS girls defeated Twinfield, 2-1, for their first-ever state soccer championship. Three years later in 1997, and again coached by Ken Nieters, they defeated Canaan by a score of 2-1. In 1999, coached by Deerfield Valley Elementary School physical education teacher, Chris Walling, they tied Proctor, 0-0, to share the state title.

In basketball, the Wilmington High School girls lost in the 1997 semi-finals by only 6 points. In 1998, they made it to the finals, where they lost to Canaan, 64-55. However, in 1999, coached by WHS grad and teacher Buddy Hayford, they defeated Canaan by two points, 46-44, for Wilmington's first ever basketball state championship.

During the 1990s, at least measured by tournament victories, the WHS softball teams struggled and did not make it into the quarter-finals.

BOYS SPORTS AND TOURNAMENT PLAY IN THE 1990S

During the 1990s, the success of the boys soccer team was remarkable, to say the least. They made it to the semi-finals six times and the finals four of those times. Their coach, Buddy Hayford, would eventually become the winningest high school soccer coach in Vermont history.

This run of soccer success began in 1992. The Warriors tied Canaan, 1-1, in regulation time of the semi-finals but lost to them, the eventual state champion, on penalty kicks. However, a year later in 1993, the boys won their first soccer championship of the nineties, defeating Twinfield, 2-1. They won two more consecutive championships. In 1994 they defeated West Rutland, 2-0, and in 1995, they bested Concord, 2-0. It was the first time in Wilmington High School history that a team had won three consecutive state championships in any sport, and in doing so they retired the state championship trophy. A year later in 1996, the boys lost to eventual state champion Proctor in the semis, 1-0, and in 1999 they lost in the semis to Black River (Ludlow), 1-0.

The boys basketball teams during this decade lost twice in the play-downs and three times in the quarterfinals.

For a three-year stretch, Wilmington High School baseball in the 1990s had some notable tournament success. Coached by WHS graduate, Roy Moyer, in 1995, they were seeded fourth, with a record of 8-7. Neighboring Whitingham High School, 8-5, was seeded first. The teams' semi-final matchup was reported by the *Brattleboro Reformer* as "the biggest baseball game in the history of the Deerfield Valley," and the game lived up to the hype.

Played at Whitingham School, the game was tied going into the seventh and final regular inning. In the top of the inning, Wilmington scored three runs and held on to defeat the Trojans, 5-2. A few days later, the Warriors lost to Proctor in the finals, 7-0. A year later in 1996, they lost to Proctor again, this time in the semi-finals, 5-0.

In 1997, the WHS baseball team was again coached by Roy Moyer. For the second time in three years, the team concluded its season in the Division IV championship game. To say that their trip to the finals that year was improbable would be an understatement.

The team consisted of just 12 players, only two of whom were seniors. With a core of six juniors, there was reason for optimism, but halfway through the season the team was winless and had already lost five games. But they recovered. After three consecutive wins against Whitingham, Proctor, and West Rutland, they alternated wins and losses to finish the regular season at 6-8. It was only a 43 percent winning percentage, but it was good enough to earn Wilmington the number three seed.

The quarter-finals that year pitted Wilmington at home against Concord, the number six seed with a record of 3-12. At the bottom of the fifth inning Concord held a commanding 16-3 lead. But by the top of the 7th inning WHS had narrowed the lead to 16-13. Then, in the bottom of the seventh inning, with a combination of costly Concord errors and timely WHS hitting and aggressive base running, Wilmington pulled out the dramatic victory, 17-16.

Four days later against home team Rochester High School, the Warriors found themselves down 6-0 in the second inning of their semi-final game. However, for the remainder of the game, they held Rochester scoreless while chipping away at their lead and sending the game into extra innings. A second comeback ended with an eight-inning 7-6 Wilmington victory.

Less than 48 hours later, the "Comeback Kids," as the *Brattleboro Reformer* labeled them, were on their way to UVM's Centennial Field to face Proctor High School again, this time in the state's Division IV finals. Proctor was the top seed in the division and featured an all-star pitcher who would go on to play college baseball. The result was a 7-1 Proctor victory.

The Wilmington loss was a difficult one, but the team and their fans took pride in how well the Warriors had played in their two previous games, overcoming total deficits of 19 runs in two games. Note: *On a personal note, it was enjoyable for me to be able to watch my son play on Centennial Field, the field where I had played exactly 30 years earlier for UVM's freshman baseball team.*

LET THERE BE LIGHT

Until the 1994 soccer season, both girls and boys soccer teams at WHS played their games in the afternoon. The May 10, 2024 issue of the *Deerfield Valley News* reported that thirty years before in 1994, "The Wilmington Athletic Booster Club started a campaign to raise money for lights at Baker Field. They hoped to reach their fundraising goal of $17,000 by the end of May, and planned to install lights by August 1."

During that summer, through the fundraising efforts, generosity, and hard work of many parents and community members, several banks of lights were purchased and installed on the soccer field before the start of the season. To this day, many of Twin Valley's girls and boys soccer games, varsity, JV, and middle school, are played under the lights on what is now Hayford Field.

GIRLS SPORTS AND TOURNAMENT PLAY - 2000-2004

In September, 2004 Wilmington High School and neighboring Whitingham High School merged to form Twin Valley High School.

Before the merger, however, the final four years of the Wilmington High School girls soccer program (2000-2003), coached by Chris Walling, were spectacular by any standard and unmatched by any Wilmington team. WHS won four consecutive state championships - five if you count the 1999 championship. Since their inception as a varsity soccer program in 1987, the WHS girls tournament record was 23 wins, 9 losses, and one tie.

The girls' record in basketball during this time reflected fewer state championships but, still, many trips to the Aud. From 2000 to 2004, and coached by WHS grad and teacher Buddy Hayford, the girls played nine games in Barre, winning four semi-finals and one state championship. They were led by several outstanding players, some of whom went on to perform impressively in the college game.

During this time, Wilmington softball endured some challenging seasons, except for 2002, when they defeated Rochester, Blue Mountain, and Whitcomb (Bethel) to make it to the finals where they lost to Canaan, 6-1.

BOYS SPORTS AND TOURNAMENT PLAY - 2000-2004

By tournament standards, the boys soccer teams from 2000-2003 did well. In 2000, they lost in the semis. However, they won state championships in 2001 and 2002. In their final season, 2003, they lost to Proctor, 1-0, in the state finals. All of these teams were coached by Buddy Hayford.

During this time, the boys basketball team's only trip to the Aud. was in 2004, where they lost in the semis to Proctor.

The WHS baseball teams struggled, winning 33 percent of their games.

Wilmington High School State Tournament Records
(Years for which there are records according to
vermontsportshistory.com)

Note: *The final WHS seasons were: soccer - fall, 2003; basketball - winter, 2003-2004; baseball and softball - spring, 2004)*

Overall, the State Tournament Record for WHS girls was:
> Field Hockey (1970-1987) 15 wins -13 losses - 2 ties
> Soccer (1989-2003) 23-9-1
> Basketball (1974-2004) 29-21
> Softball (1974-2004) 19-17

Overall, the State Tournament Record for WHS boys was:
> Soccer (1960-2003) 46 wins -21 losses
> Basketball (1938-2004) 11-31
> Baseball (1967-2004) 10-22

OTHER SPORTS

For decades before my arrival, cheerleading was consistently offered as an activity for girls at WHS. During my time at WHS (1972-2004), in addition to the traditional sports described above, other athletic opportunities were also available. Many WHS students skied competitively on a school team or under the auspices of Mount Snow, Haystack, WHS, another organization, or independently. In the 1990s and into the 2000s, several WHS students participated in competitive snowboarding.

Other sports included golf, tennis, track and field, and girls lacrosse, all on an intermittent basis dependent usually on student interest and the availability of coaches.

Intramural gymnastics was offered but only until the mid-seventies.

In 1972, cheerleading at WHS involved 13 girls, six at the varsity level and seven at the JV level. Cheerleading continued for several years until it ended as a formal activity in the late 1980s. However, in 1993 and 1994, cheerleaders once again took the floor for WHS during the basketball season.

WILMINGTON'S MASCOT

The word "mascot" is derived from French and refers to something intended to bring good luck - a lucky charm. A mascot usually represents or symbolizes a group or organization. Colleges and universities, along with professional sports teams, have had mascots for over 100 years.

To the best of my knowledge and based on my research, until 1945, Wilmington High School's athletic teams were not represented by a mascot in the traditional sense; they were known generally as Wilmington High School.

I once heard a vague reference to the Wilmington High School mascot from earlier times: the Wolves. However, it's difficult to know if, for how long, or by whom Wilmington's teams might have been known in this way. I found only one such reference in my research. In a 1945 article in the *Rutland Daily Herald,* the WHS boys basketball team was referred to as the Wolves. The headline read, "Wolves Whip Midd (Middlebury), 19-11." The article states, "The Wilmington Wolves, coached by Principal Newton Baker, were Class C tournament favorites for the three years when the playoffs were held in Waterbury."

When I heard that the Wolves once represented Wilmington's teams, I heard from the same source (who that person was I have long since forgotten) that the mascot name was dropped because of the rather unsavory connotation of the "wolf whistle."

By the mid-1950s, the existence of another mascot at Wilmington High School appears to have become official. The first reference that I found to Wilmington's "Warriors" was in the February, 1955 issue of the *Mirror*. A headline in the publication's sports section announced a WHS victory over Leland and Gray Seminary: "Warriors Scalp L.G.S."

In the spring, 1957 issue of the *Mirror,* the nature of the Warrior is clearer. The full title page of the *Mirror's* sports section depicts a cartoonish Native American with a large nose and a toothy grin, wearing a breechcloth, and wielding a stone club in one hand and a scalp in the other.

Today, the appropriateness of high school mascots in various parts of the United States, including Vermont, is still being discussed, evaluated, litigated, or legislated. In many states, mascots that evoke negative memories or images are being challenged and often replaced.

I don't recall seeing the image of a Wilmington Warrior on any school athletic uniforms. They were usually adorned with a large "W" or the words "Wilmington" or "Warriors." For example, the shirts of the boys baseball uniforms in the mid-1960s included crossed tomahawks with "Wilmington" printed underneath.

Other representations of the school's mascot, however, were more graphic. In addition to the page in the 1957 *Mirror*, in the mid-1970s, a pad of notebook paper being sold at the school store included on its cover a drawing of the Wilmington Warrior. It showed a stereotypical caricature of a Native American similar to that in the 1957 *Mirror*. The WHS band uniforms in the mid-1980s displayed on their bibs a similar image minus the tomahawk and scalp. Team gym bags in the 1970s also carried this caricature.

However, these negative depictions were a rarity and faded with time. Most of the Warrior images, for example on a WHS yearbook cover or at the center of the school's basketball court, were of a dignified Native American brave or war-bonneted chieftain, usually depicted above the shoulders. And by the time Native American images and mascot names had been recognized as unacceptable, a large blue "W" had replaced the Warrior image at the center of the school's gym floor.

The last WHS yearbook to use any Warrior image (in this case a war-bonneted chieftain) on its cover was in 1989.

It's important to note that during my time at WHS no one challenged these images. The nature of the WHS mascot was never an issue that involved the students, faculty, administration, or the community at large, either in Wilmington or beyond.

However, I do recall one discussion about the appropriateness of the Warrior nickname or the images used to represent it. When I was the student council advisor in the late seventies, the council president asked me what I thought about changing the name and image of the school's mascot to something less ethnic. I said if that was an issue the council would like to pursue, I would be glad to advise them on it. In spite of some early student interest, it quickly faded and no action ever materialized.

In 2004, as Wilmington and Whitingham (formerly the Trojans) high schools were preparing to merge into Twin Valley, the students in grades 6-12 voted to have the wildcat serve as their new mascot.

According to the March 28, 2024 issue of the *Deerfield Valley News* describing events from twenty years earlier, students preferred "Harriman" as the preferred name for the high school and "Twin Valley" for the middle school. The newspaper reported that, "The 'Twin Valley' name was also the second choice for the high school. The top school mascot names were the 'Lakers,' as in Harriman Lakers, and the 'Wildcats.' Some of the more whimsical names, such as the Wombats, the Wizards, and the Demons failed to get enough votes for future consideration." Note: *One student in my middle school advisory enthusiastically suggested that the aardvark be the new mascot. I can't recall how many votes it received, but it was ultimately and mercifully rejected.*

WILMINGTON HIGH SCHOOL'S OPPONENTS, 1972 - 2004 (SPRING)

In addition to the schools mentioned in this chapter, there are others that Wilmington teams played against. From 1972 to 2004 (spring),

Wilmington High School teams played teams from the following Division IV schools during the regular season and in tournament play.

Arlington
Austine School for the Deaf* (Brattleboro)
Black River* (Ludlow)
Blue Mountain
Cabot
Canaan
Chelsea
Concord*
Craftsbury
Danville
Enosburg Falls**
Leland and Gray**
Proctor
Rochester*
Sacred Heart (Bennington*?)
Sharon
Stowe**
South Royalton*
Thetford
Twinfield
United Christian (Newport)
Websterville Baptist Christian
West Rutland
Whitcomb* (Bethel)
Whitingham (merged with Wilmington HS, 2004)
Williamstown

*Closed and merged with neighboring school(s) as of 2020.
** Alternated between Division III and Division IV

Wilmington Competed Against Other Nearby
Non-division IV Schools
(these schools were in Vermont unless otherwise noted)
Mt. Anthony Union HS (Bennington)
Brattleboro Union HS
Bellows Falls Union HS
Burr & Burton
Clarke School for the Deaf (Clarke School for Hearing & Speech, Northampton, MA)
Drury HS (No. Adams, MA)
Green Mountain Union HS (Chester)
Green Mtn. Valley
Hinsdale HS (NH)
Marlborough HS (Marlborough, NH)
McCann Tech. HS (No. Adams, MA)
Mohawk Regional HS (MA)
Putney School
Springfield HS
Stratton Mtn. School
Thayer HS (Winchester, NH)

A PERSONAL REFECTION: COACHING JUNIOR HIGH SOCCER

During the autumn of my first and second years at Wilmington High School, I helped coach the boys junior high soccer team. In those days in the early seventies, the boys played soccer, and the girls played field hockey. In 1972, the official junior high coach, Mark Fitzpatrick, was an English teacher, and like me, he was new to Wilmington High School. Coaching was an opportunity for both of us to get to know some of our junior high boys, and vice-versa, outside of the classroom. We played schools like Stamford, Halifax, Readsboro, Leland and Gray, and our arch rival in those days, Whitingham.

By 1974, Mark had become the varsity soccer coach, and I remained as the junior high coach and would continue as such for another 13 years. Our junior high team continued to play the smaller schools and a few schools of comparable size like Whitingham, Leland and Gray, and Mohawk Regional. We also competed successfully against larger schools like Mount Anthony (Bennington) and Brattleboro.

Each junior high soccer season was unique. While it was not uncommon to have more than 20 boys on the team, our win/loss record fluctuated. Some years we went undefeated, even while playing larger schools. Other years we struggled to win one or two games, regardless of the opponent.

In the early years, I scheduled our games and arranged for officials, all of whom were volunteers. Note: *These included WHS teachers John Stetzel, Frank Spencer, Bernie Shaw, Bill Kunz, and Mark Fitzpatrick, and DVES principal, Don Finck.*

Some years there might be several eighth grade boys on the team who were physically mature and athletically gifted. In other years we might have a collection of players more typical of grades seven and eight: all shapes, sizes, and abilities.

Each game was also unique. One time we played a larger school, 45 minutes to the north, and lost decisively. Their goalie, according to some of our boys who saw him up close, had whiskers. I supposed it was possible, but I dismissed it. And then, as we were boarding our bus to return to Wilmington, I could swear we saw him get behind the wheel of a jeep and drive away.

One year in the mid-seventies, we won the Trail League championship (Wilmington, Whitingham, Readsboro, Halifax, Stamford, and Mohawk Regional). The championship game was closely contested and very exciting - a back-and-forth 7-6 overtime victory against Readsboro, coached by a good friend and neighbor, Dennis Butchko. My memories of that game remain vivid to this day.

During my time as a junior high soccer coach, I was quite competitive, as were my counterparts at some of the schools we competed against - some smaller than WHS, some larger. None of us coaches was ever a wild-eyed, screaming, frothing-at-the-mouth kind of coach. We were cordial to each other and insisted on good sportsmanship from our players. Even so, underneath our cordiality was a strong desire to win and an even stronger desire not to lose.

In those days, I could call the *Brattleboro Reformer* sports department in the early evening and give them a brief summary of each game: our opponent, the score, and which boys scored or played well. A game summary was usually published the next day in a two-to-three column-inch story.

When Mark Fitzpatrick and I began coaching the junior high boys, we concluded the season with a father and son banquet. I soon changed that to a parent and son banquet, and ultimately to a family event.

The 1975 banquet was especially memorable for me. Our season had been quite successful; we had gone undefeated. The team presented me with a wristwatch. This was a complete surprise. As a junior high coach, I had never received nor had I ever expected to receive a gift from my team. The watch was a modest piece, as it should have been. But it was special. Inscribed on the clasp of the metal band in small letters written with what I am sure was a focused but shaky 13 year-old hand, was: "SOCCOR - 1975 - WJHS - 9-0-0."

The day after our banquet, I was wearing my new watch with pride and appreciation. Between classes, two of my players, the eighth grade co-captains, approached me. They were proud of the gift they had chosen for me and pleased to see it on full display. But they had a concern and a question.

"Mr. Larsen, on the watch band did you notice that 'soccer' was misspelled?" The boys were apologetic and a little embarrassed, and one of them confessed to making the spelling error while inscribing the watch band.

"Well, yes," I said. "I did notice. But I'm not concerned. It's a really nice watch, and that's what makes it special." With smiles of satisfaction and maybe a little relief, they nodded in agreement and headed off to their next class. The watch is long gone, but I still have that piece of inscribed silver-colored metal. Special, indeed.

During the years I coached, every player received a small trophy or plaque with a small gold soccer ball mounted on it. The plaque was inscribed with, "Wilmington Junior High Soccer" and the year.

Later, we instituted the practice of awarding every participating junior high student a modest trophy, the height of which was determined by how many sports (one, two, or three) they participated in. It didn't matter who had scored the most goals, baskets, or runs. What mattered was what we as a school wanted to emphasize: participation and commitment to being a member of a team.

I know there are those who scoff at giving awards to students for simply participating or "showing up," with no priority for performance above and beyond. But this wasn't the Congressional Medal of Honor or even high school athletics. This was a matter of spending a few bucks of taxpayer money to give each kid a small memento of a time when they were a member of a meaningful group experience: all wearing the same uniform, all pulling in the same direction, and all working toward a common goal. There were and are few things more important to a young adolescent than finding success and satisfaction as a member of a group of their peers, and I thoroughly enjoyed helping them do that.

FINAL THOUGHTS

As is the case in many high schools, sports were an important core activity at WHS, and they were supported as such. Shortly after I arrived in 1972, as soccer began to grow in popularity, the school board approved without hesitation a request from a parent to fund a junior varsity soccer program, similar to the existing JV field hockey program.

In addition, whenever there was a larger-than-usual number of junior high or middle school students who wanted to play a sport, the school board and community invariably supported additional teams and coaches. This was especially true for basketball where only five players could simultaneously participate in a game. If there was sufficient student interest, I can't think of a single instance where the administration or the school board rejected a request to expand an athletic or extra-curricular activity for WHS students.

By any measure, athletic teams at Wilmington High School were consistently successful. This was due to many factors: strong family support and involvement; high-quality coaching, often by WHS faculty, WHS graduates, community members, or parents of team members; elementary-level and community feeder programs; supportive school boards and administrations; strong local interest and publicity; positive peer-to-peer influence; public and financial support for programs; and local traditions.

There was a sign in my high school locker room that read, "A boy for every sport and a sport for every boy." With 1000 students, there were certainly enough boys at my high school to easily fill every position on every team, and then some. However, there were obviously not enough "sports for every boy." The result? Tryouts and cuts.

I know that tryouts and cuts, attempts and failures, are part of life. It's not like Lake Wobegon where "all children are above average." Life is competitive, whether it's sports, getting and sometimes keeping a job or being promoted, or getting into the college of one's choice. Competition is woven into the fabric of our capitalistic economy and our democratic society. It's who we are as Americans. But when it came to sports, it didn't have to be. And that is why I so enjoyed coaching and teaching at Wilmington High School.

At Wilmington High School, whether it was in the junior high program and years later in the middle school program, or in high school, if a student wanted to play and was willing to do what was expected, they were on the team. I always enjoyed seeing students develop a sense of self by being part of a peer group - a team - that worked cooperatively toward a common goal.

There are many ways to assess the value and the success of athletic programs for middle and high school students. The two I describe in this chapter, tournament competition and overall team records, are two criteria for measuring success, mostly because they are quantifiable. But there are many other ways to assess the value of an athletic program, and most of them are more important than a team's win-loss record. They include: learning that academics come first; appreciating and enjoying the benefits of physical activity; understanding the importance of team-work; learning to accept victory with a sense humility and defeat with a sense of grace; and personal growth and self-discipline, to name a few.

Toward these ends and throughout its existence, Wilmington High School exhibited a proud tradition of athletic commitment, accom-plishment, and support.

Above and following page: The Central School gym, 1930 - 1955.

CHAPTER 20

Technology

O ne of the first references in annual town and school reports to technology at the Central School appears in 1898, when Wilmington superintendent of schools Ernest Maynard wrote, "Through the generosity of Miss Mary Heather and prominent citizens of Wilmington, the school has been equipped with a Bausch and Lomb compound microscope with two eye pieces and one-half and one-sixth inch objectives, an Abbi camera lucinda, forceps, slips, cover-glasses, scalpel and eighteen prepared slides illustrating botanical and physiological structures. The value of the apparatus is $55." Note: *According to Wikipedia, the camera lucinda was a device "used largely for copying (by hand), for reducing or for enlarging existing drawings."*

Shortly thereafter, the Old Home Week edition of the *Deerfield Valley Times* proudly proclaimed that the high school owned a Bausch and Lomb compound microscope and touted it as being "as good as any used in college work, and which renders more effective the work in zoology and botany."

In the late 1920s and into the 1930s, the technology used by high school students at the Central School included the aforementioned science equipment as well as typewriters and general science and home economics equipment consistent with the times.

In an effort to improve the school's assortment of technology, Superintendent Benjamin Hamlin in his 1932 annual report wrote, "Other needs of the Central building, tho by no means to be classified as absolute necessities, but which would still add to the effectiveness of our high school, are a duplicator such as a mimeograph or 'ditto;' a projector such as the 'Balopticon;' and even a radio..."

Note: *The Balopticon that Superintendent Hamlin refers to was the precursor to the overhead projector. It was a combination slide and opaque projector manufactured by the Bausch & Lomb Company in Rochester, New York. It got its name from the first two letters of the company's founders' last names, John Bausch and Henry Lomb. An ad for the projector stated that it, "adds interest and effectiveness to English classes" because students' essays could be projected onto a screen so that "wrong constructions, grammatical errors, misspelled words..." could be seen and critiqued by their classmates.*

Superintendent Hamlin's mention of the ditto machine was prescient. The use of this machine was a staple of school communication into the early-to-mid 1980s. In addition to being of practical use in the school's office, it was necessary for the publication of the *Mirror*, the high school's highly acclaimed literary magazine and yearbook.

In 1936, according to the *Deerfield Valley Times*, "The Wilmington High School Mirror board purchased a new mimeoscope or drawing board. Its use will make it much easier to draw pictures and headings in the Mirror and at the same time greatly improve their quality...The new mimeoscope will be their particular pride and joy if all goes well." Note: *The Mirror was published commercially in paperback from its inception in 1921 until 1933. From 1933 until 1967, it was published in-house using the school's ditto or stenciling duplicating equipment. In 1967 until the closing of WHS in 2004, the Mirror, serving as the school's yearbook, was published commercially in hard cover.*

Bill Cimonetti (WHS '48) recalled that in the late 1940s, WHS offered typing, and, he said, may have had as many as 12 typewriters in the typing classroom. Until the late '40s, typing was offered to or taken by only girls.

Mr. Cimonetti also commented on the WHS chemistry lab, or room, in the late 1940s: "We did have a course in Chemistry in 1947-48, and there was a sort of lab. I remember tables with sinks, but this might have also been the Home Ec. Room. Our chemistry experiments were really rudimentary. There were no Bunsen burners, so each lab station had a miniature alcohol fueled lamp. It seems to me that the only chemical conversion we accomplished was creating sulfur dioxide. I do remember the 'rotten egg' aroma."

School reports in the 1950s make a few specific references to the school's use of technology or, in some cases, equipment. They include in 1950, a new stove for "the Home Economic laboratory; new typewriters for the Commercial Department; and a new Spirit Duplicator machine for use by all teachers and the school office."

In 1951, principal Russell Hanson wrote that the school had purchased "11 new typewriters for the Commercial Department and an opaque projector." Two years later he reported that the school had purchased a new electric typewriter for the department. In 1954, a new fume hood was installed in the high school's science lab, and a new gas range was added to the Home Economics lab. Finally, in 1959, a new tape recorder and several new record players were purchased for general classroom use. Note: *Absent any information to the contrary, it's safe to assume that in the 1940s through the 1960s, the school's equipment and use of technology continued to improve and was consistent with the times.*

The increasing importance of technology affected, at least to some extent, the curriculum at WHS. In their 1963 annual report, the school directors wrote, "We have been seriously considering instruction in Modern Mathematics. This change seems necessary to prepare the graduate for a world of computers and IBM machines."

In support of that possibility, the superintendent wrote in his 1963 report, "A teacher workshop was held in Modern Mathematics this summer in Wilmington under the direction of Dr. George Cunningham who is the Director of the Greater Cleveland Math Project. While we have not formally entered into the structured modern math program, we are trying out some of the processes and vocabulary used in such a program."

MY EXPERIENCES WITH TECHNOLOGY AT
WILMINGTON HIGH SCHOOL: COPY THAT

When I started teaching at Wilmington High School in 1972, I had no texts or materials for two of my three courses, so I had to quickly master the skills and the equipment needed to reproduce any materials I created or could find.

If I wanted to make copies of a worksheet or an exam, I used the ditto machine. I would type the document onto a ditto master. If I made an error in typing or writing on the master, I had four choices: retype the document onto a new master; cross out the error by typing over it with a series of "Xs,"; apply a thin piece of white-out tape to the underside of the master and type on it; or scrape off the blue ink error with a scalpel-like instrument and try again. None of these was optimal. In fact, each was a giant pain in the neck.

If the duplicator fluid setting was too low, the copies would have a distinctly faded appearance. If it was too high, they'd be soaked with fluid, in which case I would blow on them to dry them off. Inadvertently inhaling instead of blowing had its risks. The duplicator fluid consisted of various alcohols and derivatives thereof. The fumes were dizzying.

When I wanted to make copies of a magazine article, I would use the Thermofax machine. I'd slide the page to be copied between two pieces of paper: one, a piece of blank tissue-like paper, and the other impregnated with blue ink. The heat from the machine produced a reverse print ditto master on the tissue paper that I would attach to the drum of the ditto machine - and crank away. Unfortunately, there was always an element of blurriness to these copies.

The folks in the main office had their own ditto machine with an electric-powered drum; no cranking necessary. But for us teachers, there was a strict hands-off policy when it came to using this crank-free piece of technology. It was for office personnel only, and appropriately so. The machine was an essential piece of equipment when it came to in-school or external communication.

Within a decade or so, the power of Xerox arrived at Wilmington High School. And by the 1990s, we had a large machine that not only made copies, it printed them back-to-back, collated, and stapled them.

In some ways the copy machine was the lifeblood of the school; it certainly was for me. From the mid-1980s until the early 1990s when I was teaching world geography and world history, I used traditional text-books. However, with the advent of the middle school, I created and chose my own materials. It was more work, but it allowed me to create, adapt, use, and regularly update materials that were consistent with our middle school themes, curriculum, and state standards. Having a modern copier made that possible.

The major downside of having a sophisticated copy machine upon which the school depended was the dreaded paper jam. Only the secretaries, and maybe our principal, were qualified and had permission to access the innards of the machine and unjam it. There was a reason for this. It was not uncommon for some of us teachers to fancy ourselves as impromptu copy machine technicians who would try to rectify the paper jam. As we started fidgeting with various wires, switches, drums, or other components, there were any number of things that could go wrong, and sometimes they did.

At that point the copier would be declared off limits and would require a service call. This happened only occasionally, but it could create havoc for office personnel or for any teacher who had not planned ahead and made copies a day or two in advance.

GOING VISUAL

During my first year of teaching, I used little or no electronic audio or visual technology. Probably my first use of a visual aid was a piece of chalk and the blackboard in my classroom.

Both my first and second classrooms at WHS were in the 1956 brick wing. Prior to 1970 and the construction of Deerfield Valley Elementary School, they had been elementary classrooms, and each had a blackboard that ran almost the entire width of the room. I appreciated having so much space to write on. However, in addition to writing legibly (my first and only "F" was in fourth grade - in handwriting), my real challenge was trying to master the act of writing on the blackboard with my back turned to my class at only a ninety degree angle. This allowed me to observe my students while I wrote, albeit with limited peripheral vision. It wasn't that I didn't trust them. I just felt that minimizing opportunities for mischief was always a prudent approach.

Since there was no established junior high social studies curriculum when I was hired at WHS, there were few, if any, relevant or up-to-date audio-visual materials available. However, rummaging through the shelves in our school's library reference closet or another closet adjacent to my classroom sometimes yielded a few older items that I could use.

Within a few years, I began to accumulate my own modest selection of filmstrips. Most were accompanied by records or small audio cassettes. The student who chose the lucky number of the day got to turn the black plastic knob on the projector that advanced the filmstrip. Any filmstrip seemed to please my students as an adequate and welcome alternative to the usual class activities.

Wilmington High School had one or two Kodak slide projectors and a few empty carousels in its technology inventory. If I traveled to an interesting locale or visited a museum, I made it a point to take photographs (slides) to share with my students. Note: *For you younger readers, to quote Wikipedia, a slide is a "specially mounted individual transparency intended for projection onto a screen using a slide projector. This allows the photograph to be viewed by a large audience at once. The most common form is the 35 mm slide, with the image framed in a 2×2 inch cardboard or plastic mount."*

I'd also take slides of pictures in books. All of these were an effective way to illustrate various concepts to my students. As was the case with the filmstrip projector, the student who chose the lucky number got to "click the clicker" on the slide projector or its attached remote and advance each slide. Either honor required me to have an excellent memory.

Otherwise, I risked hearing, "Mr. Larsen, that's not fair. I haven't done it yet, and Jimmy did it two months ago."

In 1975, I discovered a thick catalog of films from the Syracuse University library. For a fee I could order a 16mm film, keep it for up to a week, and then mail it back. This, of course, required me to learn how to thread one of the school's two 16mm sound motion picture projectors, the first of which was a gift to the school in 1963 by the Beaver Brook Parents and Teachers Club.

Each projector threaded the film automatically, which was great - until it malfunctioned. With 25 sets of eager eyes belonging to increasingly restless young adolescents focused on me, I quickly learned how to troubleshoot under pressure. This meant being adept at rethreading the film, splicing torn film with Scotch Tape, replacing a burned out bulb, or making sure the image on the film and the sound were in sync. More than any other form of technology, films, or "movies" as my students called them, were a big hit. As soon as my students entered my classroom and saw the projector I would hear, "Aw, cool. Mr. Larsen, are we gonna see a movie today?" If the answer was, "No, sorry. It's for another class," their disappointment was palpable.

Another piece of technology was the overhead projector. It was a lightweight and simple piece of equipment. I could simply lay a transparent sheet of plastic onto it, and light from a large bulb below reflected the image onto two angled mirrors. The image would then appear on a large screen in the front of the room. However, I rarely used it. The fan that cooled the hot bulb made far too much noise and rendered this piece of equipment impractical, at least for me.

Probably the largest and least useful piece of technology throughout my career was the opaque projector. This was a large metal beast of a machine - the shape of a Volkswagen Beetle and almost as large. It was capable of projecting non-transparent images such as the page of a book. To do this, it used mirrors and an intense light. The problem with this machine was, much like the overhead projector, the cooling fan made so much noise, I had to almost shout to be heard above it.

SONY MAKES A DIFFERENCE

In October, 1973 a new age of technology arrived at Wilmington High School in the form of a large color television, a VCR (video cassette recorder/player), and a video camera that recorded in black and white. The VCR recorded with sound, as long as the microphone with its long thin wire was attached to it. All were SONY products - top of the line stuff.

The television and VCR were massive by current standards. Each was stored and transported in a heavy-duty case on wheels. The cases looked like something a rock band would use for road shows. Each case had two inches of foam padding glued onto its interior. Together, the television and its case easily weighed 70 pounds. The VCR and its case weighed around the same. The camera, its tripod, microphone, and wires were stored and transported in a suitcase weighing around 30 pounds. All of it combined was a far cry from today's iPhone that has far more capabilities than this entire SONY ensemble. However, in its day, it was state of the art.

When this equipment first appeared at WHS, few of my students had ever seen themselves on videotape. I occasionally taped a class activity in which they were performing or presenting. Unfortunately, in the early years I rarely used the recordings as true teaching or learning tools. When we watched a video of the students, it was more often for the novelty of the experience than it was for teaching and learning specific skills.

However, as I became more familiar with the equipment's use and potential, this changed. In my sociology and psychology classes I used it to record various class activities. I also used it with my younger students for mock trials and oral presentations.

In addition to the occasional classroom use, the camera and recording unit had a few other applications. A year or two after acquiring the video equipment, I suggested to teacher and varsity basketball coach, Frank Spencer, that it might be fun and even instructive to videotape the boys basketball games. He agreed, and I did so for several years.

With only one camera on a shaky tripod - a camera that produced a rather fuzzy, gray image - it was difficult to watch the recordings without getting a little nauseous. There was one time, however, when a video of a game, and more to the point its aftermath, was involved in what some of our students viewed at the time as a scandal of considerable proportion.

It happened at a basketball game in the mid-1970s that took place in a packed WHS gymnasium. The game was hotly contested, with lead changes throughout. While the fans weren't necessarily unruly, they were definitely involved in cheering for their respective teams. It was intense. With just seconds remaining, Wilmington took the lead and held on for an emotional and exciting victory. Wilmington's cheerleaders and students poured onto the court to congratulate our team.

Suddenly, amid the chaos, the cheerleaders of the visiting team tore down two or three of the large "Go Warriors" posters that were taped to the gym wall. As the bedlam subsided, some of the Wilmington students began making accusations about who had done what. Denials quickly followed as the fans began clearing the gym. With no definitive proof on either side, the issue was unresolved, but it was not forgotten.

A few days later, our principal asked me if I had videotaped the game. I responded in the affirmative and commented that I had also recorded what followed. He watched the videotape and then called his counterpart at the other school. With virtually irrefutable proof (although fuzzy, gray, and shaky), the sign-tearing culprits from the visiting school were identified and, I presume, justice was served.

A LIFE CHANGER? QUITE POSSIBLY

While the SONY VCR/television/camera unit was a novel and occasionally useful teaching tool for me, for one of my former students the impact of this particular equipment was, at least according him, life changing. In the late 1970s, I taught Jeff in junior high, and having seen the equipment in operation, he was aware of its capabilities. Jeff connected with the WHS field hockey coach and ended up using the camera and VCR to record the team's home games - albeit with one or two very long extension cords.

Jeff went away for the final few years of high school, and I lost track of him until many years later when we reconnected at a meeting. By then I had heard stories about him and the career he had made for himself. He invited me to visit his place of business in a neighboring town. When I entered the old farmhouse in which it was housed, I came face to face with technology the likes of which I had never seen and could only hope to understand.

In lay terms, the main focus of Jeff's business was and continues to be to design, create, and install camera systems to record or broadcast a wide variety of major sporting and other events. The equipment he showed me looked like something from a science fiction movie: lenses and cameras - huge and minute; wires; tripods; connectors (for lack of a better term); and countless gadgets of every shape, size, and function.

As Jeff guided me through his offices, storage closets, labs, and workspaces, he described the purpose of each item, as well as where and how it was used in a wide range of events: a small camera buried in the dirt two feet in front of home plate in a World Series game; a small helmet cam used in the Running of the Bulls in Pamplona, Spain; a tiny hold card camera in competitive poker; a camera buried in the asphalt at the finish line of the Daytona 500. Each of these cameras was inconspicuous but positioned well enough to capture and transmit a truly unique image. And these examples represented only a fraction of the breadth and depth of Jeff's business and its capabilities.

A few years into retirement, I developed the practice of asking former students who had established themselves what had led them to their current jobs, careers, or professions. Because Jeff, now in his early 50s, had completed both high school and college since I had last seen him, I was curious about his answer to this question.

"Jeff, this is amazing. So impressive. I'm curious, what led you to this career path? What lit the spark? What got you started?" His answer was a surprise and one from decades in his past.

"In junior high you let me borrow the video equipment, and I recorded the field hockey games."

My immediate thought upon hearing this was, *Well, yes, I do remember that. However, there's an enormous difference between that and what I've been hearing and observing for the past hour as we've toured your business. Certainly, there's more to it than that.* And then with an element of pride, he continued. "At the end of the season, the field hockey team gave me a varsity letter for my recording work."

I nodded understandingly. But as I surveyed the vast array of equipment and the knowledge and expertise it represented, I thought, *My gosh, all of this because of a varsity letter to an eighth grade boy?*

I had no sooner processed his answer than he pointed to a blue chenille "W" proudly displayed on the wall. He said, "That varsity letter is special because it represents the beginning." But what I saw next as we finished the tour truly astonished me.

I happened to glance to my left. And there, resting inconspicuously on a window sill in all their splendor were three Emmys. Three Emmys! The real deal. Tall and stately, gold and gleaming, shining brightly in the sunlight. I asked Jeff if I could hold one. "Sure," he said with a pleased but modest smile. Note: *Jeff and his colleagues are now the proud possessors of seven Emmys!*

The SONY television and VCR made, I imagine, a small difference in my teaching and in my students' learning. But from what I observed in Jeff's business that day and from what I'd heard him say, they had started him on a truly distinct and incomparable career path.

CABLE AND CLASSROOMS

Technology in Wilmington High School continued to evolve with the times. In 1974, we connected one of the high school's classrooms to the local cable television system. As a result, any teacher who could set up the VCR and connect it to the cable system with an alligator clip could record a program being broadcast on public television or on one of the major networks. This was not cable television in the modern sense. Our channel options were limited and mainstream. However, I welcomed the documentaries and occasional relevant films or programs they offered as suitable additions to my teaching repertoire.

This cable service expanded the SONY equipment's use to beyond what the black and white video camera could provide. There was, however, one requirement. Since there was no timer on the VCR unit (I doubt they even existed then), whenever I wanted to record a program, I had to be present in that specific classroom to push all the right buttons for the duration of the program. So even on a Sunday night at 10:00, I was there, pushing the buttons. By today's standards, the entire process was primitive. But for the mid-1970s, the whole system was cutting edge.

COMPUTERS? NAH. NOT INTERESTED...YET

In 1975, the United States was preparing for its 1976 bicentennial celebration. This was a very big deal. Congress and individual states had appropriated significant funding for a wide variety of school-related events and projects. One day, several of us teachers were invited to an optional afterschool meeting to hear about possible student-designed bicentennial-related projects and how they could be created and funded. The presentation dealt essentially with computers, my knowledge and understanding of which was limited at best.

The presenter began talking about two computer-related concepts: hardware and software. Hardware was familiar to me, or so I thought. As a kid I had made countless trips to Benfante's, our neighborhood hardware store. They carried tools, sporting goods, bicycles, household goods, small appliances, and every nut, bolt, and screw known to humankind. If Benfante's hardware didn't have it, I didn't need it. But on this day, hardware was being described in a way that was completely foreign to me. I was a bit confused and not particularly interested.

And then there was this thing called software - something that made the computer function in a specific manner or perform a certain task. The presenter had me baffled. I had no clue what he was talking about. Even though the presenter assured us that money for student projects would be no object, I decided not to participate in his plan. Computers? Hardware? Software? No thanks. But within a few years, my attitude would change dramatically.

APPLE - MORE THAN JUST A FRUIT

As the early 1980s arrived, so too did the age of the personal computer. By 1983, Deerfield Elementary School (DVES), under the leadership of principal Don Finck, had purchased several Apple computers. The Apple corporation had made what appeared to be a strategic move to enter, seize, and monopolize the nationwide education computer market, and DVES was on the forefront when it came to purchasing and using its products.

Since my wife, Kathy, taught at DVES, she had access to one of the new Apple IIe computers. With permission from her principal, she brought one home over the Christmas break so we could try it out. The machine itself was captivating. But I was most intrigued by its word processing capabilities. I wrote to my parents, "This computer allows me to do something called 'word processing.' It allows me to rearrange paragraphs, correct spelling errors and other errors on the spot. And if I make an error, I can always backtrack and make the correction before actually printing the document. This whole thing (the draft of my letter) looks great on the (computer) screen." I was in awe.

The Apple IIe computer, when hooked up to the five-and-a-quarter-inch floppy disc drive and the dot matrix printer, was the ultimate in technological wizardry, and I wanted one. The Apple company had established a very favorable price for educators. So by May, Kathy and I had purchased a IIe for our home.

Our high school principal, Jurgen Combs, budgeted for the high school to purchase its own computers. However, instead of purchasing Apple computers, he opted for the Commodore 64 models. Nationally, these were popular computers, and I imagine their price and capabilities were at least as desirable as those of the Apple computers.

I took a series of Saturday morning classes offered by a non-WHS instructor to learn how to use the Commodore 64. However, instead of learning how to apply it to our teaching, we were taught the fundamentals of programming or coding. It was interesting but only to a point. Having already had some practical experience with the Apple IIe, I quickly concluded that it and its capabilities were preferable to the Commodore.

It was not long before the high school began purchasing Apple computers. A classroom was rewired and converted into a computer lab. For the next several years, different models of Apple computers came and went. While I lack the expertise or the definitive proof to accuse the Apple corporation of using a business model of planned obsolescence, it was clear that the constant introduction of new computer models and related accessories with all the latest bells and whistles put pressure on both educators and school budgets across the country to stay current. The technology was constantly evolving.

For the next twenty-one years, from 1983 until 2004, students and teachers at WHS used a long series of computers starting with the Commodore 64 and followed by a sequence of Apple products: Apple II; Apple IIe; Macintosh; Macintosh Plus; Macintosh SE; Macintosh Powerbook; iMac; Powerbook G4; and iMac Intel.

Bernie Shaw, a longtime WHS teacher (business, typing/keyboarding, accounting) recalled, "My earliest memory of computer use in my classroom was of an Apple IIe, which one of our math teachers, Doug, and I used to co-teach a one semester class. It was called 'Introduction to Computers' (1984-5). The initial introduction of computers co-taught by us was 'programming,' which found Doug and me staying a step or two ahead of our young pupils. Within a year our students were showing us newfound methods and shortcuts."

He continued, "I began using a newly-found focus on word processing, data base, and spreadsheets - this quickly led to the abandonment of typewriters. Typing 1 and 2 then were replaced with Keyboarding 1 and 2, and computers were used in all of my classes.

"Desktop Publishing was a favorite, and soon this led to the hiring of a technology teacher (at WHS) who led the way into the World Wide Web. The use of computers grew into many different fields."

As a teacher in 1983, I began creating assignments, exams, and lesson plans on our home computer. I also kept student grades and averages on it. All data and documents were saved on a five-and-a-quarter-inch piece of thin plastic encased in a slightly less thin cardboard sleeve. It was known as the "floppy disk." The cardboard sleeve was eventually replaced by a three-and-a-half-inch disk housed in a hard plastic case.

As wonderful as these computers were, their use and advertised capabilities occasionally resulted in considerable frustration. Anyone who used a desktop computer, especially those of us who used them in their infancy of popular use, experienced the loss of data. Saving information on the earliest home and school computers had to be done as a deliberate act. Nothing was saved automatically and, therefore, sometimes nothing was saved.

I cannot recall the number of times I typed for five or ten minutes or longer only to somehow lose all of my information before saving it. And, of course, even after having been saved, there were times when my data seemed to disappear altogether with no plausible explanation. The feelings of ease and excitement while using a computer were often matched by the fear and anxiety of inadvertently losing minutes or even hours of work.

It was around the year 2000 that the Internet became widely used in Wilmington High School. In the 1960s when doing research in high school or college, I had depended on the card catalog, the Guide to Periodical Literature, and general reference books and materials. Having my students simply type a word into a search engine like Google and then having dozens of resources literally at their fingertips was revolutionary. Computers and the Internet were astonishingly powerful teaching and learning tools, and they had a strong presence in the final years of Wilmington High School.

In addition to the technology of desktop computers, some students at WHS used small, hand-held spellcheckers. Just as small calculators facilitated various arithmetic and mathematical operations, these spellcheckers helped some students with spellchecker functions. The difference was, of course, with hand-held spellcheckers the student had to ask whether a word was misspelled.

In spite of the fact that these small, handheld devices could improve student performance, they had their detractors. Critics claimed that calculators precluded students from having to learn their multiplication tables. Spellcheckers did the same for learning to spell, they claimed. One of the more common criticisms often expressed as a rhetorical question was, "What happens if they run out of batteries?"

And now, of course, calculators are on our watches, our computers, and our phones. How times have changed.

THE STUDENT NETWORK

I would be remiss if I didn't acknowledge in this chapter Wilmington High School's Student Network. In the late 1990s, Bob Edwards, a 1977 graduate of Wilmington High School, established a non-profit corporation called, The Student Network (TSN). It was a school-based television studio located in Wilmington High School that offered a wide variety of opportunities to WHS students. It continued for several years after the merger with Whitingham High School that formed Twin Valley High School.

Through grants, school budgets, and contributions, a classroom was converted into a studio, and thousands of dollars worth of equipment was purchased. Under Mr. Edwards' leadership, students learned a variety of skills: writing scripts; creating skits (some humorous, some serious) that dealt with current local and state issues; interviewing local people of interest; operating the audio and visual equipment; etc. For several years it was a highly successful enterprise. Wilmington's Duncan Cable TV broadcast these programs on its local cable system, and some segments eventually found their way onto YouTube.

GOING WIRELESS: THE "AIRPORT" REVOLUTION

As the 21st century began and the end of Wilmington High School was approaching, the school's computer room, or lab as it was often called, housed around 20 desktop computers and seemingly miles of wires. If a teacher wanted their class to use computers, they had to sign up for the lab. However, within a couple of years, that changed dramatically.

The school purchased a large cabinet on wheels. And what was remarkable was what it housed: 20 Apple laptop computers. And to top that, the computers were connected to what was referred to as the "airport."

These 20 laptops could be connected to the Internet simultaneously and without that tangled mass of different colored wires that were attached to every computer in our computer lab. That meant that a teacher could roll the cart to their classroom, and every student or pair of students could have access to a computer and be connected to the Internet. It was magical!

COMING FULL CIRCLE

So within the span of my 33 years of teaching, I had seen technology morph from a simple piece of chalk to the mechanical simplicity of filmstrip and slide projectors to the excitement of videotape to the limitless potential of computers and the Internet. And then, as if to bring this sequence of advancements in technology almost full circle, this happened.

It was mid-June, 2005, in my seventh grade social studies class. It was not only the final day of school but the final day and the final class of my teaching career. We were concluding a unit on China. In the summer of 2002, I spent three weeks traveling in China with six other teachers, and I had taken slides to share with my students. And now I was preparing to do just that.

As my students entered the classroom and began to settle in, I was removing my own 1980s-model Kodak slide projector from its box and was in the process of nesting the projector's plastic carousel onto its top. Usually when they entered the classroom, my students were noticeably observant, processing what they were seeing, and looking for clues about what I had planned for the day's lesson. How were the desks arranged? Was there a VCR and TV on a cart in the room? A stranger - a guest presenter, perhaps? Were there new or interesting materials on their desks or props on my desk?

Today, the day before the students' summer vacation - my final day of school - of my career - and my final class, the room was unusually quiet and calm as my students took their seats. Was it because they knew this day marked the end of my teaching career? Were they being especially cooperative and kind to me? I wondered. Respectful? Even sad? Well, I soon had my answer. It was none of these. They were curious.

As I called the class to order, one of my students pointed to the slide projector and asked, "Hey, Mr. Larsen. What's that?"

"It's a slide projector." I responded. "It's going to project photographs up there," I said, pointing to the white reflective wall-mounted projection screen.

"Oh, sweet!" he exclaimed with enthusiastic fascination, apparently seeing this old-fashioned technology for the first time. His classmates appeared to share his excitement. And so, due at least in part to the novelty of my decades-old slide projector, my slide presentation on China - the final act of my 33-year teaching career - was a hit. And of course, I made sure that we chose a lucky number to determine for the final time in my classes who had the privilege of "clicking the clicker."

A FINAL THOUGHT

Since 2005 when I retired, technology has changed and improved in ways no one but the most gifted and creative futurists could have imagined. The impacts of smart phones and social media, some positive and some negative, were felt in schools and classrooms soon after I retired in 2005. And now, virtual reality headsets and artificial intelligence are poised to radically change teaching and learning even more. If the past is any indication, I am confident that if it were still in existence, Wilmington High School and the people who were its lifeblood would be doing their best to use these and other elements of modern technology to enhance the ways in which students are taught and the ways in which they learn.

Wilmington High School science classroom, ca. 1940s

Wilmington High School commercial classroom, ca. 1940s

CHAPTER 21

Field Trips

CANDY, GLUTEN, AND COLD HARD CASH

I remember taking three field trips during my school years, two in fourth grade and another in fifth grade, all while I attended PS #49 in Rochester, NY. The first field trip was to the Fanny Farmer candy factory on the edge of Rochester's downtown area. Why my class toured a candy factory I cannot recall.

As if to offer a balance in cuisine and nutritional value, our other fourth grade field trip was to a grist mill. We were studying the history of Rochester, and the recreated mill was reminiscent of the city's 19th century past. I remember our guide telling us that if we chewed a mouthful of grain long enough it would be transformed into gum. And she was right - kind of. It was more like a gooey paste.

A year later we were off to the main branch of the Rochester Savings Bank, probably to see firsthand where our weekly deposits of twenty-five or fifty cents (collected at school) were stored. Possibly in an effort to convince us about the benefits of saving, each of us was allowed to handle - ever so carefully - a thousand dollar bill.

So that was it, the totality of my field trip experiences in the 1950s. Savoring a freshly manufactured piece of candy; chomping on a mouthful of whole grain; and experiencing a very brief but tangible flirtation with unimaginable wealth.

But here's the point. Much like me, I still encounter students who, more than anything I might have taught them in the classroom, remember their experiences outside of that classroom - on field trips.

IN THE EARLY YEARS OF WHS

Prior to the 1960s and as early as the 1940s, and based on information gleaned from various issues of the *Mirror*, perhaps the most significant field trip experience for Wilmington High School students was Vermont's All State Music Festival. Each spring, high school choruses and bands from throughout Vermont traveled to Burlington to perform and march.

In the 1950s and 1960s, according to the *Mirror*, Wilmington High School students took science-related field trips to the Science Park in Boston, the Boston Museum of Science, New Hampshire's White Mountains, and Howe Caverns in New York State. WHS Latin classes took trips to the Museum of Fine Arts in Boston. The senior class trip, usually three or four days in a large Northeastern city, was a frequent annual event at WHS. One year the seniors spent several days in York Beach, Maine.

In the early 1960s, one WHS senior class took a rather unique trip. In 1963, the *Bennington Banner* reported that, "'Mr. Barry's Etchings,' sponsored and performed by the Wilmington High School senior class played to an appreciative audience at the Memorial Hall...About $150 was earned and will be used for a class trip to Hidden Valley Dude Ranch on Lake George in New York over Memorial Day weekend."

Regarding WHS field trips in the 1970s, Russell Hanson and Ruth Streeter wrote in the 1980 Old Home Week booklet, "Students in the Wilmington schools have been great travelers. Various high school subject classes have journeyed to Canada, England, France, Mexico, and Spain."

During the 1980s, 1990s, and into the early 2000s, WHS students and their teachers continued to take occasional trips to various foreign countries, including those listed in the article written by Russell Hanson and Ruth Streeter. In addition, one year near the end of the 20th century, a group of students from Wilmington and Whitingham high schools and their chaperones traveled to The People's Republic of China.

I recall at least one senior class trip in the 1970s to Myrtle Beach, SC. However, few, if any, subsequent senior overnight class trips occurred after the 1970s.

FIELD TRIPS: WHY?

Any teacher who plans, organizes, and then executes a field trip does so for a variety of reasons. Out-of-classroom experiences broaden student horizons. They stimulate student thinking and enhance and inform student perspectives. And, they can teach a myriad of practical life skills.

But as lofty as this sounds, my motive for taking students on field trips was probably as simple as believing it would be enjoyable and interesting - for them because they'd have new experiences, and for me because I could guide them to and through those new experiences.

"MR. LARSEN, DID YOU SEE THAT GUY'S SOCKS?"

During my second year of teaching (1973-1974) and as part of my eighth grade human rights and responsibilities course, I arranged for my students to attend an arraignment session in District Court in Brattleboro. These arraignments occurred on Monday mornings. It was the time that those who were being charged with violating one or more laws, usually over the weekend, entered a plea of guilty or not guilty.

My students were able to observe various elements of the arraignments, including some of the constitutional rights we had studied and discussed in class. While the arraignments could be somewhat routine, the students always had a variety of observations and conclusions to share when we returned to class the next day. One of these student observations stands out: "Mr. Larsen, did you see that guy's socks?"

The presiding judge that morning had seated us in the jury box, and the students had literally a front row seat to the morning's proceedings. Apparently, at least one of them had noticed the socks worn by one of the attorneys. These weren't the normal white tube socks favored by many of my students. Nor were they the more formal dark dress socks worn by most men. They were argyle socks, and apparently they were quite visible.

At the time, the fact that one or more of my students had noticed the attorney's rather unique socks meant little to me. However, as the years passed and the trips my students and I experienced together went far beyond a morning trip to Brattleboro, the argyle socks became an instructive metaphor, and they taught me an important lesson.

As much as I might plan a field trip with goals, objectives, and what I wanted my students to notice, to learn, and to remember, there was only so much of that I could control or anticipate. What happened more often than not was that students would experience a field trip with their own expectations, their own observations, their own learning, and their own memories, much as I had with candy, gluten gum, and a thousand-dollar bill.

It was also during my second year of teaching when I had my first experience with field trips beyond Windham County. In early March, 1974, I took one of my eighth grade classes to Montpelier, our state capital. The trip was organized by Casey Murrow, an experienced teacher at Deerfield Valley Elementary School (DVES). Knowing that my still-developing eighth grade curriculum focused to some extent on laws, he invited us to join him and his elementary school students to see some of those laws being made.

We visited the State House where we met with our local state representative, the lieutenant governor, and the speaker of the house. We also stopped by the governor's ceremonial State House office.

And then it was off to the Vermont Supreme Court where we were given a tour by one of the court's law clerks. He encouraged the students to sit in the justices' chairs or to sit at the bailiff's station. Knowing his audience of fourth and eighth graders, the law clerk's presentation was appropriately brief but informative, nonetheless.

We rounded out our trip with a visit to the Barre granite quarry and a fried chicken dinner at the now defunct Howard Johnson's in White River Junction.

A few weeks later, Casey invited my other eighth grade class and me to join another group of DVES students and him on their trip to Montpelier. It was essentially the same as the previous trip. However, this time we were introduced in the House chamber to the full membership and received a standing ovation.

On each trip I was so proud of my students. They dressed for the occasion and behaved appropriately. I observed how well Casey had organized both trips and how that planning paid off. Good planning by the adults and high expectations for the students paid dividends. I took note.

MR. LARSEN, CAN I SIT IN IT?

Later in my second year of teaching, as part of the eighth grade rights and responsibilities curriculum, we were studying the Eighth Amendment and its prohibition against cruel and unusual punishment. One of my students, Deb, asked if we could take a class trip to the state prison located in Windsor, Vermont. I quickly but gently dismissed the idea. I may have been smitten with the notion of field trips, but there was a world of difference between Vermont's State House and its state prison. I asked myself, *Take eighth graders to a state prison? No way!* was my answer.

A few days later, Deb asked me again, this time privately, if perhaps she and just a of couple of her classmates could go. I wasn't entirely sure why she was making the request, but she seemed earnest in making it, and I said I'd write to the prison superintendent and see what he had to say. Note: *Fifty years later, I asked Deb why she pursued this matter. She wrote, "I was fascinated by prisons and their inner workings and actually wanted to work in one someday." As it turned out, she didn't. But with young adolescents, one never knows what might light a spark and influence their future.*

I soon received a response from the prison superintendent stating that while the prison did sanction visits from students, it was exclusively for upper-level high school and college students. I shared with Deb his response to my letter and figured that would be the end of it. But to her credit, she persevered.

"What if I write to him?" she responded when I showed her the superintendent's letter. While I really didn't want to make a nuisance of myself or my students, I acquiesced and offered a few tips on how she might fashion her request. Within two weeks, the superintendent wrote back. He reiterated his original point that visits and tours of the prison were normally reserved for older students. But, he added, if Deb and two or three classmates and her teacher were truly interested, he would welcome us. So in late April, Deb and three of her eighth grade classmates climbed into her mother's roomy four-door sedan, and with me behind the wheel, we headed north to Windsor.

Windsor State Prison was an imposing brick structure. The cornerstone had been laid in 1808, when Thomas Jefferson was president. Its brick walls were three feet thick and 14 feet high. By 1974, when we visited the prison, it had gone through several renovations and additions, and it housed several hundred inmates. The students were excited and a little nervous. I was a little excited and a lot nervous. None of us had any idea what lay ahead.

We entered the administration building, already intensely aware of the security measures in place, including perfunctory personal searches for "metal objects." Fortunately, we came up clean. Before long, the superintendent met us and guided us into the prison itself. Deb would later write to me in an email, "I remember the eerie feeling I got when the prison door slammed behind us as we went inside."

We met with a prison social worker who explained the various services available to the inmates, preferably called "residents." And then much to my surprise, he gave us a tour, albeit a limited one, of the prison. We saw the prison "bubble," the control room from which all doors in the prison were controlled. We also saw a cell (through a window), the visitation room, the gymnasium, and a classroom where we met with the prison's director of education. The social worker remained with us.

While the director of education was explaining the various educational and training programs available at the prison, one of the residents entered the classroom. His name was Todd. Like a mother bear watching over her cubs, I became ultra-vigilant. "Todd," said the social worker, "you got a haircut. It looks very nice."

Todd looked us over with a smile, and asked, "Where are you kids from?" The prison's superintendent had instructed the students not to talk with any of the prison's residents, so I offered a brief response. Todd then walked over to Jane, one of my students. He cradled some strands of her long blonde hair in his hand and said, "Before my haircut, my hair was as long as hers." Jane was rigid. I was poised to intervene.

But then Todd walked over to Andy, another student, and placed something in his hand. It was a .22 caliber shell casing. "Don't let Mr. Baxter know I gave you this," he said with an innocent smile and loud enough to be heard by everyone, including the education director, Mr. Baxter.

I never believed my students to be in danger. On the other hand, I really didn't know what was going on. In retrospect, Todd was probably a well-meaning and trustworthy prison resident simply interrupting the monotony of his day by having some brief and innocent fun with my young students. But it was time to move on. Our tour continued, and I never could have anticipated what happened next.

The superintendent joined us for what turned out to be the grand finale of our visit, at least as far as my students were concerned. He guided us to the top floor of the prison's 19th century brick administration building. And there, amidst a collection of athletic equipment (baseball gloves, badminton nets and rackets, etc.), were a few plastic chairs and several feet of television cable wire. The superintendent informed us that the chairs and cable wire had been used in an attempt to escape from the prison. A resident had attached the cable wires to a chair, attempted to throw the chair over the wall, and then use the cable wires to scale the wall to freedom. The attempt, he informed us, was unsuccessful.

But then we noticed another object sitting amongst the clutter: a solid-looking wooden chair. "What's that?" one of my students asked. It was Vermont's electric chair. It had last been used 20 years earlier, in 1954, the superintendent informed us, and now it rested unceremoniously in a dark prison hallway.

Being inquisitive eighth graders, they asked a few questions but were appropriate in their content and tone. And then, the inevitable: "Mr. Larsen, can I sit in it?" one of the boys asked. As I quickly prepared my negative response, the superintendent nonchalantly replied, "Sure."

As we departed the prison, we thanked the superintendent for his hospitality and his trust - his trust that young adolescents would accept this rare opportunity in the manner in which it was offered. On the drive home, all of us processed the visit. I was so pleased with their mature and perceptive comments. While I can't recall the specifics, I do recall them saying that seeing the prison and especially interacting with Todd, challenged many of their stereotypes and preconceived notions of prisons. And, I concluded, it had added depth to their understanding of what cruel and unusual punishment was and was not - and much more.

None of this—meeting with the superintendent, talking with the social worker and educator, getting a tour, interacting with a prison resident, seeing and even sitting in Vermont's old oak electric chair—had I expected or anticipated. But that, I was beginning to understand, was one of the many benefits of these out-of-class experiences, both for my students and for me. As much as I might try to plan, whether it was seeing an attorney wearing argyle socks or sitting in our state prison's now defunct electric chair, I couldn't plan for everything. Note: *Windsor State Prison closed 16 months after our visit. It was then converted into 75 apartments. The electric chair, according to an article in the August 9, 2017 edition of VT Digger, now resides at the Vermont Historical Society where it is not on public display and where I am certain no sitting is allowed.*

"DON'T WORRY. THEY'RE NOT VIOLENT."

A few years into my teaching career, I divided my high school sociology course into three units, one of which was criminal justice. In addition to a variety of readings, discussions, and films, we attended arraignments at the Vermont District Court in Brattleboro and took a tour of the Brattleboro police station.

The unit included a subunit on corrections. With the old prison having closed, I decided to pursue another possibility. There was an operational minimum security prison farm on the outskirts of Windsor. I wrote to the prison farm superintendent and received an invitation to bring my class to the facility.

Before visiting the prison farm, the students prepared questions, and I did my best to prepare them for what they might experience. I cautioned them, please don't ask any of the residents (like the residents of the former prison, they were not referred to as inmates) about their crimes. It's personal, I told them. The students asked what those crimes might be. Although I wasn't sure, knowing this was a minimum security facility, I confidently stated that most of the residents had committed non-violent property crimes like burglary, embezzlement, theft, and bribery. I told them that these residents were not violent criminals and assured them there was nothing to worry about. Note: *In those days, drug-related crimes were not the major problem they are today.*

When we arrived at the prison farm, the superintendent met us and proceeded to give us a tour where we observed the residents at work. Some were engaged in agriculture, while others were working at small manufacturing jobs. He then accompanied us to a large meeting room where four residents sat waiting for us for a Q and A session. The superintendent described the work, the educational opportunities, and other programs available to the residents. He then asked the residents to introduce themselves.

Initially, my students were a little ill at ease, but within minutes the atmosphere became more relaxed. The four men seemed to welcome the opportunity to see some new faces and interact with new people. They came across as honest and decent guys. They gave descriptions of their lives and explained how life circumstances had eventually led them to criminal activity. As instructed, my students didn't ask about what crimes these men had committed. But they didn't have to. Each of the four men freely provided that information: burglary; armed robbery; rape; murder.

I watched as eyebrows rose, eyes widened, and heads discreetly turned my way as if to say, "Well, Mr. Larsen, so much for non-violent crimes." But the students took it in stride. They were juniors and seniors, and while they were surprised, they handled the surprise well. The visit concluded with a tour of the facility. The entire experience provided much to discuss in subsequent classes.

With each additional field trip, I realized more and more how valuable they could be. Accordingly, it wasn't long before the notion of taking my students to a more distant locale, and the experiences that would result, became increasingly appealing.

DC BOUND

My wife, Kathy and I visited Washington, DC on a brief vacation in July, 1974. I had completed only my second year of teaching and was already contemplating how I might incorporate into my teaching our visits to all the buildings, locales, and history on our DC itinerary. But then it hit me. What better way to do this than to have my eighth graders directly experience the city and all it offered. I began to plan.

With the help of eighth-grade parent and veteran Marlboro teacher, Bruce Cole, we found housing for our students. It was a motel in College Park, MD, but it also had several small cottages. Each cottage could accommodate 20 people, with five bedrooms and two bathrooms for $60 per night. That worked out to $3-$4 per student, per night. I calculated the rental cost for a large van along with gas money for Bruce's car which he had offered to drive. For each student, the cost of six days (two travel days and four full days in DC), would be less than $45. Students would manage their own food and souvenir expenses.

Being responsible for 16 eighth graders for six days and five nights was a new experience for Kathy and me. Even so, knowing that Bruce would be with us was very reassuring, and we felt prepared.

For the next several years, the DC trip was an annual event for any eighth grader who showed an interest. Bruce Cole chaperoned with us the first year. Kathy chaperoned for the first two years, and Wilmington teaching colleague, Nicki Steel, served as van driver and stalwart chaperone for all but one of the several subsequent trips. Future chaperones included three different WHS parents.

On each trip, our four-days in DC included all or most of the following: the Capitol (including visits with US Senators Robert Stafford and Patrick Leahy, and Rep. James Jeffords), the White House, Mount Vernon, Arlington National Cemetery, the presidential monuments and memorials, DC's St. Patrick's Day parade, the Vietnam Veterans Memorial, Ford's Theater, the Petersen House, the Holocaust Museum, the Bureau of Printing and Engraving, the national museums (Natural History, Air and Space, History and Technology), Hirschhorn Art Museum, Washington Star newspaper, FBI, National Archives, Supreme Court, Explorers Hall at the National Geographic headquarters, and the National Mall.

Note: *When I first presented the itinerary to the students, I included a reference to the National Mall. "Oh wow, a mall! That's awesome!" The excitement that filled my classroom was palpable. However, their disappointment was just as palpable when I explained that the National Mall consisted not of stores but of grass, sidewalks, and museums. "Don't worry," I told them. "DC is loaded with gift shops."*

GRACIOUS HOSTS

For all of our trips, Vermont's US senators and their respective staffs were gracious hosts. Beginning with our second trip in 1976, we always met with Sen. Patrick Leahy. His ability to relate to the students, and vice versa, was a pleasure to watch.

On several occasions, our visits to the US Capitol included access to special seats in the Senate gallery, a visit to the vice-president's ceremonial office in the Capitol, or a tour given by one of Senator Leahy's knowledgeable staffers. He always had time to pose with us for a group photo arranged by his office. Within a few weeks, each student would receive a signed copy of the photo.

SUPREME COURT OR FOOD COURT?

One year, we had the opportunity to sit in on a session of the U.S. Supreme Court - well, almost. As we left Sen. Leahy's office, the Court was in sight. We had studied the Supreme Court in social studies class, and much to my surprise it was now in session. Not only was it in session, the justices were hearing a case dealing with the death penalty. All I could think was, *Oh my gosh, we've hit the jackpot! The U.S. Supreme Court is in session, and it's hearing a capital punishment case. We're right here, and the kids are all dressed up because we just met with Sen. Leahy.*

We'll fit right in. This is what we've been studying. Classroom teachings related to the real world. It's the opportunity of a lifetime. The Supreme Court. The death penalty. This is incredible!

I was told by someone supervising the line of hopeful Court observers that if we waited for about an hour, we could gain admission to the Court and hear the oral arguments. I gathered the students around me. "Okay, everyone. Listen up." I explained to the group that we had a truly unique opportunity. "And if we wait in line for less than an hour (okay, I lowballed it), we'll get to see the Supreme Court in session - in action. And they're hearing a case on the death penalty!" And then, as a seemingly casual afterthought, I added, "The other option is to get some lunch."

Napoleon is said to have commented that an army marches on its stomach. In other words, no group can function effectively unless its most basic sustenance needs are being met. Well, eighth graders are no different from Napoleon's army. "What would you like to do?" I asked. I suspected that the students knew this was a big deal, at least to me. But I also understood what was important to them.

The absence of an enthusiastic response from the group was a response nonetheless. It was clear that these kids were tired, and they were hungry. They'd been up since dawn, crammed into a van, asked to wear their nicest clothing, required to walk a considerable distance, strongly urged to listen attentively to our US senator, reminded to be on their absolute best behavior as we toured the Capitol, and then made to walk some more. They had done everything I had asked. They were ready for a break, and they deserved one. The Supreme Court or a food court? The choice was easy.

STEPPIN' OUT AT NIGHT: "WE'RE FROM VERMONT"

One of the benefits of having the vans and a relatively small group of students was flexibility. Being completely in charge of everything was more work for the chaperones. However, it provided some opportunities. We often took an evening and visited the Lincoln and Jefferson Memorials. They were most impressive at night. Occasionally, I scoured the newspapers for an evening event that might appeal to eighth graders. Through the years, either as an entire group or smaller separate groups, we saw a concert, a circus, an NHL game, an NBA game, and a movie in a theater much larger than any in Vermont.

These entertainment-type evening outings were not the norm. They were spur-of-the-moment and depended on student interest, student (and chaperone) stamina, our schedule, and affordability. To address affordability, I always employed the "kids from Vermont" strategy. An example of this was when we saw the movie, "Tootsie," starring Dustin Hoffman.

When we arrived at the theater, I noticed the evening ticket price of $4.50 (early 1980s price) for anyone over the age of 11. That obviously included all of us. I approached the ticket window with my students in tow. "Hi. I have a group of kids here with me. We're from Vermont. We're on a school trip. I was wondering if we might be able to get a group rate for the movie." In situations like this the operative phrase was, of course, "kids from Vermont." The manager kindly obliged and charged each of us $2.00.

The same was true with the NHL and NBA games (with a smaller group of students) at the Capital Center in Landover, MD. The folks at the ticket windows were always accommodating.

THE SERENDIPITOUS POWER OF A NYLON JACKET

Anytime a teacher ventures with students outside the normally predictable and clearly defined physical and behavioral parameters of a classroom, interesting things are bound to happen. Such was the case on our first eighth grade trip to Washington, DC. A chance encounter significantly enriched several subsequent trips to DC.

It was April, and the city was crowded and busy. Kathy, Bruce Cole, and I, along with our 16 students, were waiting in line with probably a thousand others for a tour of the White House. The line to enter the White House was wrapped around the block, but it was moving at a reasonable pace, and our wait lasted only 45 minutes. The tour itself was self-guided, which is a nice way of saying we were herded in constant motion through a series of four or five rooms. It was a cursory experience, but I wanted my students to have at least a general notion of where their president lived.

Despite my efforts to keep all 19 of us together, we were quickly separated and scattered among the tourists wending their way between the red velour ropes and stainless steel posts that defined our path. I wasn't concerned, though. There was no way any of my students could get lost. Their route through the White House was clearly established and strictly regulated. Accordingly, I was just as confident that none of them would get into any mischief. Everything seemed under control, and my students, as far as I could tell, were behaving themselves.

But then, as I entered the East Room, the largest room in the White House, I heard the voice of Bobby, one of my students. Sounding like an eye witness identifying the perpetrator in a lineup of criminal suspects, I heard him say, "That's him!" Recognizing Bobby's voice, I sensed that my hopes for an incident-free tour of President Gerald Ford's home had just been dashed. However, Bobby was a good kid. Why in the world would he misbehave on only the second day of our trip? And in the White House, no less!

Upon hearing, "That's him," I immediately turned to see Bobby standing next to an official-looking White House guide, a neatly groomed gentleman wearing a navy blue blazer and gray slacks. And Bobby was pointing at me! It was my understanding that the guides (or guards) in the White House were Secret Service agents, and all I could think at this moment was, *Oh jeez, Bobby, there you are, standing next to a Secret Service agent. What the heck did you just do? If you're in trouble, that means I'm in trouble. And if I'm in trouble, trust me, that means you're in trouble!*

The guide was, in fact, a White House Tour Officer, a branch of the United States Secret Service. His name was Steve Eccher. He was from Readsboro, Vermont, and it turned out he was related to at least one well-known Wilmington family whose children I had taught or would teach for several years to come. Officer Eccher had recognized Bobby's Wilmington Warriors jacket and had taken him aside to confirm that, in fact, Bobby was from the Wilmington in Vermont. And, he told Bobby, he wanted to meet his teacher.

Officer Eccher and I exchanged a few pleasantries, and I began to relax, as much as one can relax with 16 eighth graders touring the White House without being attached to their chaperones. He said that if we ever returned to Washington, we should give him a call. Perhaps, he said, he could arrange for a better tour of the White House. Not knowing exactly what that meant for future visits, I thanked him, and we completed the tour without further incident.

Two or three years later and not wanting to bother Steve Eccher, in spite of his kind offer to contact him if we should return to DC, I arranged a White House tour through Senator Patrick Leahy's office. That morning, we were first in line. We were merged with another small group and were then greeted by our official White House guide. In a moment of serendipity, I realized that he was none other than Officer Steve Eccher. I reintroduced myself. We exchanged pleasantries, and soon our tour was underway.

As our tour concluded and the other members of our combined group were ushered out, Steve turned to me and said with a slight tone of anticipation, "Wait here." The students could sense my curiosity and asked me what was up. I said I had no idea.

Steve quickly returned and took us to the ground floor where the tour had begun. He peered around an opaque partition that blocked our view into the West Wing. We heard a buzzer. By this time all of us knew that this was something special. "Just a second," he said. And then, after a brief pause, "Okay, now follow me."

He led us to a door that opened to the South Lawn where the president's helicopter lands and where important White House guests are received. There were no helicopters or important guests this time. However, we did catch a glimpse of Amy Carter as her chauffeured black SUV left to take her to school. This was very exciting.

Steve took us into the Rose Garden and then into the White House Theater where he shared a few anecdotes and opinions on former presidents Nixon and Ford, and on then-president Carter. His comments were insightful, interesting, and unexpected. Note: *Officer Eccher recently wrote to me: "My first day of work at the White House was a Saturday, June 21, 1971, Tricia Nixon's wedding in the Rose Garden. In my 21 plus years with the Secret Service, I've had the privilege of witnessing a host of historic events, not to mention I got to travel globally. One example was conducting a security advance in Budapest Hungry just prior to the Fall of the Wall...clearly events that have changed the course of history."*

We finally parted ways. Steve gave us his phone number for future reference and future trips. And in a few years one of the best DC trip highlights, courtesy of Steve Eccher, would materialize.

It was the early 1980s, a Wednesday. Ronald Reagan was president. We were scheduled by Sen. Leahy's office to visit the White House on the final day of our four days in DC. I rose at 5 a.m., and the other two chaperones and I made sure everyone was up and functioning, more or less, by 5:30. We arrived at the White House by 7:30, right on time. This year I had arranged with Officer Eccher to meet us at the gate designated for tourists. We easily passed through the metal detectors and received what had become a traditional private White House tour with him. At the conclusion of our tour, we expressed our collective appreciation and began to say good-bye.

But then Steve pulled me aside and asked, "What are you doing tomorrow?"

Before responding honestly that we were planning an early departure and returning to Vermont, I replied with a vague, "Well, we're supposed to head back to Vermont." And then, sensing that something was up, I added, "At some point."

"Well, here's why I asked," Steve continued. "Tomorrow morning at 10:00 President Reagan is welcoming the president of Italy here at the White House. An official ceremony will be held on the White House grounds. There will be military bands and an honor guard, along with Vice President (George H.W.) Bush, Secretary of State (Alexander) Haig, and other officials. If the weather cooperates, the ceremony will be held outside. I can get you in."

My mind went into overdrive. Too many negatives, I thought. The weather forecast was for showers. That meant an indoor ceremony with space limitations, and that would preclude our attending, even if we managed another early morning wake-up. In addition, if we did attend the ceremony and left DC in late morning, we wouldn't arrive home until after midnight - and I had to teach the next day. And finally, I didn't have any more clean dress shirts.

I paused for a moment, and immediately dismissing the negatives, I blurted out, "That's great! Thank you! Yes, we'll be here!"

At 5:45 the next morning, I went outside and looked skyward. Clouds but no rain. I turned on my small transistor radio and was thrilled to hear the forecast: clearing and mostly sunny. Our plan was to attend the ceremony and return to our cottage dorm to change out of our good clothes (the clothes we'd brought for our meeting with Sen. Leahy) before heading home. This, I thought, just might work. After a quick breakfast snack to get us through the early morning, and one last visit to the restrooms, we were on our way to the White House.

As we had done on previous drives into the city proper when we knew parking would be at a premium, we rode in only one of our two vans. Like all vans we had used, this one was designed to hold 15 passengers. It was cramped, but a little discomfort was worth the convenience of having to find only one parking space.

Officer Eccher had told me where to park near the Ellipse, a large grassy area south of the White House. I was to look for an officer named,

"Pete." I knew this was going to be a long shot. What was the likelihood, I thought, of finding Pete, and Pete knowing who I was and then saying, "Hi, Dave. Steve Eccher told me you'd be coming. Sure you can park here in this special area. No problem. Stay at the White House as long as you want." I was hopeful but not confident. But the parking gods were smiling on us that day. We found Pete, and with his permission we parked the van within a 10-minute walk to the White House. So far, so good.

We went to three different security gates looking for Steve. Just as I often did on our trips whenever I needed or was hoping for special treatment from someone, I mentioned to the guard at one gate that, "I have a group of kids here from Vermont." If I'd been alone and asking for Steve Eccher, I'm sure it would have raised some suspicions among the uniformed officers. However, with 16 kids in tow, I might have seemed crazy, but I certainly was no threat to the president.

Steve soon met us and quickly ushered us through the metal detectors, through the East Wing of the White House and the Jacqueline Kennedy Rose Garden, and onto the South Lawn, just 40 feet from where President Reagan would soon be speaking.

As 10 a.m. approached, and as promised, Vice President Bush and Secretary of State Haig arrived. Each stood with the other VIPs. Precisely at 10 a.m., President Reagan walked out of the White House to the sound of "Hail to the Chief." Within seconds, a limo arrived at the South Portico, and out stepped the president of Italy. For the next 30 minutes, music was played, speeches were made, and a 21-gun salute was fired. And then it was over.

We extended to Steve Eccher our deepest gratitude, walked back to the van and hopped in, gave Pete the parking officer an enthusiastic and heartfelt "thank you" wave, and returned to our dorm for a change of clothes and a late checkout. By 10:30 that night we were back in Wilmington. What a day!

As I reflect on the special treatment my students and I received over the years from and because of Steve Eccher, I can't help but be amazed that all of it was due to the serendipity of Bobby's blue Wilmington Warriors jacket and the keen observational skills of one White House tour officer who spotted it.

In the fall of 1983, I was assigned to teach ninth grade world history instead of eighth grade social studies, and the DC trips ended. However, in twelve years that would change.

A NEW APPROACH

In September, 1992, Wilmington Middle School began its inaugural year, and I was one of the six core teachers in that program. That year, the eighth grade and the seventh grade took no trips. As sixth graders at Deerfield Valley Elementary School, those two classes had taken the traditional week-long class trip to a Cape Cod Nature Center, and we teachers felt that no additional seventh or eighth grade trip was necessary.

But two years later, in the fall of 1994, our middle school team received word from our principal that there was an expectation that the eighth graders would be taking a class trip in the spring. This class had spent their sixth grade year at Wilmington Middle School and had not taken the traditional Cape Cod trip. Nor had they taken a trip in seventh grade. Hence, the decision to offer an eighth grade class trip.

I suggested to the middle school team that we consider going to Washington, DC. The team and our principal agreed. However, since the plan was to take the entire class of 29 students, we'd have to make some adjustments. It had been 12 years since my last DC trip. The idea of renting vans to transport 29 students and at least four chaperones was out of the question. And, at the very least, I was sure the legal liabilities for such a trip would be prohibitive, as would the logistical challenges. I researched student tour companies, and the middle school core team settled on one with an itinerary and a price that looked reasonable.

Because we were taking the entire class, and because times and expectations had changed, our core team of teachers was obligated to provide fundraising opportunities for all of our eighth graders. It was time to call Ron, our fundraiser-in-chief from the past. I had worked success-fully with Ron during previous years on a variety of fundraisers. Note: *More on that in the next chapter.*

We hadn't worked together in several years, but I was confident that Ron could set us up with some solid fundraising plans. Sure enough, he could, and he did. In the fall, we went with the tried-and-true practice of selling magazines, books, and CDs. In the spring, we worked with Ron again, this time selling various items including candy, wrapping paper, and a wide variety of small gift items.

I invited Ron to do a downsized kickoff presentation to the eighth grade. We did it in my classroom. Having worked with Ron on previous fundraisers in the '70s and '80s, I was a veteran of these magazine sales programs, and I once again served as Ron's able assistant. When it came to getting my students excited about selling magazines, CDs, and candy, all for "amazing prizes," I could gin up adolescent enthusiasm with the best of them.

I always preferred the fundraisers that required little or no financial investment up front and that resulted in reasonable profit. These fundraisers fit the bill. Each student kept 40 percent of their sales. Our math teacher established a spreadsheet that recorded an account for each student. Collecting and recording each student's earnings took a lot of effort, but it was all part of the job, and it worked well. And by our deadline, all students had raised the necessary funds through fundrais-ing and personal arrangements with their parents.

Part of the tour company's package was transportation by charter bus, complete with restroom, video system, and professional driver. It was certainly a far cry from the rental vans Kathy, Nicki Steel, Bruce Cole, and I had used in the seventies and eighties.

Before we knew it, late May had arrived. We departed our school parking lot at 10 p.m. on the Tuesday before Memorial Day. By 11 p.m. the four of us chaperones had essentially given up hope that the students would sleep during the nighttime ride. Young adolescents are by nature highly energetic. In this situation, they were even more so.

The bus's video system included a VCR wired to several small television monitors on each side of the aisle. It was running constantly. We had told the students they could bring VCR tapes. However, they were annoyed when we said they could bring only those tapes rated "G" or "PG." By 1:30 a.m., after three-and-a-half hours of non-stop videos, we shut down the system for a little quiet time before our 7 a.m. arrival in DC.

We had planned the itinerary with the tour company, and everything went well. After one night on a bus, another in a hotel, two days of seeing the traditional sights of DC, and a nine-hour return trip, we arrived back in Wilmington tired but none the worse for wear.

The next two years we decided to forego the all-night bus ride and fly to DC from Albany, spend two full days and one night in DC, and fly back the next night. It was more expensive, and it required more fundraising work from everyone: teachers, students and parents. However, it decreased our travel time and increased our time in DC. And, we concluded, the prospect of another all-night bus ride, and then expecting our kids to be all perky and attentive for the duration of the trip, was unrealistic.

All three of these DC trips lasted two days instead of the six that constituted my DC trips in the '70s and '80s. Nevertheless, the students were able to get the flavor of DC and its most important sites. As they had done in the 1970s and 1980s, Sen. Leahy and his staff once again accommodated us with a meeting and a group photo. If his schedule permitted, Sen. James Jeffords joined us. Note: *Because the tour company was now in charge of our itinerary, I knew that trying to arrange a White House rendezvous with Steve Eccher would not be possible.*

As the fourth year of our middle school eighth grade trip rolled around, the cost of flying to and from DC became prohibitive, as did the thought of another less expensive all-night bus ride. We decided to visit New York City instead of Washington. Like the three previous DC trips, this one was arranged by the same tour company.

We departed Wilmington early on a Thursday morning, spent Thursday night in a hotel, and returned late the next day. Our two-day itinerary included the United Nations, St. Patrick's Cathedral, NBC studios, FAO Schwarz, the Empire State Building (all the way to the top), a meal at the Hard Rock Cafe, Ellis Island, the Statue of Liberty, and the Liberty Science Center in Jersey City. We also went to an evening performance of a Broadway musical, "Beauty and the Beast."

At the beginning of the 2001-2002 school year, the New York City trips had been going well, and they had the potential of becoming an annual tradition. And then 9/11 happened. Even though I believed that by May, 2002, New York City would be one the safest cities in the United States, caution prevailed, and it was time to rethink the eighth grade trip once again.

Our principal, Frank Spencer, was a Canadian Studies major at Harvard. He suggested Montreal as our next eighth grade destination. As a teacher at WHS he had taken several of his Canadian Studies classes to Canada, including Montreal. I wasn't too enthused about the idea, mostly because I didn't know much about Montreal. But, I figured, if Frank was excited about it, our students and the team would be, too. Frank agreed to help chaperone, and we teachers began our preparations.

Unlike all the other trips I had taken with our eighth graders, this trip was to a different country. It required passages through US and Canadian Customs which, due to 9/11, was especially rigorous. Accordingly, we were required to have a birth certificate for each of our students and chaperones.

In addition, the trip involved a different language and a different monetary system. It also included a half-day interactive activity, a scavenger hunt, of sorts, in Old Montreal. The students, having been prepped by the team as well as by guest appearances in our classes by Frank Spencer, seemed to thoroughly enjoy themselves. Beginning in

2002, we took four annual eighth grade trips to Montreal. The trip in May, 2005, as I approached retirement, was my last.

On the second and final day of that trip, as our tour bus departed Montreal, Frank and I sat as one or two of us chaperones always did, in the back of the bus, just to keep an eye on things. I began to reflect.

In 33 years, 32 of them at WHS and my final one at Twin Valley, my colleagues and I had organized, led, and chaperoned morning field trips to Brattleboro and six-day trips to Washington, DC, and many places in between. And now, it was over.

I stared out the large window of our bus as the views turned from urban Montreal to its suburbs to the rural landscapes of northern Vermont. The kids were calm, probably a little tired, and looking forward to their upcoming three-day Memorial Day weekend. I was grateful that the trip had gone well. Since this would be the final class trip of my teaching career, I had wanted it to go smoothly, and it had. My teaching colleagues and I, along with our principal, Frank Spencer, were a good team, and we had good kids.

FINAL THOUGHTS

Whenever we returned to the WHS parking lot after an overnight trip, whether it was six days in DC or two days in DC, New York, or Montreal, there was always an air of excitement. Lots of good-byes from students to teachers, and some thank-you's, as well, which was always nice.

Upon picking up their kids at the end of the trip, it was common, according to parents through the years, to have a conversation something like this:

Parent: "So how was the trip?"

Student: "Great!"

Parent: "What did you see?"

Student: "I don't know. All kinds of stuff."

Parent: "Well, was there anything in particular that stood out, something you really liked?"

Student: "Yeah. Everything."

The parent was likely thinking, *Jeez, my kid's been away for one day, two days, or even six days, and this is the best he can do?*

However, these mildly frustrated or confused parents would soon discover something. For the next several weeks, months, or maybe longer, an item their student saw on television, on the news, read in the newspaper, heard their parents discussing, or learned about in school, would trigger a memory of something that had occurred on their trip.

With all of these trips, I tried to glean from my students what had most impressed or influenced them and why. However, it was impossible to truly assess how they had been affected. For some, a field trip might have been an incentive to purchase a pair of argyle socks. For others, a field trip might have served as an inspiration to pursue a specific career. For most students, I suspect, it was somewhere in between.

CHAPTER 22

Fundraising

1910 - 1971

The 1910 Annual Report written by Wilmington's superintendent of schools, Rev. A.N. Blackford, includes an early reference to fundraising by the high school classes of Wilmington's Central School. He was not a fan of having students raise money to support school activities. Among several recommendations he made for improving the operation of the high school was one that "the town pay part of the graduating expenses, and that the money making schemes in the high school be done away with for raising money for the same."

In spite of Reverend Blackford's recommendation against school-related "money-making schemes," by the 1920s, students at Wilmington High School were engaged in selling various items as a way to pay for a variety of activities. According to issues of the *Mirror*, throughout the 1920s, fundraising through sales and dances was a frequent activity undertaken by junior high and senior high classes.

The December, 1923 issue of the *Mirror* reported that, "During the month of November, members of the High School solicited subscriptions for the Ladies Home Journal. The school was divided into two teams, the Barney Googles and the Spark Plugs. Those procuring the most subscriptions, Madeline Pike, Frank Farrington, and Lincoln Haynes, received fountain pens. The school made about sixty-two dollars, part of which was spent on a new basketball, two new baskets, and a football." Note: *Barney Google was a cartoon character that originated in 1919. Spark Plug was his horse. They were the subject of a popular song in the early 1920s.*

Some classes raised money by selling homemade candies at the weekend movies shown at Memorial Hall. Classes also sold refreshments at school or at community events. For example, the *Mirror* reported in the early 1920s that, "The junior class held a Valley Fair in the Town Hall. Candy, cake, hot dogs, and grabs were sold." The *Mirror* also reported that, "Fortunes were told," presumably by students as a lighthearted activity.

The November, 1934 issue of the *Mirror* reported that, "On October 31, at Wilmington High School, Mr. E.B. Vanderpool, representative of the Curtis Publishing Company, presented plans for the magazine contest...It is hoped to raise enough money to pay for the field hockey uniforms and for new basketballs."

The November 4, 1934 issue of the *Deerfield Valley Times* indicated that for the magazine drive that year the student body was divided into the green and gold teams. The team that raised the lesser amount would host a party for the winning team.

In the early 1940s, the Central School's band was apparently viewed as an extra-curricular activity and, as such, it was not funded by the school's budget. It was, therefore, in danger of elimination unless it could be supported through fundraising. In his February, 1940 Annual Report, Superintendent of Schools Edward Boak wrote, "The biggest trouble was financial. Money management of the band was regarded as outside the school appropriation and all support had to be provided by school operettas, band engagements, etc. This was too great a financial strain and resulted in irregular rehearsals." Fortunately, the situation improved when the school was able to hire and pay for what was referred to as a "bandmaster," or director.

There were times during World War Two that students were involved in fundraising, of sorts, for the greater good. In this case it was supporting the war effort. Wilmington High School graduate ('48) Bill Cimonetti recalled those times: "I remember that during the war there was constant urging to buy war bonds. As school kids we all had stamp books and perhaps once a month there was a school day where we exchanged our cash savings for stamps that would eventually become bonds."

Mr. Cimonetti described another similar activity which could have involved the Central School or its students: "There were town sponsored scrap drives in which scrap metal was collected, with an emphasis on aluminum. I recall seeing piles of pots and pans gathered next to Parmelee & Howe and the village bridge. There was also a drive one year to collect milkweed pods. Cork was unavailable and milkweed fluff was being used in making life vests."

Magazine drives continued into the fifties and sixties. During a magazine drive in 1958, Central School students sold a reported $1218.91 worth of magazines. Prizes were awarded to the top sellers, and the school netted a profit of $400, about 33 percent of the total sales. A 1960 issue of the *Mirror* announced that the school's magazine drive that year earned $33 over the $1200 goal. The 1968 WHS yearbook included photos of a magazine drive assembly.

Occasionally, a specific group or team would engage in fundraising. Cliff Duncan (WHS '67) recalled one such instance: "Our baseball team canvassed businesses throughout the Valley for the funding of an 'Iron Mike' pitching machine in the spring of '67. Unfortunately, we fell $700 short of what the machine cost. Without hesitation, our coach, Mike Dymon, took that amount out of his own pocket to enable its purchase. He knew that machine could throw close to 90 mile-an-hour fastballs, so if we could hit off the machine, it was very unlikely any pitcher we might face could 'blow one by us!'"

1972 - 2004

During my 33 years of teaching, fundraising was an essential element of student life. It served a variety of purposes. It saved the taxpayers a little money here and there. But most importantly, having money in a class or organization treasury allowed students to sponsor or participate in a variety of activities.

KABOOM!

During my first year of teaching in 1972, another teacher and I served as class advisors to the eighth grade. One of our responsibilities was to assist with fundraising. Fundraising for what, I wasn't quite sure. Some students said it was for a senior class gift to the school upon graduation. Others insisted it could be used for a senior class trip. I was still trying to survive my first year of teaching, and the notion of eighth graders planning for a senior class gift or a senior class trip was the least of my concerns. Even so, helping my students raise money appeared to be the thing to do, so I agreed to assist.

My first experience with such an activity was a hunters breakfast held the first day of deer season. I awoke at 4:30 a.m. that Saturday morning in November and was at the school by 5:00. Some of the students were from families that owned and operated inns, and they seemed to know more than I did about what was involved with the breakfast. They supplied the pancake mix and other elements of a meal designed to satisfy the appetites of hungry hunters as they prepared for the season's opening day.

My lasting memory of that early morning involved the oven. The school's cafeteria kitchen had a large, six-burner gas stove that included two large ovens. The stovetop burners were easy to light because they ignited automatically. However, no one was familiar with how to light the oven. After a few tries we got it lit, exactly how, I can't recall. However, as we did so, there was a minor explosion inside the oven, and the heavy metal door flew open with a loud and forceful "whoosh."

Fortunately, no one was injured. However, it was a lesson to this new teacher that it's always best to solicit advice from experienced class advisors and teaching colleagues (as opposed to depending on overly confident eighth graders), to carefully plan events like this, and then prepare accordingly. After the oven explosion passed with no harm done, the hunters breakfast went off without a hitch.

Future go-to fundraisers for this class included bingo, more hunters breakfasts, and other activities that required low overhead and minimal up-front costs and that usually guaranteed a profit. At our ninth grade bingo night we cleared almost $100. An impressive return for an evening's work in 1973.

LET'S MAKE A DEAL: KICKING OFF THE MAGAZINE DRIVE

Two or three years into our respective teaching careers, my social studies colleague Frank Spencer and I became student council advisors. Among other roles, the student council was expected to organize a fundraising event to pay for the school field days, a dance or two, or other similar school-wide events. Traditionally, the big moneymaker at school had been the magazine drive, and we decided to continue it. The drive was an activity that we hoped would involve all of our students in grades 7-12.

As new student council advisors and to begin the magazine drive, Frank and I met with a small committee of council members. We decided to focus on selling magazines and 8-track tapes. Frank and I, along with the committee, met separately with representatives Walt and Ron, each from a different fundraising company. Magazines, 8-track cassette tapes, gift wrapping paper, flower seeds, candy, and assorted knickknacks. You name it - they sold it. Still, our focus remained on magazines and 8-track tapes - the big sellers.

After hearing pitches from the two representatives, the students chose to work with Walt and his company. It fell to me to contact Ron and explain that we had chosen Walt. I assumed the phone call would be a simple one. "Hi, Ron. Look, the kids decided they wanted to work with Walt," and that would be it. Not a chance. Our phone call lasted over a half hour. It was then that I realized how competitive and sometimes personal this fundraising business could be.

A few days later, Walt arrived at our school to make a presentation to the student body. His goal was to motivate the kids to get out there and sell, sell, sell. I guided him to the gym where he began to set up his display and then returned to my class. At the appointed hour, all students reported to the gym for a special assembly. As I entered the gym, my jaw dropped and my eyes opened wide.

Walt had arranged several cafeteria tables in front of the gym's bleachers, each loaded with an array of merchandise that would make even the most unresponsive and skeptical teenager perk up and take notice. Adorning the tables and the floor in front of them were radios, giant stuffed animals, boom boxes, radio controlled cars, tape recorders and cassettes, and all kinds of items that reflected the latest in teen fads, trends, fashions and must-haves. Everything, it seemed, sparkled and bedazzled. For every large item, there were also assorted smaller items - tchotchkes that were designed to stimulate an adolescent's irresistible desire for flashy trinkets. As the students took their seats in the bleachers, their excitement was palpable.

Frank and I began the assembly by addressing the students and setting the context for what was to follow, even though we had only the vaguest notion of what that might be. We described the magazine drive and its purpose. We then explained how the school would keep forty percent of our gross sales. Sixty percent, of course, would go to the magazine and fundraising companies. And then, Walt took center stage as the master of ceremonies. Monty Hall of "Let's Make a Deal" fame and Bob Barker (Drew Carey, these days) of "The Price is Right" had nothing on this guy. Walt was a pro, and he definitely knew his audience.

First, he explained to the students that if they sold five magazine subscriptions they'd get a small, stuffed animal. If they sold 10, 15, or 20, the value of the prizes would increase proportionately - all the way up to a fabulous stereo system, the maximum volume of which could, I was certain, crack plaster and shatter glass. Selling certain magazines like *TV Guide* or *Newsweek* yielded special prizes like five cassette tapes. Frank and I weren't sure (we'd never discussed it with Walt), but we assumed these sales-related prizes would be paid for out of our profits - the forty percent of all sales that we were keeping. We were okay with that. It was, we figured, just the cost of doing business.

One particular prize, in retrospect, should have made every adult in the room wince. Walt announced that for every ten sales, a student would receive a large mug with the Wilmington High School name and the school's warrior logo emblazoned on it. It was most definitely the design and shape of a Bavarian beer mug, but Walt described it with a smirk and a wink as a "milk mug." Frank and I soon put the kibosh on that particular prize.

With the details of the sales and prizes out of the way, it was time to get the kids even more enthused. For the next half-hour, Walt created a boisterous WHS rendition of "Let's Make a Deal." He began giving out prizes left and right. Most of them were tacky items like keychains, pens, and tiny furry creatures with weird features and catchy names. Other items were things that the fundraising company's analysts of trending adolescent tastes and preferences had determined were "hot." The kids loved them. Heck, anything for free was a good deal.

Frank and I observed from the sidelines, alternately shaking our heads in disbelief or smiling at the enthusiasm shown by our students. This guy Walt, I was thinking, man, he's like the Pied Piper. What an extravaganza! And then came the grand finale.

Walt called down a random student from the bleachers and engaged him in some sort of game, the specifics of which I cannot recall. However, what I can recall is that the kid won $50 cash, courtesy of Walt. Fifty years ago, that was a lot of money! The kids were incredulous. Wow! Fifty bucks! This guy, Walt. He's awesome! Note: *According to the Internet, $50 in 1975 would be worth almost $300 in 2025.*

The assembly concluded, and some students returned to their classes while others headed down the hall to lunch. Frank and I helped Walt pack the most valuable prizes and returned them to his station wagon for safe keeping. I took the rest of the prizes, extra order forms, sales booklets, etc. back to my classroom. Walt said he'd be in touch.

During the two-week campaign, if daily sales seemed to be slowing, Frank and I, channeling our inner Walt, would create modest two-day contests to generate enthusiasm and encourage an increase in sales, either among all the students or between different classes. All in all, it went well, and as the sale concluded, we were pleased with the results.

When Walt returned to school to retrieve the unused prizes and to settle our account, Frank and I were about to learn a valuable lesson in the business of school-related fundraising. We knew that the cost of the regular prizes related to student sales would be subtracted from our profits. We were okay with that. If the kids sold more magazines, the additional profits would pay for the prizes. That made sense.

However, what we didn't know and were too naive to ask when we should have was who was going to pay for Walt's impressive largesse at the kickoff assembly. Turns out, we were. Not Walt. No splitting the cost fifty/fifty. The cost of all those prizes Walt awarded at the assembly, including the fifty bucks to that lucky student, would be deducted from our profits - right off the top.

Frank and I felt chagrined. We'd been duped, or at least we believed we had. But we'd learned a valuable lesson, and as a result, Walt's days at Wilmington High School were over.

For the next 30 years, whether it was magazines or any number of different products, whenever it came to raising funds for the student council or middle school class trips, we worked with Walt's competition, Ron. He was high energy and a salesman's salesman. But most of all, he was fair, transparent, and he always took good care of us.

DONKEY FUNDRAISERS

In the 1940s, donkeys were an integral part of a local sporting event: donkey baseball. George Van Wyke, a 1946 WHS graduate, described this event: "I remember when a donkey baseball team came to Wilmington to play one evening. It was well advertised in advance and a big crowd turned out - maybe 200-300. Everyone, except the pitcher, catcher, and batter, had to be on a donkey. One play could take a long time. The game lasted until dark, and I think less than two innings had been played." Whether this was a school-sponsored event is unclear.

For several years, sometimes for a specific class at Wilmington High School but usually for the school's student council, the early spring brought another beast-of-burden fundraiser: donkey basketball, courtesy of the Buckeye Donkey Ball Company located in Sterling, Ohio.

According to the *Hancock County Journal-Pilot* in Carthage, Illinois, "Donkey basketball was seen as affordable Depression-era entertainment. It was invented in the 1930s and is still (as of 2024) alive and well in rural America. The game has morphed through the years into a popular fundraising vehicle for schools."

When donkey basketball first appeared at WHS is unclear. However, in the mid-1960s an issue of the *Mirror* and an article in the *Bennington Banner* reported on a donkey basketball fundraiser game between the WHS seniors and the faculty.

Until I began my teaching career, I had never played donkey basketball nor did I know it even existed. What it involved were 10-12 donkeys that traveled in a truck to various schools with their handlers. All of them, (the donkeys, not the handlers) wore special rubber "shoes" so as not to damage the gym floor. A few were trained to buck and were essentially unrideable. Others were trained not to move no matter how hard their rider stood in front of them and pulled on the reins. Other donkeys were docile and rideable. Each of them was given a name that was consistent with their temperament.

Usually the faculty played against the class or group doing the fundraising. All participants wore helmets. At the urging of the crowd, certain teachers were assigned to specific donkeys. The teacher who was given the bucking donkey, often named something like "Dynamite," was in for a long night. And the teacher who, along with their donkey was given a shovel to "clean up" with, well, you get the picture.

It was like a regular basketball game, but a player had to be on the donkey or in contact with their donkey's reins in order to possess the ball or score. For most players (and their donkeys), sinking a basket was a rare and celebrated occurrence. Note: *I do recall participating in this event, once with a donkey that would not under any circumstances allow me to sit on his back. After two unsuccessful and downright risky attempts to do so, I decided simply to walk around on the court, reins in hand, trying to be relevant.*

I haven't seen or heard of donkey basketball in our schools for many years. Given the travel and game conditions endured by the donkeys, it's probably just as well. However, according to Buckeye's Facebook page, Buckeye Donkey Ball, LLC is still in business.

THE ALL-AMERICAN REDHEADS

Another school-wide fundraiser was the All-American Redheads. The Redheads were six or seven women with above average basketball skills and with hair colored various shades of red. Fashioned after the Harlem Globetrotters, the Redheads played against a co-ed team of faculty members. During a game one year, "Rusty," the Redhead I was guarding, advised me as to what she and her teammates were about to do.

"Okay, Dave, I'm gonna do a dribbling exhibition now. Try to get the ball from me, but don't try too hard. Know what I mean?"

"Yup. Okay, Rusty."

Other Redheads gave similar instructions to my teammates. This cooperative arrangement was important and actually necessary for the success of the show. The Wilmington High School faculty in the 1970s included some young, athletic, and competitive males. We sometimes played against the older high school boys in informal games of baseball, basketball, and soccer. On weekends, it was flag football. If the Redheads hadn't advised the other male teachers and me that we were simply part of the show and that we were not *the* show, the spirit of the game could easily have been ruined. Instead, we teachers played along and played the fools. It was easily done and all in good fun.

THE HARLEM WIZARDS

The Harlem Wizards were a minor league version of the Harlem Globetrotters. Much like the Redheads, they traveled in a van, going from town to town, somewhat like the baseball barnstorming tours of the 1930s, '40s, and '50s. The Wizards were accomplished former college or high school basketball players - and they were good. Their victims were, as usual, members of the high school faculty, male and female, and sometimes members of the crowd. The Wizards entertained with tricks and trick plays, and the faculty always did an appropriate job of serving as their foils.

COMPUTER MATCHES

In the years before the presence of computers in schools was the norm, a school class or organization would sponsor a computer match fundraiser. It was usually held several weeks before Valentine's Day. For a dollar or two anyone at school - students, faculty, and staff - could complete a paper questionnaire by filling in bubbles with a number two pencil. The bubbles were associated with multiple choice questions dealing with one's preferences in hobbies, friends and personality type(s), pets, music, movies, weather or seasons, TV shows, sports, etc. The completed questionnaires would then be collected and sent to a company that would purportedly use the latest in computer technology to find for each participant the "perfect" match(es) in the school. It was a lighthearted way to raise money and often created a buzz and maybe even a little good-natured controversy around school for a few days.

CAR WASHES AND BAKE SALES

For many school groups, car washes and bake sales were go-to fundraisers throughout my time at WHS. Originally, specific prices were assigned to having one's car washed or purchasing a baked good. However, as time went on, these events were advertised as "free," and donations "were welcome." Profits usually demonstrated that the "free" approach was as lucrative if not more so than the specific-price approach.

RAFFLES

A few times each year, one group or another would conduct a raffle. Prizes were often donated by area businesses. Sometimes, if the parents of a student owned a local business, a ski shop, for example, they would donate one or two valuable prizes to be awarded to the raffle winners. Raffles could be quite lucrative, especially if the prizes were donated. I remember one in the spring, 1981, when the seniors raised with relative ease $180 (a lot of money back then) to pay for attending "Senior Night" at the Riverside Amusement Park in Agawam, MA.

A FINAL THOUGHT

So in spite of Rev. Blackford's 1910 recommendation against fundraising at Wilmington High School, for the next ninety-plus years it was a common and in some cases necessary way for students to pay for a wide variety of worthwhile activities at the school. In addition, fundraising activities could be fun, and they connected a group of students in working toward a common goal, in this case earning money and then enjoying the fruits of their collective labor.

CHAPTER 23

Student Activities

S chools in Vermont and nationwide have long supplemented their curricular offerings with extra-curricular programs, also known as student activities. Throughout its history, Wilmington High School offered its students a wide variety of these activities.

In the first three decades of its existence, Wilmington's Central School and its high school classes sponsored a variety of student activities. One such activity was an essay and public speaking contest called, "Prize Speaking." One of these contests was described in the November 20, 1903 edition of the *Vermont Phoenix* newspaper. There were several contestants who were evaluated by five judges, all members of the local clergy. "Valuable books," according to the newspaper, were presented to the winners by the school's principal.

Seven years later in 1910, a similar competition was reported in the *Deerfield Valley Times*. First, second, and third prizes of five dollars, three dollars, and two dollars respectively were awarded to the winners. The high school also held an "information contest" in which students answered 100 questions on various subjects.

In her February, 1920 annual report, Central School principal Hazel Whitney reported the pending formation of a "girl scout organization" and the reorganization of the "Junior Red Cross."

The *Mirror*, a student newspaper that would become the high school's acclaimed periodical, was first published in January, 1921. Written by generations of students throughout its more than eight decades of publication, the *Mirror* would evolve as a student activity and be referred to as a newspaper, a magazine, and finally, as a yearbook.

Originally, the *Mirror* was published three times a year. Early issues included student editorials, school news, original essays and poetry, attendance records of note, the honor rolls, and community obituaries. Many issues contained a section of humorous riddles and jokes entitled, "Think and Grin." They also included alumni notes of local interest such as: "Floyd Davis (WHS '11) has been doing his meat business alone this winter, hiring a man occasionally to do delivering," or, "Harold Whitney (WHS '20) says he likes his new radio but that it doesn't always work."

The third and final issue of each year included several items related to the seniors' upcoming graduation: valedictory; salutatory; class history; class will; class prophecy; and class song. The class poll was called, "Character Analysis" and included categories such as haughtiest, biggest flirt, biggest bluff, most vivacious, best contriver, most giraffe-like, biggest vamp, and rosiest complected.

By 1925, members of the *Mirror* staff were proudly exchanging copies of their publication with dozens of schools in New England and with schools as far away as Kentucky, Florida, Kansas, Washington, and the Philippines.

Other student activities in the 1920s included school socials, dances, the Senior play, baseball, basketball, and school picnics. In 1923, according to the *Mirror*, the school had an orchestra consisting of individual students playing the piano, the mandolin, and the drum, and two students playing the violin.

In 1928, Wilmington High School offered weekly entertainment by and for its students. Each Friday morning a class presented a program to the rest of the school. As principal Arthur L. Welcome stated in his February 1, 1929 report, these programs included "short plays, readings, musical numbers, both vocal and instrumental. These are only a few of the types of entertainment, but they serve to illustrate the variety of programs from which no small amount of benefit is derived."

The 1929 annual report described Friday morning assemblies a little differently, more like recess periods when classes would organize and supervise a variety of games.

1930S

In the early-to-mid 1930s, student activities at Wilmington High School, in addition to those above, expanded to include University of Vermont statewide writing contests, a musical performance at Memorial Hall involving more than 30 students, the Windham County Historical Essay contests, box socials, an end-of-school picnic, class-sponsored dances, a harmonica band, an astronomy club, a horseshoe pitching team, round and square dances, class parties, field days, and student council.

By the 1930s, the *Mirror* was a quarterly publication. It included a broad assortment of offerings including plays, short stories, essays, jokes, book reports, social notes, alumni notes from as far back as 1906, an operetta, sports news, and ads - all of these written by the students.

The January, 1933 issue of the *Mirror* marked a change in its production and appearance. With a nod to frugality brought on by the Great Depression, the decision was made to forego professional printing for a *Mirror* published in school on purple ditto masters. As the *Mirror* staff explained, "This is the first issue of the *Mirror* in its new dress. Because of the depression we felt if the *Mirror* was to be continued it would be necessary to reduce the expense...The cost of printing alone has been over one-hundred eighty dollars annually or forty-one cents per copy."

The WHS principal at this time was Col. Charles A. Meserve. According to the *Mirror*, he had once been the editor of "Foreign Service," a monthly magazine with a circulation of 100,000. He was the moving force behind the decision to print the *Mirror* in-house. He was also instrumental in assisting the students with the purchase of an S.M.M. Co. rotary duplicator and all the supplies necessary for its operation.

The main goal of student activities during these years, as described by the Central School's principal, Arthur Welcome (Col. Meserve's successor), was to provide the "type of education often referred to as character building, social development, and citizenship training." However, echoing the words of Central School principals before him and as a gentle reminder to parents, he added, "It must be remembered that the boys and girls spend only one-fourth of their time in school and that the home is responsible for seventy-five per cent of these desirable qualities."

1940S

The early 1940s at Wilmington High School saw, among other things, the re-emergence of the high school band. Many of the band's veteran members had graduated, and according to Edward Boak, the superintendent of schools, "...capable new members were so slow in appearing that for the past year or two we've had no band that could put on a public performance."

However, according to Mr. Boak, the situation improved with the hiring of a bandmaster who held instrumental "instruction periods each Tuesday evening, right through vacations, fair weather or foul." And, to bolster the band's numbers, students in grades 5-8 were encouraged to join, as were WHS alums.

Musical supervisor Ethel Strawser and bandmaster Warren Brigham were credited by Superintendent Boak with rescuing and resuscitating the band program. He wrote, "The result has been truly astonishing."

Another student activity that was celebrated during this time was the *Mirror*, now completing its second decade. In his 1940 annual report, Newton Baker, the highly regarded WHS principal, teacher, and coach wrote, "For the fifth time in six years our school paper, the *Mirror*, was judged the best among the small high school papers of Vermont. For this the school was again awarded a scholarship of one hundred twenty five dollars to the University of Vermont. This honor has been won so often that some may think it has become a habit. If there is any 'habit' to it, it is surely that of devoting much time and energy (and perhaps a little genius) to producing a worth-while publication." Note: *Parentheses added by Mr. Baker.*

From 1941-1945, virtually every issue of the *Mirror* included references to the war: letters from soldiers, photos of WHS graduates serving in the military, war-related student-drawn political cartoons, and similar student-written poems and articles.

After the war, the *Mirror* reflected somewhat lighter times, including material that was similar to that before the war. Typical post-war issues of the *Mirror* included editorials, essays, short stories, book reports, ballads, school sports news, an alumni section, a report on social activities, and ads.

Certainly there were student activities at WHS in addition to the *Mirror*. In his unpublished memoir housed at the Historical Society of Wilmington, George Van Wyke offered a detailed and insightful look into the various student-centered social gatherings that in the latter 1940s were held throughout the year. He wrote, "The small towns, school and churches provided most of the entertainment. In the fall, there was a 'School Party' held each Friday night at the school until the basketball season started. Each was 'sponsored' by a different class and everyone from Junior High age and up were welcome to come.

"The sponsoring class had to supply the music, including records and a record player, and the refreshments, often sweet cider and donuts. The 'party' consisted of dancing in the gym and then refreshments upstairs in the Home-Ec room. It lasted until 10:30. Of course this was before the time of long-playing records, etc. so someone had to man the phonograph - either changing or turning the records over as the song finished.

"Our class advisors, a different teacher for each class, were in charge when their class was sponsoring, and most of them let us turn off the gym lights when Dancing in the Dark was played. However, they only let us play it once a night."

Note: *The "Dancing in the Dark" that Mr. Van Wyke refers to is, of course, not the fast-paced Bruce Springsteen song, "Dancing in the Dark," composed by Springsteen himself. The 1940s song of that name was a foxtrot recorded by artists such as Frank Sinatra and Artie Shaw and his orchestra. It has a lilting rhythm similar to the slow dancing of my high school years (1962-1966). That slow dancing could be described as more of a prolonged embrace. There was an informal "rule" at my high school dances that chaperones had to see "daylight" between the couple. Whether the chaperones at the dances described by Mr. Van Wyke enforced the same rule is difficult to determine.*

However, one answer to that question might be provided by WHS teaching colleague and former Jacksonville resident, Bernie Shaw. He told me about Carrie Roberts, born in 1893, who lived in Jacksonville, Vermont. At times during her adult life (presumably in her 20s and 30s), Mrs. Roberts was involved in organizing and supervising various youth activities, including teen dances at the school (now the Municipal Center) in Jacksonville. She'd monitor the kids during the evening. It was customary, he said, for her to ring a small bell during a slow dance. This would signify that it was time to switch partners. However, if any couple was dancing too closely on a slow dance, she'd ring that bell with exceptional vigor!

Mr. Van Wyke also wrote about the junior prom, a more formal dance held each spring: "The big dance of the year was the Junior Prom. A real live band was hired for this and it was held in Memorial Hall. In our junior year we paid $100 for the band which I thought was awfully high, but it had at least ten members and a good female vocalist and was an excellent band. This was one affair not covered by our 'Student Activities' ticket so we managed to break even on it.

"Dates were common at this affair, whereas no one formally dated at the other affairs. Girls wore long dresses, boys wore suits and were expected to buy a corsage for their dates. A special car came from Brattleboro to Wilmington on 'Prom Day' delivering flowers since there was no florist in town. With all this a guy could blow up to $8-10 on one night's date.

"Of course at midnight the band stopped and everyone took their dates home - there was no place else to go in town and most of us had no car for transportation."

By the late 1940s, in addition to the spring prom, WHS was offering a variety of additional student activities. Among them were: the Edmunds Historical Essay Contest; the Vermont State Music Festival in Burlington; the Student Safety Patrol; glee club; a variety of formal and informal team sports; cheerleading; school parties; and a Christmastime Senior Hop.

Eventually there was a student council. One former WHS student reported that until 1947, at least during his time at WHS in the early 1940s, there was no student council. However, in 1947, at the urging of several students, one was created. He reported that, "The council had a modest but meaningful impact in its first two years."

1950S

Similar student activities continued into the 1950s. According to the January, 1951 report of newly-hired Principal Russell Hanson, "Evening dance classes were held each week with an average attendance of forty pupils. They meet for an hour one night a week and are given instruction in various forms of ballroom dancing, folk dancing, and the social graces."

Mr. Hanson continued, "Social activities have been devoted mainly to school parties in the gymnasium on Friday nights previous to the opening of the basketball season. The parties have been well attended and have served to provide much needed wholesome recreation."

In the mid-1950s, the WHS Latin classes sponsored an event called a Roman banquet. In addition, throughout the decade, various groups such as WHS's senior class offered performances of dramas and comedies. One year during the fifties, the senior class presented its play, "January Thaw."

During this decade there were four choral groups: the girls glee club, the boys glee club, the mixed chorus, and a sextette. Forty of the high school's 77 students were members of the glee club, proudly wearing their blue choir robes for their concerts. They performed locally and also at the Tri-State Musical Festival in Williamstown, MA and at the Southern Vermont Music Festival in Brattleboro. According to the principal's report in 1953, to raise funds to send a group to the All State Musical festival in Burlington, the glee club was featured in a local variety show.

The band, like the glee club, consisted of 40 students and performed both locally and at regional music festivals. David Wheeler, a World War II veteran, served as a volunteer drillmaster to assist the band in its marching performances. Priscilla Lackey and Bruce Willard, in their article, "Class of 1955 Wilmington High School - Home of the Warriors," added that, "We had a great music program that included a great band. We attended many music festivals which many of our class members took part in." Note: *David Wheeler served as a WHS science teacher and later, in the late 1990s and early 2000s, as a dedicated member of the Wilmington School Board.*

The school also supported a student orchestra that performed at a variety of school and community events.

Under the supervision of Helen Allen and Ralph Shindler, the *Mirror* continued its reputation as a high-quality publication. The May 8, 1953 edition of the *Rutland Daily Herald* announced that Wilmington High School and its publication, the *Mirror*, placed first in the fourth annual Vermont High School Stencil Duplicated Paper Competition sponsored by the McAuliffe Paper Company of Burlington. According to the Herald, newspapers from 15 high schools were judged on "general attractiveness, neatness of duplicating, originality of artwork, and general rules of composition and setup." Note: *The WHS chapter of the National Honor Society was later named for Helen Allen.*

For obvious reasons, the *Mirror* was a source of immense pride for its staff and for Wilmington High School as a whole. According to former WHS students Harriet Maynard, Priscilla Lumbra Lackey, and Pat Crawford Morris in a newsletter article published by the Historical Society of Wilmington, "The *Mirror* was published 4 times a year, charging 35 cents per copy. The *Mirror* staff dedicated the 1952 fall issue to Dwight D. Eisenhower and mailed a copy to him in Washington, DC. His return letter of appreciation said, 'a well presented magazine' and it became the first page in the February 1953 *Mirror* issue."

The article also highlighted the fact that for three years in a row the *Mirror* received one of the Columbia Scholastic Press Association's "three medalist ratings in its class of senior high schools among 1300 entries." It continued, "This medal for 'publications of distinction' was even higher than 'first place' in any of several classes. It meant a 'superior' rating due to the fine printing, design, coloring, and literary publications."

1960S

During the early 1960s, Wilmington High School students participated in a wide variety of student activities. The *Mirror*, itself, continued to be a significant activity, and in the 1960-1961 school year its publication required the efforts of more than 30 students in grades 10-12. Additional activities included dances/record hops, holiday parties, and student council.

A review of WHS yearbooks from the later 1960s reveals an expanded variety of student activities that were offered during the decade. Among them were student council, Student Government in Action, the *Mirror*, National Honor Society, Future Nurses of America, Future Homemakers of America, Industrial Arts Association, a pancake supper, winter carnival and spring field day, interscholastic sports, proms with queens and kings, annual Christmas parties, Boys and Girls States, class plays, intramural competitions, glee club, debate club, gym team, a "ski instruction program" (presumably at Mount Snow) involving 100 students, "'The Hawkeye,' a new (in 1969) venture in journalism for our school - a one or two page insert report of student activities and opinions in a local weekly publication," and a performance of "Brigadoon" for which rehearsals "began immediately after school closed in June and continued until the final production in the fall."

Editions of the *Mirror* in the few years prior to 1967 (when the *Mirror* was first published as a hard-cover yearbook) were being printed on the school's mimeograph machine. They included a format and items that often and to this day continue in high school yearbooks. They included glossy pages that included a black and white photo of each senior along with information such as their school activities, favorite saying, pet peeve, and birth date.

STUDENTS AND SOCIAL CHANGE

The 1960s, especially near the end of the decade, saw significant changes in various American institutions. Some changes were the result of youthful rebellion and what was called "the generation gap" caused, according to some, by "the communication gap" between adolescents and adults. This was the case in many of America's high schools, including Wilmington High School where some student activities took on a more serious tone than those in previous years.

WHS principal Russell Hanson's 1969 annual report reflected the changing times. He wrote, "The past year has seen many changes in our school directly attributable to better communication between students and faculty. The student council was primarily responsible for initiating the improvement in these lines of reasoning together."

Mr. Hanson reported that one change agreed to by the students and faculty was the "elimination of the dress code." Note: *While I found no evidence to the contrary, it's probably safe to assume that while a dress code the students believed to be overly restrictive was eliminated, at least some version of a dress code or expectations at WHS remained.*

Another change at WHS was a privilege system that allowed some students to be in specified areas of the school or school grounds during study periods (study halls). The privilege system, according to Mr. Hanson's report, was "for the purposes of study and/or communication; a lengthened school lunch period, and changed noon dismissal procedures."

Mr. Hanson's report also mentioned, "...there have been a number of student-faculty meetings for an exchange of viewpoints. These will continue."

In addition to calling for change within their own high school, Mr. Hanson wrote that some WHS students were involved in similar activities beyond their school. "Some students have represented the school in various statewide and county gatherings designed for the purpose of airing student problems and concerns. Locally, a number of students have made up a panel of discussants on youth problems related to drug use and abuse and generation gap communication problems. These have been well-received by the adults and students in attendance at the discussion sessions."

EARLY 1970S - AN UNEXPECTED BENEFIT

In 1960 at the age of 11, I traveled with my family to Mount Snow for a four-day ski vacation. The drive from Rochester, New York was a reasonable six hours. We stayed at the Sun and Ski Lodge on Route 100 in West Dover. In those days Mount Snow was known for, among other attractions, an indoor skating rink and an outdoor swimming pool. The cost of a lift ticket was around $5.00

In 1972, when I was hired to teach in Wilmington, the cost of a lift ticket had increased to $11.00. For a first year teacher, as well as for many others, this was a lot of money. The thought of skiing remained only a thought - until one day in December.

In those days, like today, Mount Snow and Haystack ski areas were under separate ownership. However, they were equally generous when it came to the opportunities they offered Wilmington's children and their teachers.

Each corporation sent its representative to the school, and each brought with them a piece of equipment that photographed students and faculty. And then, on the spot, everyone was presented with a laminated season pass for each ski area - free! By the end of the day, the students were proudly wearing their passes hanging from narrow chains around their necks. This was a generous benefit offered by both Mount Snow and Haystack. However, within a few years due possibly to economic challenges, both Mount Snow and Haystack ceased the practice.

Soon, however, all students in area elementary schools were offered either free or discounted passes. Students at the high school who achieved certain academic honors were rewarded in a similar fashion.

1972 - 2004: A BRIEF LOOK AT STUDENT ACTIVITIES

During my 32 years at WHS, the majority of teachers and administrators at Wilmington High School, along with school staff, parents, and community members, gave generously of their time and energy to support a wide variety of student activities.

According to the WHS *Mirror* yearbooks from 1972-2004, there were dozens of such activities. Some were associated with the official curriculum; others were not. Some activities were offered by WHS organizations while others were connected to local, statewide, or even national groups. Some activities, like the yearbook and student council, lasted throughout my time at WHS. Other activities lasted for only a year or two depending on student interest or the availability of an advisor.

Listed by decade, a survey of WHS yearbooks reveals the following student activities offered to WHS students. Note: *It's certainly possible that other activities were offered but simply did not appear in the yearbooks. Sports are not included in these lists because they are included in a previous chapter.*

1972-1979

Activities included: the yearbook; student council; National Honor Society; varsity club, stamp collectors, drama club, Boys and Girls State, All-State chorus/band; American Legion essay contests; French club; Senior Honors English colloquium; International club; debate team; Spanish club; Canadian Studies club.

1980-1989

In addition to many of the activities and organizations in the 1970s, these were offered in the 1980s: school newspaper; Hospitality & Tourism program; mock trial state competition; Governor's Institutes of Vermont; Vermont Legislative Page program; US Senate Page program; Youth Partnership Program; Students Against Drunk Driving (SADD); astronomy club; German club; UVM Junior Conference.

1990-1999

In addition to many of the above activities, other student activities included: Jobs/Choices for Vermont Graduates; Third Floor West literary magazine; weather club; Scholars Bowl state competition; school store; Leadership Project; Hugh O'Brien Scholarship; Daughters of the American Revolution; UVM Writing contest; Teens as Teachers; Pendium (assisting students with special needs); S.T.E.M.; statewide middle school spelling bee; senior internships; middle school National Geographic Geo-Bee; Independent art club; outing club; environmental club; Vision 2000; Upward Bound; Green Mountain Teen Institute; peer mediators; the Student Network.

2000-2004

Additional activities included: outdoor adventure club; Focus Forum; 1-2-1 Mentors; Child Labor Education Action; Vermont Kids

Against Tobacco; chess club; Foundation for Excellent Schools; Congressional Arts Competition.

LOOKING BACK: STUDENT EVENTS

In addition to student activities which tended to be established programs, there were school-wide events that occurred once, twice, or several times a year.

During my years at Wilmington High School, the student council and classes, either academic (e.g. Spanish class) or year (e.g. juniors), sponsored and organized various events such as dances, proms, meals, Halloween dress-ups, theme days when students dressed as teachers and vice-versa, pajama days, etc. Students and/or faculty also organized contests (dance) or tournaments (volleyball, basketball) between classes or home rooms/advisories.

Two of the longer-lasting annual events at WHS, the winter and spring field days, began before my arrival at WHS. An article in the February 16, 1934 edition of the *Brattleboro Reformer* describes "the first winter sports meet to be conducted by Wilmington High School under the direction of Coach N.B. (Newton) Baker." The event was held on a Saturday on what was then called the "baseball grounds." Events included an obstacle course, snowshoe races, and "informal jumping on skis."

School-wide field days were organized by the student council as far back as the 1930s. They were also held in 1971-1972, the year before my arrival, and lasted well into the 1990s. During my time at WHS, grades competed against each other, usually in three divisions: seventh vs. eighth, ninth vs. tenth, and eleventh vs. twelfth.

Winter field day indoor events included volleyball, basketball foul shooting, sprints, and races on small four-wheeled carts used to move large pieces of furniture. Outdoor events included snow sculptures, snowball throwing for distance, and races on cross-country skis or snowshoes. Events were also held on the hill behind the house at the end of Whitney Lane, owned at the time by WHS parents Dr. Milton "Mickey" Wolf and his wife and then-school board member, Betty. The students raced down Wolf's hill either on jack jumpers, skis, inner tubes, or cafeteria trays. Thick brush at the bottom of the hill, and I suppose occasionally a teacher, prevented participants from sliding into Beaver Brook.

The spring field days were held on the school's athletic fields and in the gymnasium. Events included three-legged races, sprint and distance running races, foul shooting, three-on-three basketball, tennis, sack races, the egg toss, tug of war, Frisbee throwing, pyramid building, and skateboard and bicycle races.

The spring field days always included a barbecue of some sort. Some years it was chicken, other years it was hot dogs and hamburgers. The barbecue was quite a logistical undertaking, but there were always some stalwart faculty members and staff who pulled it off.

These field days took an enormous amount of work, both in planning and execution. The faculty, staff, and students coordinated the events and always worked together to make them a success.

LOOKING BACK: THE HISTORY OF THE *MIRROR*

In its inaugural edition, the *Mirror*'s editor-in-chief, senior Eleanor C. Brown, wrote in the newspaper's first editorial, "We wish to warn you not to expect too much in this first attempt. Entirely lacking in experience, we're starting on a pathway where there are no footsteps of former venturers in which to follow." Suffice it to say that Miss Brown probably had no idea how successful the *Mirror* would be. It continued in its original form for another 45 years and received many accolades and awards. Eventually, in 1967, it became the hardcover, commercially-produced WHS yearbook that lasted until the school's end in 2004.

At its inception in 1921, the *Mirror* measured 9 inches by 6 inches in size. It was printed commercially by the Vermont Printing Company located in Brattleboro, and two years later by the Springfield Printing

Company in Springfield, Vermont. In the early 1930s, its size expanded to 8.5 by 11 inches, and it was printed at the school using blue ditto masters. In the latter 1930s, and until its final soft cover edition in 1966, stencils were used.

At its height in the 1940s, 1950s, and until 1966, each of the issues of the *Mirror* was 80 to 100-plus pages in length. To emphasize the challenges of the technology used by the *Mirror* students and staff, authors Harriet Maynard, Priscilla Lackey, and Pat Morris wrote in their newsletter article cited above, "Now keep in mind, the *Mirror* staff in this era had to type the pages onto stencils, run the pages off on a hand crank drum mimeograph, then hand staple the copies in an assembly line fashion. This form of production happened with every *Mirror* issue from 1921 to 1966 when, in 1967, the school yearbook became a hard copy."

During its time, each issue of the *Mirror* contained sections that included original student-written literature, student art, alumni news, school news, sports, humor, news exchanges with other schools, editorials, and other examples of student work and creativity. It also included hundreds of ads promoting businesses in Wilmington, Whitingham, Dover, Wardsboro, Marlboro, Brattleboro, Bennington, Townshend, Londonderry, Newfane, and North Adams, MA. These ads reflected considerable effort on the part of the students who sold and created them. They were also a testament to broad community support for the school and the *Mirror*. And to this day, the ads provide a comprehensive and fascinating picture of the area's economy during those years.

Top: The first publication of the WHS Mirror, January 1921
Bottom: Final publication of the WHS Mirror, June, 2004

Certainly during the 45 years of its in-school publication, the *Mirror* provided an opportunity for WHS students to improve their writing skills. In addition, they also learned and improved the many skills that were and continue to be necessary to successfully complete any major project: creativity, organization, teamwork, time management, personal responsibility, leadership, initiative, problem solving...the list in endless.

In the *Mirror*'s very first editorial in January, 1921, editor-in-chief, student Eleanor C. Brown, wrote about the *Mirror* name: "This isn't the usual kind of mirror, a look into which satisfies or wounds one's vanity...This 'Mirror' is going to reflect the life and actions of our school and we hope and pray a look into it can hold your attention for a moment or two."

Note: *I would say unequivocally that Eleanor Brown's hopes were realized and her prayers were answered. Each issue of the "Mirror," especially during its years of traditional publication prior to 1967, is truly unique as a primary source. I cannot imagine a better, more accurate and vivid representation of the unfiltered student voices, attitudes, values, skills, interests, opinions, and culture that filled the classrooms of Wilmington High School. Issues of the "Mirror," whether explored individually or collectively, are an invaluable resource for anyone wanting to learn about the history of Wilmington High School. Copies of the* Mirror *can be viewed at Wilmington's Pettee Memorial Library and the Historical Society of Wilmington.*

LOOKING BACK: A UNIQUE STUDENT EVENT AT WILMINGTON HIGH SCHOOL

As described in previous chapters, the WHS student council was normally involved in raising money, sponsoring dances, representing the student body in dealings with the administration, and organizing field days and various student activities. However, there was one time when council members, along with some other students, waded deep into controversy with some surprising results. The controversy? The presence of the Ku Klux Klan.

In early May, 1982, the Grand Dragon of the Connecticut chapter of the Ku Klux Klan publicly announced (I cannot recall exactly how) that about a dozen or so Klan members were coming to Vermont to, as he stated, "test the waters." They chose Wilmington as their test site because allegedly there were two or three Klan members who lived here. However, the word around town (which I believe was shown to be accurate) was that they were second-home owners and not true citizens of Wilmington.

I was our school's student council advisor at the time. The council members wanted desperately to hold their own counterprotest to demonstrate their opposition to the Klan's presence and what it represented. However, the police chief had requested that we stay away. In fact, he had requested that everyone in town stay away.

The Klan had originally requested a permit to hold their rally in Wilmington's downtown district where Vermont Routes 9 and 100 intersect. They said they planned to have only a dozen members present. However, this event had the potential for a major challenge for law enforcement and downtown merchants. To make matters worse, there were rumors that a few radical or militant groups from Keene, New Hampshire and Albany, New York were coming to town to hold their own counterprotests and to confront the Klan.

Wilmington's police chief suggested an alternative location: at the high school on the baseball field. However, the thought of the Klan using school property to promote its philosophy was especially objectionable to the students. To respond to the students' concerns and their desire to make them known, the police chief asked to meet with some student council members, a few teachers, and me. He explained the potential for violence and reiterated his request that everyone stay away from the Klan and their gathering.

He then suggested that the students create anti-Klan fliers. The student council accepted his suggestion and got to work. In the meantime, the anticipated presence of the Klan was creating quite a stir throughout the school. Accordingly, I spent some time in my classes, as did other teachers in their classes, focusing on the history of the Klan.

As the police chief had suggested, the students designed and printed a batch of fliers and then posted them throughout the downtown area.

In addition, some student council members were excused from their study halls to spread the word. They signed out of school with the principal's permission and stood at the village's four corners asking people to sign anti-Klan petitions. The petitions stated, in essence, that, "While we the undersigned acknowledge the right of Klan members to assemble peacefully, we unequivocally condemn and reject the Klan's beliefs and past actions."

In addition to circulating the petitions and making and posting the fliers, the students made a large poster with the same anti-Klan statement and had students sign it. The day before the rally, the students displayed, with the owner's permission, the poster and the signed petitions in a large window of a downtown business.

Finally, on that same Friday, the student council attached a huge white banner to the soccer kickboard. Painted on the banner was "KKK" in large black letters. The letters were surrounded by a thick red circle and bisected by an equally thick red line running from the upper left to the lower right, essentially negating the "KKK." The kickboard was immediately adjacent to the field where the rally was to occur the next day. The banner's presence was impossible to ignore, and the import of its message was clear.

By Friday afternoon, with fliers posted, petitions signed and on display, and a large anti-Klan banner hanging prominently at the school's field, we were ready.

That Saturday morning, I walked down from my Ray Hill home to school to do some work. On the way, I saw some community members hanging a banner across East Main Street in the middle of town. It read, "Hate does not grow well in the rocky soil of Vermont." I also saw people in town wearing black arm bands as an expression against the presence of the Klan.

By 11 a.m., after completing my work in my classroom, I knew I had a decision to make. Should I honor the police chief's request to stay away from the ball field, or should I submit to temptation and view firsthand what could be an offensive yet momentous event. I compromised.

From my classroom on the eastern end of the school I walked to the other end of the building, the old wooden section. I walked up the stairs to the classroom located on the third floor in the southwest corner of the school. From there I could survey the entire event while still honoring the chief's request not to attend the rally.

What I saw was an overwhelming presence of law enforcement: Wilmington police officers, Windham County sheriffs, and Vermont State Police. And there may have been additional law enforcement under cover. The Klan had yet to arrive. However, the Young Communists League from Keene State College soon arrived and began chanting, "Cops, courts, and Klan...All part of the boss's plan."

A few minutes later, about 17 Klan members, males and females, arrived in two or three pickup trucks accompanied by a police escort. Some members rode in the cabs while others rode in the cargo beds. They wore their white robes and pointed hats but nothing covering their faces. They tried to speak but were shouted down by anti-Klan groups that were present.

At noon or so I headed home for lunch. Media accounts stated that by 3 p.m. the Klan members and everyone else had left, all without incident. No one had been injured or arrested. The ball field was clean and nothing, including the students' large anti-Klan banner, had been disturbed. But we would soon learn that there was more to the story.

According to the UPI (United Press International) Archives website describing that Saturday, "Four Connecticut-based Klansmen, including Imperial Wizard James Farrands, were arrested in Wilmington at 5 a.m. on charges of possessing loaded long-armed weapons - a fish and game violation. The four are being held in the Brattleboro lockup for lack of 500 dollars bail."

As it turned out, according to the *Rutland Daily Herald*, four of the Klansmen had been in Wilmington's village early Saturday morning before their planned demonstration. They were observed tearing down the students' anti-Klan fliers and, I suppose, possibly littering. As part of a resulting police-Klan interaction, an officer spotted a rifle in the back of a Klansman's car. The rifle was loaded. This led to an arrest, and the Klansmen were held in jail until their release after the demonstration.

The *New York Times* reported that, "Earlier (meaning before the demonstration) four Klansmen were arrested on weapons charges." As a result, these four Klansmen, including their leader, the Imperial Wizard, never made it to the rally.

The police chief came to school on Monday, and in a school-wide assembly relayed this story to the students. He thanked them for protesting in a way that was peaceful, responsible, non-confrontational, and surprisingly productive. He described how the fliers the students had made and posted had been torn down by the Klan. This had led to the Klan interaction with the police and their subsequent arrest. And that had led to some of the Klansmen, including their leader, missing their rally.

For their part, the students were excited, pleased, and proud of the manner in which they had responded to the Klan's presence. In their own way, Wilmington High School's student council and students in general had foiled the Klan. They had let everyone know that the Klan and their ilk were not welcome at their school, in their town, in their state, or beyond. The students had sent the Klan a message and had sent them packing.

A FINAL THOUGHT

Despite its small size or perhaps because of it, students at Wilmington High School were fortunate. During the school's existence, most student activities were available on a predictable and sustained basis. A few student activities at WHS lasted less than a year or only intermittently. Another, the *Mirror*, lasted more than 80 years. But by any measure, from 1899 to 2004, Wilmington's Central School and High School consistently offered its students an impressive array of activities both in the school building and beyond.

WHS Band, ca. 1941

Wilmington High School students protesting against the Ku Klux Klan

CONCLUSION

A school building serves many functions. It defines and represents the value a community places on educating its children. As such, its purpose is to provide a safe, healthy, comfortable, and stimulating place for effective teaching and active learning.

Ultimately, however, a school serves as a physical and tangible focus when we want to reminisce about our lives as children and adolescents. In some ways it serves as a repository of our memories. Memories of learning, growing, developing, even flourishing. Memories of experiencing countless human emotions and thoughts. Memories of learning through failure and becoming confident through success. Memories of lessons taught and lessons learned.

Let there be no doubt that Wilmington Central/High School as a building and as an institution provided such memories for more than 100 years and will continue to do so for many years to come.

Sources

HSWV = housed at the Historical Society of Wilmington, VT.

PML = available at Pettee Memorial Library, Wilmington

All photos courtesy of Historical Society of Wilmington (except two Larsen family photos and photo of WHS students and anti-KKK banner).

* * *

"A Tale of Two Towns." Jan. 31, 1990 John Taft. (HSWV)

"Auditors' Report and Annual Exhibit of the Finances of the Town of Wilmington," as cited in the text. (PML)

Bennington Banner. Various articles as cited in the text.

Brattleboro Reformer. Various articles as cited in the text.

"Building the Mountain Mills School - 1918." Historical Society of Wilmington, VT newsletter. 1975-2024.

"Burlington's Venetian Ginger Ale." *History Connections.* Vermont Historical Society. Spring, 2023.

"Class of 1955 Wilmington High School Home of the Warriors." Priscilla Lackey & Bruce Willard. Historical Society of Wilmington, VT newsletter. 1975-2024.

Deerfield Valley News as cited in the text.

Deerfield Valley Times. Various articles as cited in the text.

Deerfield Valley Times Reunion Edition. Compiled by J.H. Walbridge - The Times Press - Wilmington, VT. August 17, 1900.

dictionary.com.

findagrave.com.

Greenfield Recorder. March, 2014.

"Growing Up In Wilmington." Bernice Barnett. *The Cracker Barrel.* Spring-Summer, 1990.

"The Growth of Education in Wilmington." Virginia Howe. The *Mirror.* May/June, 1934.

Historical Society of Wilmington Newsletter, 2009. (HSWV)

History of Education in Vermont, George Gary Bush, Ph. D. 1900.

Images of America - Wilmington. Julie Moore and Nathan Moore. Arcadia Publishing. 2020

"I remember...or The First Eighteen Years." George Van Wyke (WHS '46) Unpublished memoir housed at the Historical Society of Wilmington. (HSWV)

John Lazelle's Facebook & "Old Post Cards" websites.

"The Late Nineteenth-Century One-Room School." *https://www.heritageall.org/wp-content/uploads/2013/03/Americas-One-Room-Schools-of-the-1890s.pdf.*

Letter from Wilmington School directors to Fred Thomas, chair, Wilmington Selectmen. April 22, 1954. HSWV.

"Letter to town voters." School Directors of Wilmington. June 25, 1947.

"Little White Schoolhouse on the Lake - A Hoot Toot and Whistle for Vermont's Lost Valley." Video produced by Martin Kasindorf, 2010-2011.

"Marriage Bar" on Wikipedia.

"Memo to Expediting Committee." Henry W. Meyer, Jr. November 1, 1954. (PML)

The *Mirror* - Wilmington High School's literary and yearbook publication, 1921 - 2005. (PML & HSWV) As cited in the text.

"Mountain Mills." Marcia Green & Myrna Green. Historical Society of Wilmington, VT newsletter. 1975 - 2024.

National Bureau of Economic Research. (*nebr.org*)

newspapers.com.

Old School Enrichment Council website.

"One Hundred and Ninety Years of Progress." Barbara Haskins. 1941. (HSWV)

"Only a Teacher." Public Broadcasting System. *https://www.pbs.org/onlyateacher/time-line.html* 1992

Philip Hoff: How Red Turned Blue in the Green Mountain State. Samuel Hand, Anthony Marro, and Stephen Terry. University Press of New England, Lebanon, NH. 2011

"Recalling Educators from the '50"s" at WHS." Harriet Maynard, Priscilla Lumbra Lackey, and Pat Crawford Morris. *Historical Society of Wilmington - 1975-2018* newsletter. (HSWV)

Record of Articles 3 and 4 of the Record of Special Town Meeting held May 1st, 1934. (HSWV)

"Rules for Teachers in 1872." Washington Post.com. June 2, 2011. Valerie Strauss.

"School Consolidation: Farewell to the One-Room School House, 1986." *Green Mountain Chronicles* radio broadcast, 1988-1989. Vermont Historical Society website.

"School Days." Evelyn Fitch Keefe. (HSWV)

"Schools in Wilmington." Marilyn Howe. March 4, 1941 (PML)

"Title IX and the Evolution of High School Sports." Betsey Stevenson. December, 2007.

Title 16 Vermont Statutes Annotated.

"To the Auditors and Voters of Wilmington." *Auditors' Report and Annual Exhibit of the Finances.* Wilmington School Directors.

Town Record Books (Town Meeting minutes, etc.), 1974-1981

"The Town of Wilmington Annual Report." (PML)

"Vermont Female Schoolteachers in the Nineteenth Century." Margaret Nelson. *Vermont History.* Vermont Historical Society. Winter, 1981.

Vermont Phoenix. Various articles as cited in the text.

"The Vermont Schoolmarm and the Contemporary One-Room Schoolhouse." Jody Kenny. 1990.

"What it Will Look Like When Finished - Floor Plans as Drawn by the Architect." *Deerfield Valley Times.* February 17, 1899. (PML)

"What Lies Beneath the Lost Town of Mountain Mills." Eric Stanway.(sentinel-source.com - *the Keene Sentinel.* 8/6/2019.

"When Children Were Property." Joanna Tebbs Young. *Rutland Herald.* May 18, 2024

Wikipedia. Various articles as cited in the text.

"Wilmington High School and Central School." Louise A. (Terzie) Hall - a collection of photos, programs and newspaper clippings from her time as a teacher in Wilmington High School. (HSWV)

Wilmington Old Home Week booklet. August, 1980.

"Wilmington's Rural or District Schools." Margaret Greene & Rita Staib. June 2, 1982. (HSWV)

Wilmington Schools, Vols. 1-5 - A Collection of Information. Margaret Greene. (PML)

"Wilmington Schools." Russell Hanson & Ruth Streeter. *Wilmington Old Home Week* booklet. 1980.

"Wilmington Schools." Mary Van Wyck Patch. (HSWV)

Wilmington Town Reports as cited in the text. (PML)

Acknowledgements

I would like to acknowledge and thank the Historical Society of Wilmington and Julie Crafts Moore (WHS '81), its president. Julie was most generous with her time as she guided me and made available to me the vast inventory of materials at the Historical Society that is related to Wilmington's district, central, and high schools. Thank you to Julie and the Historical Society for their work in preserving the past of our town and the Deerfield Valley.

Another invaluable source of information was Bill Cimonetti, WHS '48. Bill and I served together in the Vermont House of Representatives for a few years in the early 1990s. We reconnected at Wilmington's Old Home Week in 2021. Bill has shared with me various photos and countless memories of his time as a student at Wilmington's Central/High School. I very much appreciate his interest and assistance.

I would also like to acknowledge and extend my gratitude to the many local writers whose work appears in the publications cited in this book, many of whom have passed away. Their recorded memories or research-based writing were invaluable sources of information for this book.

Finally, I would like to thank the people whose names appear below. They were most generous in responding to my questions and requests for information, some several years ago, others more recently.

*Betty Adams	Cindy Hayford
*Bill Adams	Kyrra Howard
*Sharon Adams	Bill Kunz
*Arnie Bernard	Ken Lady
*Bob Boyd	*John Lazelle
*Deb Boyd	*Bonnie Aubertine Lorimer
*John Boyd	Therese Lounsbury
*Vicki Raymo Capitani	Allison Maynard

*Bill Cimonetti   Karen Molina
*Cliff Duncan   *Julie Crafts Moore
Steve Eccher   *Tallu Meade
*Bob Edwards   *Rebecca Schoonmaker
Mike Eldred   Bernie Shaw
*Bob Greene   Jeff Silverman
*Evelyn Greene   Pat Spencer
*Jessica Greene Hammond Nicki Steel
*Buddy Hayford   *Meg Streeter

• Graduate of Wilmington High School